The truth.
It's not always pretty.
It is always essential.

THE MASTER TERRORIST
THE TRUE STORY OF ABU NIDAL

"THOROUGH RESEARCH AND A
SEVERELY DISPASSIONATE ANALY-
SIS . . . SKILLFULLY DISSECTS THE
PATHOLOGY OF ANTI-ISRAELI AND
ANTI-AMERICAN VIOLENCE . . ."
Dr. Ray S. Cline,
Former Deputy Director,
CIA, Department of Terrorism

THE MASTER TERRORIST

THE TRUE STORY OF ABU-NIDAL

Yossi Melman

AVON
PUBLISHERS OF BARD, CAMELOT, DISCUS AND FLARE BOOKS

AVON BOOKS
A division of
The Hearst Corporation
105 Madison Avenue
New York, New York 10016

The Adama Books edition contains the following Library of Congress Cataloging in
Publication Data:

Melman, Yossi.
  The master terrorist.

  Bibliography.
  1. Abu-Nidal.   2. Terrorists—Biography.   3. Terrorism.   4. Palestinian
Arabs—Biography.   I. Title.
HV6431.A28M45   1986   303.6′25′0924 [B]   86-10820

First Avon Printing: July 1987

Table of Contents

THE MASTER TERRORIST

Foreword

Since World War II, terror has become one of the major problems of our time. This is all the more true of Palestinian terrorism, to such an extent that the words "terror" and "Palestinian" have come to be almost synonymous. And indeed, since the end of the 1960's the Palestinian terror organizations have not only disturbed the delicate balance in the Middle East, but have become a burden on the entire world.

The founding in the late 1950's of the Fatah organization by a young Palestinian engineer in Kuwait named Yasser Arafat helped to shape the new direction of the Palestinian movement. Within a few years, Arafat and his Fatah took over the Palestine Liberation Organization (P.L.O.)—the umbrella organization of the Palestinian groups—and became the dominant force within it.

Though the actions of the various Palestinian organizations provided clear evidence of the continued existence of the Arab-Israeli conflict, the problem seemed to be declining between the 1973 Yom Kippur and 1982 Lebanese wars. This was due to an extent to the fact that the world has learned to live with terror, and has developed certain preventive measures against it. Part of the reason for this decline, however, was that the majority of the Palestinian organizations had reduced their reliance on armed struggle against Israel as the only way to achieve their goal: the establishment of a Palestinian state. The number of terrorist acts accordingly decreased considerably. Instead of, or more correctly, together with, the use of force, the Palestinian organizations began to stress the use of political and diplomatic means to achieve their end. And even if they did not lay that great a stress on diplomacy, they at least tried to combine both methods.

In the nature of events, though, just as there are proponents of replacing or supplementing terrorism with political actions, there are others who feel that, on the contrary, terrorism must be increased. Thus, as the majority of Palestinian organizations began laying less emphasis on terrorism as a vehicle, other new, more radical organizations sprang up whose goal was to continue the armed struggle against the "Zionist enemy" at any price, under any conditions, and without caring about changing political circumstances on the international scene. The more the P.L.O. under Arafat attempted to moderate its image, the greater the number of radicals who emerged to reject this stance.

One of the most notorious of the radical organizations, possibly the most dangerous and certainly the most active, is the one known as the Abu Nidal group. It is a very small band, numbering no more than a few hundred members and supporters. Setting out from its headquarters in (successively) Iraq, Syria, and Libya, its members have undertaken some of the most daring and bloody attacks against Israeli, American and Western European Jewish targets, as well as against moderate Arab leaders, including important members of the P.L.O. The group's name is derived from the alias adopted by its founder and leader, Sabri al-Banna. Since it was formed in the early 1970's, a great number of myths have surrounded the group, and especially its leader. Both the group and its leader have tried to become "living legends"—and may well have succeeded.

Reports have claimed that Abu Nidal died years ago in Baghdad, but the Syrians and Libyans continue to claim he is alive. Other reports, based on Israeli and United States intelligence, state that he has undergone two open-heart operations, but is still alive and functioning. Both the Italian and American governments have outstanding arrest warrants for him.

Al-Banna is praised highly by his supporters and damned by his opponents (and he has an extremely large number of the latter). He continues to be inaccessible, not only—obviously—to those who would harm him, but even to those journalists who beat a path to his door. One has the impression that Sabri al-Banna rejects any personal publicity and prefers to work in the dark, far away from the spotlight of the media. The organization which he built from scratch is indeed relatively small, but its strength lies in its clandestine nature and the secrecy which surrounds it.

The Abu Nidal group has an extensive and checkered past, with a great number of skeletons buried in its closets. Israeli intelligence attributes more than one hundred terrorist acts to it in the twelve years since it was established in 1973. Its actions on three continents—Africa, Europe and Asia—were aimed at twelve different targets: the United States, Israel, Jordan, Kuwait, the United Arab Emirates (UAE), the P.L.O., Egypt, Saudi Arabia, Britain, Austria, Italy, and France; and were carried out on the soil of no less than eighteen countries: Greece, Malta, Austria, Italy, Rumania, Poland, Yugoslavia, India, Egypt, Pakistan, Jordan, Syria, Kuwait, France, Britain, the UAE, Lebanon, and the Netherlands.

Israel's incursion into Lebanon increased the organization's visibility. The liquidation of the P.L.O.'s military infrastructure in southern Lebanon and the expulsion of Yasser Arafat and his men from Beirut in September 1982 only served to strengthen Abu Nidal's terrorist organization, and indirectly aided it in becoming one of the most dangerous groups to Israel, as well as to such pro-western Arab states as Jordan, Saudi Arabia and the United Arab Emirates (UAE), and the entire West. Its attacks on land and in the air have resulted in the deaths of about two hundred people and the wounding of a similar number.

Like a chameleon changing its skin color, these attacks have been made under the guise of ten different organizational names, but all carry Abu Nidal's fingerprints. In a rare interview in the West German weekly *Der Spiegel*, Abu Nidal stated that "I am the evil spirit of the secret services. I am the evil spirit which moves around only at night causing them nightmares." He boasts that his daughter, Bisan, has no idea who he is and what he is really up to, and that he will have no hesitation killing— as he has done in the past—his own relatives. He regrets that someone else killed President Sadat, and hopes to be consoled by assassinating President Reagan, Queen Elizabeth II, Prime Minister Thatcher, Egyptian President Husni Mubarak, Jordan's King Hussein, and Yasser Arafat, leader of the P.L.O.

He has proclaimed, "I am Abu Nidal—the answer to all Arab suffering and misfortunes." The late Dr. Issam Sartawi, a member of the P.L.O., labelled him a "psychopath." Others, relating to his boast, "Give me $400,000,000 and I will change the face of the Middle East," see him as an insane megalomaniac.

When Dr. Wadi Haddad, who had been the operations officer of the Popular Front of the Liberation of Palestine (P.F.L.P.) and the planner of the spectacular air hijackings of that period, died in 1978, the world media began searching for a new terrorist on whom to focus attention. It was then that Sabri al-Banna together with the Venezuelan terrorist Ilich Ramirez Sanchez (better known as Carlos) rose to fame as "the greatest terrorists of our time." In recent years, though, Sabri al-Banna has become sole possessor of that notorious title. His attacks on the El Al counters in Vienna and Rome in December 1985 have made him one of the most brazen terrorists in the world. Compared to him Carlos is a mere boy scout.

The actions of his group in the past decade have been mentioned in the same breath as other terrorist acts which shook the world, such as the murder of the former Italian premier, Aldo Moro, by the Red Brigades. There are those who claim that Abu Nidal has been behind the activities of the Brigades in Italy and the Baader-Meinhof group in West Germany. As is usually the case in such matters, fact and gross speculation, truth and untruth, have been woven together into a crazy patchwork in which the actual facts blur into legend and myth.

In June 1982, by almost killing the Israeli ambassador to the United Kingdom, Abu Nidal furnished Israel with the excuse to invade Lebanon. On Sunday, June 6, 1982, three days after the attack, the Israeli cabinet met for its weekly meeting. The head of the General Security Service (the Shin Bet) was invited to report to the ministers on the events in London. The head of the Shin Bet, whose responsibilities include protecting Israeli institutions and representatives abroad, described how the attackers had ambushed the ambassador as he left a dinner party at the Dorchester Hotel in the British capital. He stated that the most likely terrorist group responsible for the assault was Abu Nidal. He therefore suggested that the Prime Minister's deputy advisor on counter-terrorism, the late General Gideon Mahanaymi, who had accompanied him, should describe the nature of the organization. But before Mahanaymi had a chance to say a word, the Prime Minister, Menachem Begin, cut him short, and exclaimed: "There's no need for that. They are all P.L.O." The Chief of Staff, General Rafael Eitan, also denigrated the need for such an explanation. Even before entering the meeting, he had already known that the Abu Nidal group had been responsible for the attack. "Abu Nidal, Abu Shmidal, they're all the same," he declared.

A similar response was heard three and a half years later. After the attacks in Rome and Vienna, the head of the security service reported that this time, too, the Abu Nidal group was responsible. The minister for industry and trade, Ariel Sharon, who had been Defense Minister and chief planner of the invasion of Lebanon in 1982, expressed his opposition in a few words. "There is no need to differentiate among the organizations," was the way he put it. One aim of this book, though, is to clarify the distinctions between the various Palestinian terrorist organizations, and, specifically, to establish the special characteristics of Abu Nidal and his group. It is essential for us in the West to understand that all Palestinian organizations are **not** alike. The more they are blurred together in our minds, the less clearly we are able to think about them, or to find an appropriate way to respond to the different problems and challenges they pose.

I imagine that there is no need to stress how difficult it is to write about any contemporary organization. These difficulties increase geometrically when the organization is composed of terrorists, and especially when it is one which lays great store on obscuring reality, deliberately employing deception and secrecy. This is compounded by the fact that whatever little "hard" information is available is mainly to be found among the security services of various Western countries—and these services are not known for any magnanimity in volunteering information.

I doubt if it will ever be possible to reveal the whole truth about this organization. This book, then, is an interim report on the Abu Nidal group, and as such is obviously incomplete. It is meant to portray a Palestinian terrorist organization and to give as detailed information as possible on the circumstances surrounding its establishment, operational environment and aims. It does not claim to tell the whole story and relate all the facts. I know that I don't know everything about the group. More than trying to answer all the questions, I have tried to ask them and to bring them to the attention of the readers.

In summary, these are the most prominent characteristics of the Abu Nidal group, as far as they can be ascertained:

1. A certain dependence on Arab intelligence organizations, as well, possibly, as some in the Eastern bloc; carrying out actions for them in return for financial and logistic aid.

2. A certain independence in choosing targets and goals, primarily in regard to Israel, the Jews, Fatah, and the P.L.O.

3. Compartmentalization and a high degree of isolation and secretiveness, which limits the danger of hostile elements penetrating the organization.

4. A solid infrastructure and branches on three continents: Europe, Asia (including India and Pakistan), and Africa (Egypt and Libya).

5. A relatively high degree of professionalism and boldness.

6. Cruelty (including the murder of a relative of Abu Nidal's, Sa'id Hamami, and an attack on a group of British cripples in an Athens hotel).

7. Elimination of group members accused of treason, deviation, or desertion (a number of members of the group were murdered, primarily in Spain, as well as in Amman, at the end of 1985 over a financial dispute).

8. Use of many different aliases.

9. Use of terrorist acts to obtain "protection" money, mainly from Saudi Arabia, Kuwait, and the United Arab Emirates.

10. Readiness to send its men as mercenaries for actions on behalf of other organizations, such as the Shi'ites in southern Lebanon.

11. Actions against many targets: Israeli and Jewish targets in Western Europe, the P.L.O., Fatah, Jordan, moderate and conservative Arab countries, Egypt, and earlier against Syria as well.

12. Use of a broad range of terrorist tactics, such as hijacking planes, explosions in the air, assassinations, random shooting at institutions or individuals, blowing up cars, booby-trapped packages, etc.

13. Threats and actions against states holding members of the group in prison. These include, among others, Jordan, Kuwait, the United Arab Emirates, and Britain.

14. Presumably, no attacks in Israel itself or in the territories occupied by it.

15. Membership is restricted to Palestinians. Unlike the terrorist organizations of Habash, Hawatmah, and others, who recruit Syrian, Iraqi, Libyan, and other citizens, Abu Nidal relies only on Palestinians, primarily highly motivated young students.

This book has its origins in my work as a correspondent in London. I had the good fortune to be present on a number of occasions at the Old Bailey courtroom in London, where, between January and March 1983, three terrorists who were members of the Abu Nidal group were tried for attempting to murder Shlomo Argov, the Israeli ambassador to the United Kingdom. A large number of surprising details were revealed during the trial, not only on the attempted assassination, but also on the structure of the organization, its methods, its targets and its doctrine. The courtroom proceedings served as the primary source for the writing of this book, but are far from being my only source. Scores of meetings, interviews with the antiterrorist squad of the London police force, Israeli intelligence sources, and the staff of the Israeli embassy in Britain also aided me in my research.

As an Israeli, it was difficult for me not to take a stand or to express my feelings. I have nevertheless tried, to the best of my ability, to be an objective observer.

The general aim of this volume is to describe the Abu Nidal organization—its ideology and structure, and the character of its leader, the guiding force behind it—and at the same time to present it within a historical perspective and in its general context, given the background of the developments within the different Palestinian terrorist organizations, the disagreements between them, and the involvement of the various Arab countries and their secret services. I hope that I have succeeded in this task.

London, December 1983—Tel Aviv, December 1985

1

The Man Behind the Scenes

The telephone rang at 4:30 P.M., on June 3, 1982. A
young woman who lived on the ground floor of 52 Evelyn Gardens, in the Kensington neighborhood of London,
picked up the phone. The voice at the other end asked for
the tenant on the second floor. The young woman ran up
the stairs and knocked on the door. Na'if Rosan, half
asleep after his midday nap, opened the door and hurried
down to the public phone on the ground floor. Comrade
"al-Sayf," in a short three minute conversation, ordered
Comrade "Thabit" to act that very night. Rosan—Thabit—immediately packed all his belongings, put on a dark
sports jacket, and went to the Hilton Hotel in the center
of London. There he made a number of telephone calls,
including one to the Y.M.C.A. in Wimbledon. Marwan
al-Banna was directed to be in the lobby of the hotel
promptly at 9:30 P.M. With the next call, Hussein Sa'id—
Abduh—was also told to be at the same place and at the
same time. The two other members of the group appeared
as directed by their commander at the stated time. "The
target is the Israeli ambassador," explained Rosan. "He
is at a dinner at the Dorchester Hotel nearby. When he
leaves the hotel, we have to shoot and kill him." The
ambassador, Shlomo Argov, was indeed at a dinner tend-
ered by the Thomas de La Rue company, printer of bank-
notes. There were 83 other ambassadors at that dinner, as
well as many members of London society: police com-
missioners, ministers, senior officials, bankers, and prominent businessmen. Marwan al-Banna went back to his

9

car, which was parked in a nearby alley, and took a small brown bag from his luggage. He returned to the lobby of the hotel and immediately went into the men's room. Hussein Sa'id followed him in. When they were alone, al-Banna handed Hussein Sa'id a Polish W.Z.63 submachine gun and two magazines for the gun. Sa'id immediately hid them in a large bag hung over his shoulder. While Rosan and al-Banna were trying to relieve their tension by walking about aimlessly in the nearby streets, Hussein Sa'id briskly walked the short distance on Park Lane from the Hilton Hotel to the Dorchester. He took up a position in front of a B.M.W. showroom and waited tensely on the pavement. At exactly 11:04 P.M., Ambassador Argov stepped out of the front door of the hotel. He was engrossed in conversation with a friend, who had also attended the dinner. As with other ambassadors who were in danger of being attacked, the London police had assigned a special and permanent guard to ensure the ambassador's safety. The person assigned that night was Colin Simpson.

Simpson recalled that night: "I got to our Volvo, which was parked right near the entrance. Michael Silver, our driver, was already standing by the car and was turning off the alarm. In accordance with our drill I opened both doors on the curb side and stood between them. At that moment the ambassador arrived. He bent down somewhat and was about to enter the car. When he was about to put his head inside, I heard a noise behind me. The ambassador fell to the pavement. I looked down at him and saw what appeared then as an extremely serious wound." Simpson also noticed the slight assailant, who was running from the area. He began chasing him. The fugitive ran northward toward Marble Arch, and soon veered right toward South Street. Simpson followed him into the dark street. When they were about fifteen yards apart, he saw that the man was aiming his gun at him. Simpson drew his gun. Two shots were fired. The assailant fell onto the street. His first shot with the Polish submachine gun had missed Simpson's head by inches. Simpson's bullet, though, had hit Sa'id, entering below his right ear. The police investigators later found that the submachine gun had been set for firing single rounds, otherwise Simpson would probably have been struck several times by the twenty-four bullets remaining in the magazine.

By the time the guard retraced his steps a doctor was already attending to the gravely injured man. A few minutes later two ambulances arrived. The first brought Shlomo Argov to a special hospital in Queen Square. The second took Hussein Sa'id away. After long operations, both men survived. The ambassador remains paralyzed and in serious condition, while the Palestinian terrorist recovered and was able to stand trial with his two comrades, al-Banna and Rosan, both of whom were caught that night when they attempted to flee in their Fiat. They were each sentenced to thirty-five years in jail. The prosecutor, Roy Amlot, referred to the trial as "the Baghdad connection," and claimed in his summation that by exposing this group of Abu Nidal's men, capturing them and then sentencing them to prison, "we have managed to open a window—even if only a small one—into the secret world of this terrorist secret organization." However, even after the verdicts at the Old Bailey, there are still a number of unanswered questions.

If terror is drama and terrorists are playing in the "theater of real life," neither the court nor the police managed to learn what had happened behind the scenes of the play. The disguise has not been stripped off totally from the faces of the Abu Nidal group. Much of what had been in darkness was not subjected to the spotlights on the stage.

There was nothing surprising about what happened to Marwan Yusuf Mahmud al-Banna. Each detail of his past was a signpost to his ultimate fate, or—to be more precise—to the way he would navigate his way through life. Throughout his life it was possible to discern where the seeds of terrorism had been sown, to the extent that the tall, mustached young man who tried to put up a front of detachment and self-confidence at his trial could not possibly have chosen any other path.

He was born in Nablus, the major city on the west bank of the Jordan River, which had already been a center of political and social ferment and the molder of Palestinian nationalism as far back as the Arab uprising of 1936–1939. In Nablus, one finds almost every party and ideology of the Palestinian national movement. This extends from Ba'athists to Nasserites, from monarchists who support the Hashemite kingdom of Jordan to advocates of the Communist Party. Of course the various Palestinian terrorist organizations are also represented.

Marwan was born into this seething political cauldron in 1962. His family was a middle class one, which had lived in Jaffa during the British mandate. His father, Yusuf, owned a small fabric store by which he supported his family, modestly but adequately.

When Marwan was sixteen, some serious disturbances took place throughout the West Bank in general, and in Nablus in particular. The cause of these disturbances was President Sadat's peace initiative and his readiness to reach a settlement with Israel. Most inhabitants of the West Bank regarded this as "treason" and as "giving in to the Zionist enemy." Incited by the radio stations of Jordan, Syria, and especially the P.L.O., the inhabitants were urged to come out into the streets. And they obeyed. Demonstrations in the central square of Nablus, its market, and its schools, became daily fare. It is worth emphasizing that Sadat's initiative, which offered the hope that peace was achievable, was regarded by many in the Middle East as a total betrayal of the Palestinian cause. For the hard-line terrorists there is no possible reconciliation of differences, no conceivable peace except through the destruction of their enemies.

Among those Nablus students throwing stones was Marwan al-Banna. Whoever knew him then is convinced that President Sadat's peace initiative to Jerusalem in November 1977 was the final element in the formation of the handsome young man's ideology. Members of his family recall that it was in the winter of 1978 that Marwan decided to become more politically involved. While his father, Yusuf, wanted Marwan to continue with his studies and acquire a university degree, he saw no reason to oppose his son's plans to do otherwise.

The al-Banna family had traditionally been politically oriented. This was especially true for Yusuf's first cousins, Mahmud and Sabri. Mahmud was an exceptionally successful wholesaler of fruits and vegetables, who was known throughout the West Bank and even in Jordan for his business acumen. But in addition to being a successful businessman, Mahmud was also the brother of Sabri al-Banna, the leader of the Abu Nidal group.

When the police asked Marwan immediately after his arrest about his relatives, he at first tried to deny his family ties with Sabri. The name "al-Banna," he answered ingenuously, is a common one in the Arab world. When questioned if the name Sabri al-Banna meant anything to him, he answered laconically, "Yes, I've heard of someone like that. I think he's a distant relative." When the police pressed him as to whether he had ever met Sabri, Marwan told them emphatically that he had never done so. The truth was, of course, the exact opposite.

After Marwan al-Banna completed his high school studies in Nablus, he applied for admission to one of the colleges in Damascus. For unknown reasons, he was turned down. His despondency was soon known to many members of his family. His second cousin, Sabri al-Banna, also soon found out that Marwan had not been admitted to college. Using intermediaries, Sabri al-Banna invited Marwan to Baghdad. On November 5, 1979, Marwan left Nablus and crossed one of the Jordan River bridges, arriving eventually in the Iraqi capital. This was a trip that changed his life.

In his testimony before the British court, in which he was convicted in March 1983 of involvement in the attempt to assassinate the Israeli ambassador to Britain, Marwan stated that the aim of his visit to Baghdad had been to enroll in the technological university there. But the British police had information on his actions in that city. They regarded his story as an alibi meant to conceal the real reason for his visit: to meet Sabri al-Banna.

The meeting took place at the group's headquarters in Baghdad. Sabri suggested that Marwan join the group, undergo a series of training exercises, and then leave for a mission in London. Even though at that time Marwan knew almost nothing about the history of the group except what he had found out from his family, the idea was most appealing. Without having to worry about supporting himself, he would be able to improve his English and study computer science and physics, all of these being subjects he had loved while still in high school in Nablus. And while studying, he would be able to make his contribution to the "Palestinian revolution."

Marwan agreed to the proposal almost immediately. The balance of his week's stay in Baghdad was spent in receiving preliminary briefings from members of the group. He was given short introductions on the principles underlying the clandestine activities of the organization and the life style required to those belonging to it. The history of the group was sketched out for him, and he was sternly warned not to use the telephone unnecessarily. It was agreed that immediately following the week's instruction, he would fly to Britain, where he would stay a number of months until he could establish himself and set up a secret cell of the group in London.

The organization bought Marwan luggage, new clothes and a return-trip plane ticket. It also arranged for him to receive a visa from the British consulate in Baghdad. Exactly seven days after arriving, Marwan flew from Baghdad to London on the Iraqi national airline. The "special treatment" that he received was due not only to the fact that he was related to the leader. That might have helped, but having a representative in Britain was part of the group's overall plan.

Throughout 1979 the group carried out only three terrorist attacks, and most of that year was devoted to making plans based on the new tactics formulated by the group's leadership. That year can be seen, from this aspect, as the turning point in the history of the Abu Nidal group. During the discussions throughout that crucial year, it was decided that the focus of the group's operational activities would be shifted from the Middle East to Western Europe. This required the establishment of a suitable organizational infrastructure. The result was a decision to set up secret cells in a number of Western

European capitals, especially in London, Paris, Vienna, Rome, and Madrid.

Marwan was assigned the role of establishing the group's cell in London and of being its contact in that city. It was his responsibility to set up "safe houses" in London for future activities and to begin gathering information on security arrangements and the difficulties of smuggling arms and explosives into the country. Above all, the organization wanted him to firmly establish himself in the city with a decent cover, so that when the time came, he would be able to act without difficulty.

The major activity of such a cell was to gather intelligence information about those institutions, organizations, or individuals which might eventually become potential targets. This referred, first and foremost, to Israeli and Jewish institutions and individuals. "Mapping the terrain" was meant to pave the way for terrorist actions when headquarters decided that these should be carried out.

The leader of such a cell—and this was Marwan's role in London—was meant to serve as combination intelligence officer, quartermaster, and logistic expert. In other words, his responsibilities would include setting up a transportation system, storing arms, receiving and transmitting messages, taking care of finances, and other such duties.

Knowing the assignments that awaited him, Marwan al-Banna was relieved to find that he was able to go through passport control and the customs authorities at Heathrow without any special problems. After spending the first few days in a small, cheap hotel near the airport, he began searching for a school that would meet his needs. He finally settled on Bedford College, a small and unknown school for the English language in Bedfordshire, north of London.

About three months later, al-Banna decided to move to another school. The great advantage of Southeast London College, which he eventually chose, was that it was located in the city itself. While Bedfordshire is a beautiful green area and has all the benefits of a country setting, it has little to offer a person hoping to set up a terrorist cell. A large city, on the other hand, offers much better conditions for clandestine activity.

The British security services know full well that the scores of language schools throughout London serve as convenient centers for members of foreign terrorist groups, including, of course, those from the Middle East. Registering in such a school enables almost anyone to enter the country without having to supply the various documents needed for enrollment in an official academic institution.

But before al-Banna began his studies at the new school, he was asked to report back to Baghdad to deliver an interim report. On February 20, 1980, about three months after first arriving in Britain, he flew back to Iraq. As with his previous visit to the city, the explanation given was his desire to be accepted to the technological university in Baghdad. In reality, though, his nine-day visit was used for a feverish series of training exercises in a secret camp belonging to the organization, near the Ramadi quarter, a suburb west of the capital. It was that training, in the company of other Palestinians, that finally turned the young man into a true terrorist.

Abu Nidal's training camps are different from those of the other Palestinian organizations in Syria, Libya, Lebanon, South Yemen, or Algeria. The training is often held in small apartments. The students drill in groups of two to three. Stress is laid on loyalty, obedience to the leader, and a great degree of compartmentalization, whereby one is familiar only with a very few others in the organization.

The first Abu Nidal students were trained in Iraq, but later groups trained in Syria. Their coursework included the use of weapons, beginning with the Soviet Kalachnikov, through the use of rocket launchers and the Polish W.Z.63 submachine gun. The latter is a small weapon with a folding butt and a 25 bullet magazine, and is extremely effective. It can be used as a single-shot weapon, or can be converted to use as a submachine gun. Its 25 bullet magazine contains 9 mm. shells manufactured by the Soviet Makarov plant. Its delivery is impressive, at 600 shells per minute. The machine pistol, as it is known in Britain, is almost unobtainable in the West, but is standard issue among the Abu Nidal group. The group's squads have used this gun for many terrorist attacks in Europe and the Middle East.

In addition to instruction in the use of weapons and explosives, the Abu Nidal recruits receive lectures, actually intense indoctrination, on political topics. Many hours are devoted to condemning the Zionist enemy and the reactionary Arab regimes. The students are warned against the long arm of the Israeli Mossad, and an attempt is made to instill in them the need to use extreme caution to ensure that their identity is not exposed.

One of the rare deserters from the group, a low-level recruit named Nidal Muhammad, provided interesting insights into the training he had undergone. As reported by *Newsweek* on April 7, 1986, the training took place in a desolate Abu Nidal camp in southwestern Iraq. During the six-month course, the recruits took a six-mile run each morning, followed by four hours of physical training and daily weapons practice. In the advanced sessions, "we learned how to kill people with a variety of methods, how to enter buildings quietly, stalk people through the streets, and then escape," he said. "There were daily indoctrination classes as well. Actually we were brainwashed at the end." Muhammad now lives in a Middle Eastern capital in fear for his life. "If Abu Nidal catches me," he confessed, "I am finished."

According to British intelligence officers, the training received by Marwan al-Banna was shorter, though in general it conformed to the pattern we have just described. Like the other members of the group, he received an alias, "Iman," and was warned not to contact other members of the group except via authorized couriers, who would identify themselves only by previously-assigned passwords, code names, and aliases. No meeting was to be held without prior secret arrangement, and meetings could only take place in a public area such as a railroad station, bar, restaurant, or large department store. Time and again during their training, the new recruits were reminded that secrecy is the terrorist's best friend.

At the conclusion of these nine days of training, which was always given in small groups and inside locked courtyards by trainers who wore masks so that they could not be identified, al-Banna took a short vacation in Amman. There he met other members of the group, who were all introduced by their aliases, for further briefings.

Before returning to London, al-Banna crossed one of the Jordan River bridges and travelled to Nablus to visit his family. But as he testified, this was not before he had been "treated demeaningly" by the Israeli security officials. He was imprisoned in a tiny cell for eight hours, his belongings were checked with a fine-tooth comb, and only after an extended investigation was he allowed to proceed.

When he came home, he told his family of this event, and admitted that it had stiffened his resolve against the Israeli occupation even further. He told them—and the news was greeted with joy—of his intention to travel to London to study, but without, of course, revealing his membership in the Abu Nidal group and the real reason for his trip.

After spending a pleasant few days with his family and friends, Marwan returned to Baghdad to continue with his training. Furnished with a small piece of paper with various codes and passwords by which he would be able to identify couriers of the organization and his contacts, Marwan al-Banna was ready to return to London. He was also supplied with two numbers, one a telephone number and the other a post office box in Baghdad. He was warned that these numbers were not to be used unless a real emergency developed, in which he and his friends faced death. In his testimony, Marwan claimed that during the thirty months he was in England, he had only used the phone number four times. When questioned about two names, Ibrahim al-Banna and Ali al-Banna, which appeared next to these numbers, Marwan testified that they were friends from the technological university in Baghdad.

The prosecutor, Roy Amlot, had a different version. Using confidential information he had received from the security services, he claimed that the two numbers belonged to the Abu Nidal headquarters in Baghdad, and that the names were those of commanders of the organization, who also happened to be relatives.

Equipped with his instructions and the secret paper, Marwan al-Banna flew back to London, as he had done before, by a direct flight of the Iraqi national airline. As soon as he returned, he enrolled in a different school, Waxhall College, which is situated near the south bank of the Thames, quite close to the South Bank cultural and art center. This school prepares students—primarily foreigners—for the entrance examinations of British institutions for higher education. The classes were to begin only in September; until then he continued studying English at the Southeast London College, and resumed his social life.

As those who knew him in those days tell it, al-Banna enjoyed the good life. He spent his time in bars and pubs, where he met fellow Palestinian students. He was especially fond of a bar named the Prince of Wales, which is near the Wimbledon underground station, in the area to which he now moved. Wimbledon is a comfortable neighborhood on the western fringes of London. It is full of small shingle-roofed homes, and its residents are basically middle class. But what has made Wimbledon world famous is its tennis club. Each year, in June, the unofficial world tennis championship is held on its grass courts.

The police believe that al-Banna chose that neighborhood because of its proximity to Heathrow airport, a fact that would make it easier for couriers of the organization, who arrived periodically with money and instructions, to contact him. He found a small room that met his needs at the Y.M.C.A. hostel on Broadway, only minutes from the underground station. His room on the third floor and the pub near the station became his "offices," where he met couriers from the organization.

Marwan al-Banna, who was described by his attorney Michael Kennedy as "a talented, sensitive and intelligent young man," proved during the period of time he lived in Wimbledon that he deserved such compliments. The hostel secretary, Roger Saunders, testified in court: "Our hostel has 190 rooms, and when Marwan al-Banna arrived, we had three or four Arab students. Marwan showed a strong desire to succeed in his studies. We had a number of very general discussions. He had a fine command of English. I do not remember having any political discussions with him. In general, our Arab students were quiet and we never had any problems. Marwan was no different than the other lodgers in the hostel.''

In spite, however, of al-Banna's desire not to attract attention and to maintain a low profile, he was not able to resist fierce debates with his fellow lodgers in the hostel. In those discussions he made no attempt to hide his political ideology. In one of their discussions, he got into an extended debate with a young student from Canada, Marcus Dankley. ''He was a proud Palestinian, who would often visit Hyde Park Corner and speak there against what he termed Israeli oppression. Marwan once told me,'' said the Canadian student, ''that he had hidden a knife under his mattress. But even though he was a Palestinian, he never appeared to me to be a fanatic.'' It is possible that al-Banna was not one. But one day in the summer of 1981, he admitted to another Arab student named Ahmad Kaflazal, who also lived in the hostel, that he would be willing to commit murder if he thought the aim was just. According to him, the struggle against Zionism was within this category. Even if al-Banna tried to mask his hatred of Israel, he was not able to do so. This was even the case when his attorney literally pleaded with him not to make any controversial political statements that were liable to harm his case. ''Will it be correct to say,'' asked the prosecutor in his cross-examination, ''that you consider the Israelis to be your enemies?''

''That is correct, sir,'' was al-Banna's answer.

''And the Israeli ambassador would then also be considered your enemy?''

''Yes, that is correct, sir.'' And he continued to maintain this even though he claimed that he had not been involved in any way in the attack.

Yet, together with his strong hatred of Israel, it was quite clear in his testimony that he had ambivalent feel-

ings about the country. He veered between fierce hatred
of Israel and a certain appreciation, mixed with fear, of
the country. The extensive use that al-Banna made of all
the conspiratorial techniques he had been taught in Baghdad was due not only to his desire to protect himself from
revealing his actions, but also because of his fear of
Israel's long arm.

When he attempted to explain to the court why the
police had found documents with codes and passwords,
Marwan answered, "I wrote different notes in code to
preserve secrecy. So that anyone visiting me could do so
without worrying about his safety. So that I would know
that the people I met were friends and not enemies. People came to talk to me about the situation in Palestine,
but we were afraid that people from the wrong side would
also come to me. Here in London there is much activity
of foreign intelligence services, and it has happened more
than once that information gathered on us, the Palestinians living in Britain, was transferred by the British services to Israel, and when we visited the West Bank we
were imprisoned there by the Israeli authorities. I know
that there is close cooperation between Israeli intelligence
and British intelligence. We therefore had to use aliases
so that the intelligence services which wanted information
on us couldn't obtain it. You want to know what intelligence organization? The Israeli intelligence of course."
(Incidentally, the members of the group, including Abu
Nidal himself, are obsessed with fears of the Mossad, the
Israeli intelligence—which they regard as being almost
omnipotent—and with the international ties of the different intelligence services.)

During the five months between April and September
1981, Marwan expanded his secret work. His major aim
during that period was to gather background information
on Jewish and Israeli institutions in London. The material
was obtained from official announcements in the Jewish
and general press, and by stakeouts of these institutions,
carried out by al-Banna and other members of the London
cell, whose identity is still not known to the police.

After al-Banna was arrested on the night of the attack,
police were sent to search his room at the hostel. In addi-

tion to his schoolbooks, they also found a file on individuals, organizations, companies, stores, and Israeli and British Jewish institutions. These included newspaper clippings and photographs of the Israeli ambassador, Shlomo Argov, taken from the *Jewish Chronicle*, and a long list which resembled a "who's who" of the Jewish community. The list contained almost three hundred names, mainly of British Jews and Israelis, but also included a number of Arabs and Palestinians. Among others, the listings included the Jewish Blind Society and the license plates of all its vehicles, the Jewish college in Golders Green, and the Tel Hai Club in Compaine Gardens, West Hampstead.

Individuals listed included Sir Immanuel Jacobowitz, Chief Rabbi of Great Britain; the chief chaplain of the Israel Defense Forces, Brigadier-General Gad Navon; the chairman of the Jewish Appeal in Britain, Trevor Chin; the director-general (in Israel) of the Israel Tourism Office, Rafael Farber; the head of the Israel Tourism Bureau in Britain, Aaron Dishon; the chairman of the board of directors of the *Jewish Chronicle*, David Kessler; and the Israeli ambassador to the U.N., Yehudah Blum (with a note indicating that he was coming to London to speak at a dinner of the Jewish Appeal).

The list also included Lord Nicholas Bethel, a member of the European Parliament, noting that he was the author of the book *The Palestinian Triangle*, "a pro-Zionist and anti-Palestinian book." Also listed was an address in the Kensington neighborhood, which was that of Lady Avon, widow of Anthony Eden, the British prime minister for a number of years in the 1950's. That was the same address at which Chaim Weizmann, later to be the first president of Israel, had lived during the First World War. The fact that a small plaque indicating Weizmann's stay had been unveiled in 1981 made the location of interest to the Abu Nidal group, possibly because the former Israeli foreign minister, Abba Eban, and Ambassador Argov had been present at the unveiling. The documents included the address of Greville Janner, a Member of Parliament who also served as president of the Jewish Board of Deputies.

Organizations on the list included the Institute of Jewish Affairs, founded by the World Jewish Congress, and the Habad school, established by the Lubavich Rabbi of Brooklyn (including the license plates of all the vehicles used in transporting its children to school).

But that wasn't all. Together with the Jewish and Israeli notations, there were important Arab names. Among others, these included the addresses of the Jordanian, Moroccan, Saudi, Egyptian, Kuwaiti and UAE embassies. Dr. Henry Kissinger appeared, as did Muhammad Milhim, who by then had been ousted by the Israeli military from his position as mayor of Halhul, and who was later appointed to the P.L.O. Executive Committee.

Finally, there was the name of a Saudi newspaper published in London, listing its office address near Fleet Street. Was it merely coincidence that barely two months after the attack on Ambassador Argov a bomb exploded in these offices in August 1982, miraculously injuring no one and causing no property damage? The British intelligence services do not think so. They believe that the Abu Nidal group, using Marwan al-Banna's cell, gathered information on the newspaper. This information was sent in coded form to Baghdad, from which instructions were later sent to bomb the offices. This was meant to be the fate of the other individuals and institutions on the list.

Al-Banna's explanation for the existence of these extensive lists was simplicity itself. He repeated his version of this twice, in his interrogation and within the courtroom. "I gathered the information about the institutions and individuals over a number of months. I did this so that it could be used by the political wing of the Palestinian National Liberation Movement, to which I belonged. I am active, but not a registered member of the organization, and did what I did only for political aims. I gathered the material for the purpose of collecting information. We wanted to strip the mask from these institutions and places. We know that many of them are actually fronts for the Mossad, the Israeli secret service, or are potential centers for Israeli intelligence. We only wanted to reveal their true identity and publish it, so as to warn the Arabs away from these people and places, and so that they would not to come into contact with them.''

When al-Banna was asked why Palestinian Arabs needed to gather information on Arab institutions as well, he answered, ''There are many groups that are ostensibly on our side but are in reality against us, such as Saudi Arabia. The wealthy men of Saudi Arabia supervise that newspaper in London.''

The British sensationalist press latched onto the list found in the Y.M.C.A., as if it had discovered a long-lost treasure. The press soon dubbed it the ''hit list.'' But the police investigators were highly dubious of this. According to them, the list was primarily meant for background information, to be filed within the intelligence archives of the Abu Nidal group, and was certainly not meant for immediate use. This was raw data for future actions. It is reasonable to assume that copies of al-Banna's list were shipped by couriers to the group's headquarters in Baghdad, and from there to the operations department of the organization.

Marwan al-Banna himself admitted in the Old Bailey: ''I began collecting the material about half a year after I arrived in Britain. During these two years [May 1980 to June 1982] I sent out about seven or eight such documents. It was political material sent to political friends in Jordan.''

The couriers who collected the materials from Comrade ''Iman'' also brought him in return coded messages and funds sent by the direct orders of the leader of the group, Sabri al-Banna. Marwan's meetings with these couriers took place in public areas, exactly as outlined in the course he had taken. Al-Banna revealed a little of the workings of these mysterious contacts in the police investigation. He mentioned that the courier would generally call from his hotel to the Y.M.C.A. hostel. After identifying himself with the correct password and thus proving that he was an official messenger, he would ask al-Banna to come to his hotel. There, preferably in the lobby or in a restroom, ''Iman'' would hand over the documentation or information he had been asked to provide, and would receive in return cash or even arms or explosives. The cash was meant to pay for his living expenses and for various expenses relating to the London cell's activities, such as purchasing a car, paying the rent of the cell members, buying newspapers, etc.

One such meeting took place in May, just before the attack on the Israeli ambassador. Marwan al-Banna received a telephone message and came to the Hilton Hotel, in the center of London. In his courtroom testimony, he tried to hide the true character of this meeting, and claimed that he had met with a family friend who brought him cash and regards from his father.[1]

"How did you receive the money?" asked the prosecutor.

"From my father; he sent it to me."

"Your father is very generous, right?"

"He loves me."

"Who brought you the money?"

"Friends of my father. These people would bring me cash. Sometimes they brought me $2000 they carried on them."

"From your father?"

"That is correct. For example, in May I received money from Jamal al-Shahruri, my father's friend, at the Hilton Hotel."

"Where is he now?"

"In the West Bank. He is a businessman."

"How does your father have enough savings to send you money in London?"

"He sent it to me, but I ask the court not to reveal the sources of my father's income, because it may affect his safety and that of my family."

"The truth is your movement sent you money," stated the prosecutor.

"That isn't true, that doesn't happen in the Palestinian camp!" screamed Marwan al-Banna.

What Marwan did not know was that the Israelis already knew of his actions. His father, Yusuf, was visited the day after the attack by a man named Abu Ghazal, who, according to the *Guardian*, was employed by the

---

[1] Translated from the author's Hebrew notes taken at the trial.

Israeli General Security Service. The week before, Marwan al-Banna had contacted his father in Nablus and had asked him to send 500 pounds sterling, promising that he would return home for a vacation in July, after completing his examinations at Waxhall College. But al-Banna never wrote the examinations. And even had he taken them, it is doubtful if he would have passed because his extensive involvement in his work for the organization took most of his time.

In fact, even before beginning his first year of formal college studies, al-Banna had left Britain. Unlike most of his trips, which were to Baghdad, this one in August 1980 was to Jordan. Intelligence sources believe that this trip combined a mission on behalf of the group with a private visit to his family.

When he returned to London, he began studying physics, but at the same time continued with his clandestine work. In April 1982 the group's leaders asked him to go to Paris. The police have no evidence of the purpose of this hasty two-day trip. Al-Banna himself volunteered the explanation that he went with a friend named Ahmad to spend a short vacation in the French capital. But the police don't believe his explanation. It is more likely that he was sent on behalf of the organization, possibly to transfer money, conceivably even weapons, or to meet with a senior member of the group. While they have no clear proof of it, the investigators do not exclude the possiblity that it was in Paris that Comrade "Iman" met Comrade "Thabit," who would, about two months thereafter, play a decisive role in his life. What is clear is that when he returned from Paris to London, he became even more involved in his clandestine work, and strengthened his ties with "Abduh."

2

"Abduh"

"Abduh" was slight, short and pale. His eyes were prominent, and his nose was slightly aquiline. He was a Palestinian who dreamed secretly of taking vengeance on the Zionists who had stolen his homeland, and concocted plans for waging war against the imperialist agents. Hussein Ahmad Ghasan Sa'id was born in 1959 in Jaba, a large village of 5000 souls, halfway between Nablus and Jenin on the West Bank. The village had achieved considerable fame in the past because of its olive groves. Its stone homes are built on the rocky hill slopes, overlooking the valley below.

For hundreds of years, the Sa'id family were farmers, seemingly like all the other villagers. In reality, however, they also served other functions. Secret agents of the Hashemite Kingdom would visit the family relatively frequently in the middle of the night, to root out those suspected of hostile acts against King Hussein's government. Later, when the village passed into Israeli control in 1967, the family's name continued cropping up at the military administration as a supporter of the Palestinian organizations.

Hussein Sa'id's childhood was normal in every respect, as he wrote in a letter to the attorney who defended him on charges of having attacked Ambassador Argov. He went to the local village school. His father had two wives, and Hussein was the oldest child. His father later had two more sons and two daughters from his first wife and a daughter and two sons from his second wife.

When he was eight years old, Hussein witnessed what he claimed later was to become the decisive event in his life, and to affect his future more than any other. An Israeli tank column entered Jaba after the 1967 war. "I had no special political opinions, except for the fact that I had known from earliest childhood that our country had been conquered, and I didn't like that," he wrote in his letter to his attorney.

After graduating from the local elementary school, he continued at a high school in Nablus. Two years later Marwan al-Banna would also study in that same school, but they probably did not know each other well. Yet, as fate would have it, they both eventually took part in a common mission thousands of miles from Nablus.

When he completed his high school studies, Hussein travelled to Amman, hoping to enter the university there. His father, who had moved to Abu Dhabi earlier in order to do better than he could as a farmer, promised to pay for Hussein's studies. But to his great chagrin, he failed the entrance examinations and had to return to his native village. "When I was told I had failed the entrance examinations, it appeared to me that my entire world had collapsed. I was depressed and didn't know what to do with myself."

For a number of months he earned his livelihood at various odd jobs in his village and in Nablus itself. He then decided to follow in his father's footsteps and move to Abu Dhabi. Literally at the last minute, as he was set to leave, friends told him of another possibility. It seemed that there were Spanish universities that were willing to accept Arab and Palestinian students without raising any major obstacles.

Hussein Sa'id left home in September 1978, and after arriving in Amman, used the meager savings he had left to buy a plane ticket to Madrid. At first he had considerable problems adjusting, and spent much time simply walking back and forth in the city. He finally met a group of Palestinian students who showed him the ropes. He found himself a small and cheap room near the Plaza del Sol in the Old City, and began attending an intensive course in Spanish for beginners.

Spain of the end of the 1970's, when constitutional monarchy under King Juan Carlos was still fighting for its life, was wide open for the activities of the Palestinian organizations. The absence of diplomatic relations between Spain and Israel, and the hopes of the young Spanish democracy to serve as a bridge between Europe and the Arab world, enabled the Palestinian organizations to act almost undisturbed within the country. Such actions, of course, drew the attention of the Israeli security services. In January 1973, Baruch Cohen was killed on Jose Antonio Avenue, one of the most important and beautiful streets of the Spanish capital. Eyewitnesses claimed that they had seen two men "of Arab appearance" speeding away from the scene. The Spanish police transferred to Israel all the information they had accumulated about the murder, but there was not much.

Baruch Cohen was a member of the Israeli security services, whose mission had been to operate a network of Arab informers. He managed to recruit a number of Palestinian students who passed on to him important information on the actions of the Palestinian organizations. The Black September organization (which was set up by the Fatah leadership) evidently found out the identity of the Israeli agent and decided to set a death trap for him.

The Spanish security services were indeed concerned about the large contingent of Palestinian students in their country. They knew that the Palestinian terrorist organizations were aiding the Basque separatist movement, E.T.A., with both arms and training, but the government preferred to ignore this and to continue its lenient policies toward the Arab states and the Palestinians. This was the Spain that Hussein Sa'id found. It was a friendly country and offered him also an exciting social life.

At the university, Sa'id met a young woman named Isabel, and through her got to know other students, most of them of either Arab or Palestinian origin. During long meetings extending into the wee hours at the small cafes near the university, most of their discussions revolved around politics, Palestine, and the struggle against Israel. From these discussions, Sa'id became convinced that he had to do more for his people, and it was proposed that he join the Abu Nidal group.

According to a number of security services in Western Europe, Madrid serves as one of the major centers of the Abu Nidal group in Europe. A British intelligence officer who asked to remain anonymous told the author that "according to reliable information in our possession, it has been clearly proven that the Spanish capital was an important source for recruiting young Arab students of Palestinian origin to the Abu Nidal organization. Madrid was also its forward command post in Europe, and it was from there that instructions and couriers went out ordering terrorist acts throughout the continent."

Was it only coincidental, the prosecutor in the trial in London asked, that "Abduh" and "Thabit," whom we will meet later, both came on the same day, January 15, 1982, to the Spanish consulate in London? And why did they both fill out visa application forms whose numbers are consecutive (539 and 540)? And was it again a coincidence that both marked down the same day (February 15, 1982), as the date they expected to make their trip to Spain? Police investigators believe that this is additional proof of the importance of Spain as a center for the group's actions.

The London police are convinced that Hussein visited Baghdad at least once during the eighteen months he was in Spain. At that time he took an intensive course, similar to that taken by al-Banna, at the group's training camps.

Over the course of time, Hussein Sa'id proved that this indoctrination had not been in vain. In his testimony in the Old Bailey he admitted that "the Israeli ambassador is my enemy, and I am not sorry about what happened to him." As for the Jews, he stated, "The Jews have many activities and I wanted to know about them. I wanted to investigate the actions of the Jewish organizations. One cannot forget that the Jews have a certain involvement in whatever happens in Palestine. I therefore wanted to expose their actions and to prove that not only are the Israelis against us, against the Palestinian people, but also the Jews in every place."

It is difficult, of course, to establish what exactly Hussein did in Madrid. The police investigators do not have any clear report on what he was up to there. The only incontrovertible fact is that he left the Spanish capital in March 1980. "The courses were too hard," he explained in court, "so I decided to return to Jordan." But it is difficult to ignore the following coincidence. In that same month, a Spanish lawyer, Adolfo Cottelo, was gunned down in front of his wife and children, as he got out of his car in the parking lot of a building in the middle of Madrid. The attackers had mistaken him for Max Mazin, a Jewish businessman, whose offices are also in that building. A young Palestinian, who admitted to belonging to the Abu Nidal group, was sentenced in a Madrid court to 29 years' imprisonment. The police were not able to elicit from him the names of the other members of the gang involved. The London and Madrid police believe, however, that Hussein Sa'id left Spain because he had been involved in the murder.

It is known that Hussein flew from Madrid to Amman, and from there found his way to his home village, and that a few months later he was ordered to appear at the organization's headquarters in Baghdad. After a tiring bus ride from Amman through the desert to Baghdad, he arrived at the group's command post, to be given a new assignment. He was told that in a fortnight he was to fly to London and enroll in an English language school, following which he was to try to enter a local university. The aim of the organization was to "plant" him in the British capital for a lengthy period of time, and to activate him when the appropriate moment arrived.

Hussein Sa'id remained in Baghdad for a few more days, until a British visa was arranged for him. The organization's treasurer gave him new suitcases, a round trip ticket, and a few hundred pounds sterling, which were meant to support him for a number of months.

On September 17, 1980, Hussein flew to London. He went through passport control at Heathrow without any difficulty. Unlike Marwan al-Banna, he soon had financial problems; this, coupled with the need for secrecy, made him move from one residence to the next. He was registered in, and left, a number of schools for the English language, first the Regent School of English on Oxford Street, afterwards Francis College in Wimbledon. But he couldn't afford to live in that area, and was forced to seek accommodations in the cheaper neighborhoods of Totting and Brixton. As opposed to Marwan al-Banna, who was related to the leader of the organization and thus enjoyed a constant infusion of funds and financial aid, Hussein Sa'id received only minimal sums. He tried to obtain a work permit, but the British immigration authorities turned down his request. Having little choice, he tried to find employment at a Lebanese restaurant in the center of the city. He was fired after the first month. His despondent mood can be seen in his diary at the time, the central themes of which are despair, self-criticism, and disappointment. "Five months have passed," he writes, "and what have I done until now? Nothing. I am following a path whose beginning I don't know and whose end is unclear to me. I must stop and think. I must act. The intellectual emptiness is killing me. I must set a daily agenda and a program. I don't have a steady girl friend, and that is also a serious problem, for which only the future will have a solution."

Sa'id's lawyer, Rock Tanzi, a well-known criminal lawyer, tried to submit the diary as evidence of the intellectual doubts of a student and the soul-searching of a sensitive young man. His other lawyer, Michel Tayci, claimed that his client had the soul of a poet. The irony is that the lawyer's name also appeared in the list of cell members. Michel Tayci is a member of a Palestinian family from East Jerusalem which moved to Britain at the end of the 1950's. Michel received a superior education in the best private schools in the country. When he completed his studies and passed the bar, his nationalist sentiments were awakened, and he offered his services to the P.L.O. at reduced fees. For a number of years he was one of the lawyers helping the P.L.O. office in London. Tayci received the news of his inclusion on Abu Nidal's lists without raising an eyebrow, and as a seasoned lawyer continued to defend Hussein Sa'id to the best of his ability.

It is possible that Tayci was correct when he asserted that Hussein Sa'id had intellectual pretensions, which were expressed in his efforts to read poetry and study music. The very day, however, that his diary seemed to portray Hussein as a sensitive young man, there were other entries in it about his other activities, which were less bohemian and more clandestine. "As to work, I must begin to concentrate on an embassy, an airline company, and a newspaper," he wrote. These were, respectively, the Israeli embassy, El Al, and the *Jewish Chronicle*.

Together with his underground work, Hussein continued studying English, and enrolled in a preparatory course for the entrance examinations to the university. In September 1981 he began to study at Waxhall College. While his financial situation hadn't improved, his spirits did. He found more than enough time for his studies, his work for the group, and a tempestuous social life. He spent his time among friends, primarily female friends, in pubs near the college and at International House, a school and social club for foreign students located on Picadilly Street in the heart of the city. He was seen there, often vigorously pursuing the female students. His knowledge of Spanish helped him with young women from the Iberian Peninsula.

The fact that he was a womanizer came through clearly during his trial. In addition to his girl friend Isabel from Barcelona, another six young women whose company he used to keep were mentioned in the trial, including two young Frenchwomen named Pascal and Mercedes, with whom he had spent time at a small pub on Tottenham Court Road, just hours before the attack on the ambassador.

In spite of his life style, however, Hussein Sa'id never forgot the goal for which he had been sent to London. Couriers from Baghdad or Amman contacted him, using passwords, and met him on a regular basis. The meetings were held in railroad stations, pubs, or hotels, and were meant to provide information or small sums of money from the movement, and for him to deliver progress reports to the central command, via the couriers.

As mentioned earlier, Sa'id would frequently move from one room to the next, reducing the danger of his being trailed and obscuring his tracks. Later, when both he and al-Banna were enrolled at Waxhall College, they had an excellent cover for what appeared to be chance meetings. In encounters in the college cafeteria or library, "Iman" and "Abduh" traded information and evaluated the progress of their clandestine work.

At a given point, Sa'id was ordered to follow the movements of certain specific individuals: Israelis, Jews, and even Palestinians. The P.L.O. representative in London, Dr. Nabil Ramlawi, whose name was also on al-Banna's list, recalled how he had spoken to Sa'id during a Palestinian students' conference in November 1981. After the fact, the P.L.O. representative reached the conclusion that Sa'id's aim at that meeting had been to gain information on Ramlawi's daily routine, so that the Abu Nidal group could attempt to murder him when the time came.

The surveillance of the Israeli ambassador was more complex. There is no doubt that Sa'id, together with other members of the group whose identity the London police have not been able to uncover, kept the embassy on High Street in Kensington under scrutiny.

The Israeli embassy is a magnificent three-story Edwardian-style building, which was built at the turn of the century and later refurbished. It had belonged to the Montefiore family, which presented it as a gift to the Israeli government. A little further along the street is King Hussein's private home. According to various sources, a number of secret meetings took place in this residence between King Hussein and various Israeli ministers and senior officials during the 1970's. In October 1985 there was a meeting there between the king and Shimon Peres, the Israeli prime minister, on the peace process in the Middle East.

Both buildings were put under surveillance by Sa'id and his comrades in the organization. The detailed information which was gleaned, including the security arrangements of the buildings both indoors and out, were sent by Sa'id, via al-Banna and different couriers, to the Abu

Nidal intelligence department in Baghdad, where it was
sorted and evaluated, to be used in operations against both
targets.

But "Iman" and "Abduh" were not always careful in
their work. Sa'id's fingerprints were found on textbooks
and on documents of the movement found in al-Banna's
room at the Y.M.C.A. hostel, while Sa'id's personal
phone book, found in his room on Brixton Road, contained the phone number of Marwan al-Banna, immediately after the numbers of three of Sa'id's girl friends.
Other documents were also found in his room. When Roy
Amlot, the prosecutor, asked Sa'id about the phone numbers, he answered that he had taken them out of the London phone directory. "They asked me to do it, and I
therefore copied out the addresses and phone numbers."

"Did you think they might be targets for terrorist
attacks?"

"No. I didn't think about that."

"Who asked you to gather the material?"

"Someone named Abd al-Rahim Sa'id."

3

The Commander

Abd al-Rahim Sa'id was either a figment of the imagination or was known to many by another name, "Thabit." He was the commander. The very appearance of the solidly built man, of medium height and with black hair, proclaimed this. His expressionless face never gave away what he was thinking. When he was on the witness stand he said what he had to say in a quiet voice, clearly and confidently. Mustafa al-Mahruki, a tall, young bespectacled Egyptian who serves as a court interpreter from Arabic to English at the Central Criminal Court in the Old Bailey, London, spent forty days at the side of "Thabit." He was very taken by his strong presence: "It was easy to be impressed by him. He had the authoritative personality of a military commander."

And these were the very qualities that Na'if Najib Miflal Rosan tried to conceal from those who came in contact with him. He was in many ways an actor, but as John Le Carré wrote, his theater was that of real life. He tried to mask his callous nature by displaying the helplessness of one who has been abused by life. "I was born in Deir Yasin and that is in essence the story of my life," he said in his courtroom testimony. "I was born in 1946 in a small village near Ramla. Its name was Deir Yasin. The village no longer exists. It was destroyed off the face of the earth by Mr. Menahem Begin and his fellow terrorists. Mr. Begin is now the prime minister of Israel. In its place the Israelis put up a new settlement. I am a Palestinian, and at the age of two my family, whose home had been destroyed, was forced to move to a refugee camp on the West Bank, and after living there a number of months in poverty, we moved to east of the Jordan. There we settled in a small village named Rosan, near Irbid.''

The suspect, who denied any involvement in the attempted assassination, stopped speaking in his monotonous tone for a while. After a short pause to impress the judge and jury, he continued with his life story, or what he claimed was his life story. ''I am a Palestinian, son of a refugee family, which suffered its entire life. I went to school in the village where we lived. This was a small village of Palestinian refugees, and most families there adopted the name 'Rosan' as their family name. After completing elementary school, I continued in high school. In 1966 I tried to find work in Jordan. But economic conditions were very bad, and I couldn't find a job. I therefore travelled to Iraq. I was there for about four years, and in 1971 returned to Jordan, with renewed hope of finding work. But when this time as well my hopes were dashed, I went to Algeria to study mechanics at the national aeronautics school. I was awarded a study scholarship and a stipend for my living expenses. I finished the course within a year, and have a diploma to show this.

''From Algeria I moved to Damascus, hoping again to find a livelihood. When I couldn't find this in the Syrian capital, I decided to return to Iraq in 1973. I was fortunate in obtaining a job, in those years which were prosperous ones. I worked within my field, as a mechanic in a small store near the Baghdad market until 1981. At that time I decided to change my life-style and to infuse it with greater content and significance. I therefore came to England, where I was arrested even though I am innocent. This is the true story of my life. This and no other.''

It appears that Rosan's attempt to sketch out his life in broad strokes as the son of penniless refugees whose life was one long struggle to find employment, was at least partially correct. Even a respected paper such as the London *Times* tended to believe it, as did his attorney, Lord Anthony Gifford, known among his fellow professionals

for his radical views. As a member of a wealthy aristo-
cratic family, Gifford inherited the title "Lord" from his
father. Unlike many of his class and his profession, however, he became a socialist. His contacts with leftist cir-
cles made him take an interest in and identify with the
Palestinian problem. After the Lebanese war, he served
as the legal advisor to the "International Committee"
which investigated Israel's actions and found it guilty of
war crimes.

Even though he was appointed by the court like the
other defense lawyers, it was clear that, unlike his colleagues, Lord Gifford identified to a great extent with his
client and with the cause he represented. It is therefore
not surprising that he tried to make the trial political, and
continued with the line of defense used by his client in
portraying him as a victim of the political circumstances
in the Middle East. "Rosan is an honest man," stated
Lord Gifford in his summation, "and you the members of
the jury must weigh in his case the terrible background
behind this trial. The terrible suffering of the Palestinians.
The history of the establishment of the State of Israel. The
annexation of the West Bank to Israel. The eviction of
people from their land. The childhood of my client was
lived under the cloud of the destruction of his village.
Deir Yasin was wiped off the face of the earth by a terrorist organization led by Mr. Begin. When Rosan told
this court that he supports the Palestinian guerrillas who
are fighting the Zionist enemy, this is the political statement of a person whose land was conquered by a foreign
power. One can understand this as the instinctive reaction
of a person who has suffered so much."

All in all, Rosan appeared to have led a hard life, and
everyone should have been filled with pity at his sad saga.
The truth, though, is totally different. Whoever was in the
court and knows a little of the geography of Israel would
immediately realize that he wasn't born in Deir Yasin.
Would anyone born in that village, which is on the outskirts of Jerusalem in what is now known as Givat Sha'ul,
claim that his birthplace was near Ramla, which is about
twenty miles west of Jerusalem? When this was pointed
out to Lord Gifford after the trial, he answered with char-

acteristic cynicism, tinged with a trace of embarrassment: "So, what can we do if Rosan doesn't know the geography of his homeland?" The fact is that the story of being born in Deir Yasin was invented out of whole cloth, meant to serve Rosan's defense. It was too good a story to miss—especially as the use of Deir Yasin as a rallying cry is a common technique of the Abu Nidal group. As was discovered after the trial, Palestine was not his homeland.

Actually, contrary to what he told the court in the Old Bailey, Na'if Rosan was one of the highest commanders of the Abu Nidal group. In spite of his passport, Rosan was not an Iraqi. He was born in the village of Rosan, near Irbid in north Jordan. He was a member of a large and influential Bedouin family which was part of the traditional Hashemite establishment of the Jordanian administration. This was an establishment that always supported the monarchy, and which sided with it in its battles against the Palestinians, who constitute more than half the total population in the kingdom. The Rosan family was no exception. Its sons were loyal to the monarchy and served faithfully in the Arab Legion of King Abdallah and his grandson, King Hussein.

As others in his family, Na'if also volunteered to serve in his king's army. He entered the air force in the mid-1960's, and was employed at the Mafraq base as a mechanic. At a certain point, however, he became the "black sheep" of the family. In 1969 a change occurred in his life. His loyalty to the monarchy waned during that period. For three years King Hussein used an iron fist in his battle against Fatah and other terrorist organizations—an iron fist enforced by his Bedouins and complemented by an efficient intelligence service.

However, after the 1967 war Hussein's iron fist had been clothed in a velvet glove. He had succumbed to pressure by both Egypt and Syria to allow the Palestinian organizations to ensconce themselves in the eastern part of Jordan (the western part had been occupied by Israel in the 1967 war), and to set up a "terrorist state," in reality a quasi-independent entity, which quarreled constantly with the central government in Amman. The Palestinian organizations began entrenching themselves in Jordan soon after the 1967 war. Having failed in their attempts to establish a strong base on the Israeli-occupied West Bank, they decided to set up shop on the east bank of the Jordan. They enjoyed a certain degree of power there and maintained a territorial base in the Jordan valley, close to the border with Israel.

After Israel struck their main base in Karameh in March 1968, most of the Palestinian organizations decided to spread their forces throughout Jordan, rather than concentrate them close to the Israeli border. For two years they used Hussein's hospitality to strengthen their position in the country, in essence creating a state within a state.

The radical organizations among these, such as Dr. George Habash's Popular Front for the Liberation of Palestine (P.F.L.P.) and Na'if Hawatmah's Democratic Front for the Liberation of Palestine (D.F.L.P.), began to question the very legitimacy of the central government. They coined the slogan, "The road to Tel Aviv runs through Amman." Perceiving Jordan as a weak state, they hoped to foment a revolution, which would be the first stage in "the liberation of Palestine."

The P.F.L.P. was founded on July 12, 1967, as three small terrorist groups, the Youth of Vengeance, which was the military arm of the Pan-Arab "Nationalist Arabs" headed by Dr. George Habash; the Return Heroes, a pro-Egyptian organization composed of opponents of Ahmad al-Shuqayri, the then chairman of the P.L.O.; and the Palestinian Liberation Front, sponsored by Syria and led by Ahmad Jibril and Ahmad Za'rur, all combined. The leader of the combined organization was Habash.

From the beginning the Popular Front adopted a Marxist ideology, as well as the slogans and terminology of that ideology. Its aim was to fight not only Zionism, but also "international imperialism" and the "reactionary forces" in the Arab world. According to the Popular Front and the Democratic Front established by Na'if Hawatmah in October 1968 when he broke away from Habash, Hussein was a "reactionary who serves American imperialism," and thus should be toppled. This view echoed that of the "popular war" which Fatah had preached, under Syria's influence, in the years preceding the Six Day War.

After the war, the radical organizations influenced by the Vietcong doctrine and the lesson learned from Vietnam, believed that their short-term goal had to be the establishment of a type of "Arab Hanoi," from which the struggle could be launched against Israel, utilizing the armed Arab revolt that would break out in the "Israeli Saigon," or the occupied territories. Thus, just as North Vietnam had helped the Vietcong forces by setting up within its own borders logistic and training camps from which the Vietcong had attacked the south, Jordan had to serve as the Palestinian base, or the springboard for attacking Israel and destroying Zionism.

One should point out, though, that over a period of time another element was added to the equation. Not only did these organizations engage in undermining the Hussein government as part of their own doctrine, they also became the tools of different Arab regimes. Almost all of them developed ties with one or another of the Arab states. These ties enabled them to obtain arms, volunteers, and funds, to the extent that a number of them became not only the executors of the orders of their patrons, but actually their agents.

Radical states such as Iraq, Syria, and Libya used the Palestinian organizations to settle accounts with their enemies, or, as in the case with Hussein, to undermine other regimes. In reality, in the period between 1967 and 1970, the Palestinian organizations became totally subservient to the secret services of different Arab regimes, the most active of which was Iraq. The Iraqi division stationed in the Jordan valley, ostensibly assigned to protect Hussein against Israel, had a separate Palestinian commando unit within it. While the function of the division, when first deployed just before the 1967 war as part of a display of Arab unity, had indeed been the protection of the king, the commando unit had become a center of support for the Palestinian organizations determined to overthrow Hussein. The intelligence officers of this unit in particular, and of the division as a whole, were in direct contact with the Iraqi embassy in Amman, and were involved in incitement against and the undermining of the regime. The unit also recruited agents to oppose the Hashemite kingdom.

It was during that time that Iraqi intelligence recruited Na'if Rosan to betray his own country and serve another. As with others, his motives were probably a mixture of a desire to earn easy money, political naiveté, personal frustration, and ideological belief. In any event, Rosan was persuaded to throw in his lot with the Iraqis.

For approximately two years Rosan passed on vital information about the Jordanian air force and its war plans to the Iraqis. When King Hussein crushed the Palestinian organizations in September 1970 ("Black September"), Na'if Rosan deserted the Jordanian air force and fled to Iraq. As a reward for the services he had rendered them, Rosan's superiors sent him to study at the national aeronautical school in Algeria. When he completed the course in 1972, he was sent for further training in the Soviet Union.

Having completed that course as well, Rosan returned to Baghdad, where the intelligence command helped him receive a genuine Iraqi passport, which deliberately falsified facts and listed his birthplace as Baghdad. When the Jordanian authorities found out Rosan's treachery, they were livid with rage. First, he had betrayed King Hussein while still serving in the Jordanian army. This was compounded by his being a member of a renowned Bedouin family which had long been loyal to the king. He was sentenced to death in *absentia*.

Either at the end of 1974 or the beginning of 1975, when the Abu Nidal organization was being set up, Rosan's superiors in the Iraqi secret service decided that he was to join this organization and to act as one of its contacts within the new group. The British *Guardian*, quoting Jordanian and Palestinian sources, claimed immediately after his trial in London that Na'if Rosan had over the years become the number two man in the special operations department of the Abu Nidal organization, and had, in this capacity, been responsible for planning the terrorist attack on the Intercontinental Hotel in Amman in November 1976.

In March 1981 Rosan was sent to Paris, where he remained for four months, supervising efforts to set up an underground cell of the Abu Nidal organization in the city and attempting to build contacts with the local *Action Direct* (Direct Action) terrorist group.

Rosan's ability to plan and execute difficult operations so impressed his superiors in Iraqi intelligence that they granted him the honorary rank of colonel in the Iraqi army. To this day, his family in Irbid continues receiving monthly salary payments from the Palestinian department of Iraqi intelligence.

When Rosan arrived in London on October 21, 1981, he had come to take charge of the underground cell established during the previous two years by Marwan al-Banna and Hussein Sa'id.

Of course, the immigration control officers at Heathrow airport knew nothing of his past. There was no apparent reason for him not to be what he purported to be. He carried a genuine Iraqi passport issued in March 1980, which stated clearly that he had been born in Baghdad. Claiming that he was a carpet merchant who had come to Britain to both further his business interests and learn English, Rosan produced Iraqi bank receipts showing that he possessed the respectable sum of $13,000. He was thus immediately admitted to the country.

After arriving in London, "Thabit," as he was known in the underground, contacted "Iman" and "Abduh." They both suggested he enroll at the Regent School of English, where Sa'id was studying. A short time later, however, Rosan decided to move to Wimbledon and to Francis College. In court, Rosan claimed that he had never met Hussein Sa'id and had no idea who he was. The fact, however, that his room contained English textbooks with Sa'id's stamp in them persuaded the police investigators, the judge, and the jury that he was lying. His notebooks also contained words which are not part of the normal vocabulary of a carpet merchant, such as "infidel," "kidnapping," and "assault."

At the end of March, the "merchant"/terrorist moved to a new apartment at 52 Evelyn Gardens in South Kensington, a common neighborhood for Middle Easterners staying in the British capital. His room, from which he planned and organized the Abu Nidal cell's actions in London, had a special advantage. It was close to the Iraqi embassy. As Rosan told the court, he had often met friends and acquaintances in the lobbies of fancy hotels such as the Intercontinental and Hilton, in whose vicinity he would also be on the night of the attack on the Israeli ambassador.

As a former soldier, Rosan wanted to remain physically fit, and he and al-Banna together used the sports facilities of the Y.M.C.A. in Wimbledon. Above all, however, Rosan was involved in organizing the cell and preparing it for action. To be able to do so, he was in constant contact with the offices of the military attaché of the Iraqi embassy on Queen's Gate. The office staff there were always ready to help him. Whatever information was gleaned from al-Banna and Sa'id was always sent to him before being forwarded for evaluation by the group's command.

Rosan's task was to choose a target among the three hundred names of individuals and organizations which had been gathered. When he was arrested, the police investigators found in Rosan's room at Evelyn Gardens an article from the *Daily Telegraph* on the Israeli Mossad, as well as a detailed list of a number of Israeli institutions. That list also had on it the fingerprints of both al-Banna and Sa'id. It included the Israeli embassy in Britain, the El Al offices, two branches of Bank Leumi, the Israeli Tourist Office, and the address of the representative of the Israeli Broadcasting Authority in London.

The English translation of the document, as presented in court, showed clearly that the first plan involved "the Zionist embassy." Next to it was a list—whose detail amazed the security experts—of the security arrangements in the embassy. A sketch showed the entranceway to the embassy from Kensington High Street. The sketch also showed the exact locations of doors leading into the embassy. A note on the side stated that "at the entranceway from the street is a barrier, and next to it is a guard-house, where a guard operates the barrier. Fifteen yards beyond that, opposite the embassy building, is another guardhouse made of glass, where an armed policeman is located, even though he carries no heavy arms. The policeman observes all those who pass back and forth in front of him.'' Details followed on the number of British and Israeli guards protecting the building. ''Closed-circuit television and an alarm system protect the embassy build-ing,'' the note went on, ''together with heavy wooden, steel-plated doors.'' Further on, all the internal security devices were listed, as well as the location of doors inside the building.

Rosan's room also turned up similar detailed descrip-tions of the Israeli Tourist Bureau, the El Al offices, and those of the Jewish weekly, the *Jewish Chronicle*, with a note that the latter was an excellent target, and could well serve as the next one.

It thus appears that Rosan and his cell planned to act against one of the seven targets on the short list found in his room. When they considered where to strike, how-ever, they did not limit themselves to possible Israeli or Jewish targets; they also included Arab targets in their plans. Almost all the Arab embassies of those regimes considered to be ''moderate'' or pro-Western were on Rosan's list. Only the embassies of the radical Arab states, such as Libya, Syria, South Yemen, and of course Iraq, were not included.

The documents that were found also gave details about the military attachés, ambassadors, consuls, and embas-sies of Egypt, Jordan, Saudi Arabia and Kuwait, as well as of the P.L.O. representatives and their offices in Lon-don. Three weeks before the attack on Ambassador Argov, comrade ''Thabit'' received orders to act ''with-out mercy'' against various targets in London which rep-resented the United Arab Emirates (see Appendix A).

The orders, which arrived together with cash, by ''the courier Wasfi,'' instructed Rosan to act primarily against the embassy or its staff, and ''to liquidate it.'' ''Comrade Mutana,'' who had signed the orders, noted that the action was meant to teach the UAE government a lesson, because it had broken a promise and handed over members of the group to Jordan. This was an excellent example of how the organization functioned. Even before this letter, the group had threatened, and actually carried out, attacks against the UAE and Kuwait, whenever it felt these had acted against it in a hostile manner. For some reason the orders this time were never carried out. Instead, Rosan was asked to await new directives. London police intelligence officers and the Special Branch believe that another courier named "Jabar" arrived in London from Baghdad at the end of May, with new instructions for Rosan, informing him to concentrate on only two targets, either the Israel embassy or the ambassador himself. He was further told to be ready to act at a moment's notice. The final orders would be arriving from the organization headquarters.

After Rosan was sentenced to 35 years in prison, the Abu Nidal group announced that he had been appointed a member of the Revolutionary Council—the highest body in the organization.[1] This appointment was meant to increase Rosan's importance. Indeed, in the years since his imprisonment, Abu Nidal's group has increased its attacks against British targets. Clearly, these attacks were meant to bring about the release of the three members of the group imprisoned for the attempted assassination of Ambassador Argov and two others in prison for smuggling arms into the country.

[1] The Revolutionary Council numbers between ten and fifteen members, and is considered to be the policy-making body of the organization. Its most prominent members are Abd al-Rahman Isa, the organization spokesman; Atif Abu Bakr; Akizo Abu Amar (who was interviewed in the group's publication in June 1985); Ka'id Yusuf; Walid Uza; Wasfi Abd al-Rahim.

4

The Leader

If there is such a thing as a "one man organization," the Abu Nidal group is an excellent example, because its entire existence revolves about a single person, Sabri al-Banna. Al-Banna boasts of being a "true revolutionary," and the most faithful representative in the entire world of the Palestinian movement. In the literature dealing with terror, much is made of "the pretentious revolutionary character of the terrorist." Typically, terrorism is the art of the gesture, and is based entirely on mannerisms. Even if Sabri al-Banna is not especially acquainted with this literary genre, his actions and the interviews he has given to the international media remind one of the image of the terrorist as being totally involved in role-playing. The concepts of disguise and pretense are especially relevant to him. His entire terrorist experience has been an extended effort to obscure his past, disguise his personal history, and "embellish" the facts, while constantly trying to conceal those elements which he finds distasteful. He keeps trying to don a mask which will conceal his actual past and to turn his entire background into an enigma. It is thus not surprising that the most mundane details are clouded in mystery: his year of birth, his real name, the positions he has held, and the schools where he studied.

It is extremely difficult to find out any details about his private life and his habits because such information would help the secret services who are looking for him.

Abu Nidal is cautious to the point of paranoia. He never speaks on the phone or radio, for fear that he might be traced or even liquidated by a remote-controlled explosive charge, such as those used by Israeli agents to kill a number of Black September members in Western Europe in the early 1970's. He is so terrified of being assassinated that he refuses to drink anything served to him by others—even in friendly countries such as Syria and Libya. Abu Jihad, Yasser Arafat's top military chief, once said that "Abu Nidal is so distrustful that he even suspects his wife of being an agent of the C.I.A."

While there is no evidence that he has personally killed anyone, he is known for his cruelty. Many of his attacks have been distinguished by a ruthless viciousness which almost seems to be his trademark. As the result of a dispute with one of his relatives at the end of 1985, he ordered a hit team to booby-trap the cooking-gas canister in his nephew's home in Amman. The resulting explosion killed his nephew's Czech wife and two children. "We used to joke," confessed the defector from the organization, Abu Samer, "that if he had a bad dream, one had to watch out the next morning, because he would target someone else to be killed."

It is known that he used to be a heavy smoker, but that recently his doctors ordered him either to stop smoking or to cut down drastically. They also insisted he follow a rigorous diet.

Sabri al-Banna takes pains concerning his appearance and that of his men. One of the few foreigners to have met him was Robert Hitchens, a British journalist. He was very favorably impressed by the cleanliness of Abu Nidal's headquarters in Baghdad, and by the immaculate dress of his men. They were all clean-shaven and properly dressed. During their conversation, no one interrupted them, not even a single time. "The difference between the quiet in al-Banna's office and the market clamor and sloppy clothes in a great number of the Palestinian institutions was especially striking," was the impression of another visitor to the headquarters in Baghdad in the 1970's.

In spite of the slogans and the boasts which he likes using during interviews, he tries to be modest when receiving visitors. As opposed to Yasser Arafat, he does not carry arms, but relies on the trustworthiness of his guards. Sabri al-Banna's close relatives—his wife and children—continue to live in Baghdad, in spite of the fact that the head of the household now presumably shuttles frequently between Iraq, Syria, and Libya.

But beyond these details and personal observations, speculation about the character and personal history of the terrorist leader run riot. Little it would seem is known for sure. There is even disagreement about his exact name. The London *Daily Telegraph* wrote that his name is Hasan Sabri al-Banna. The *Middle East International* (which appears in London in English) spoke of Muhammad Sabri al-Banna. Stewart Steven's book on the Mossad gives two possible versions: Sabri Khalil al-Banna, or, alternatively, Mazan Sabri al-Banna.

The British *Guardian* stated he was born in 1939, while the London *Times* gave his year of birth as 1940. The Truman Institute of the Hebrew University, Jerusalem, has yet a third version: 1934; and Dr. Issam Sartawi (in a conversation with the author) declared that Sabri al-Banna was born in 1936. There are also differences of opinion as to where he was born. A document of the Israel Defense Forces' spokesman lists him mistakenly as having been born in Haifa.

After extensive research, it is possible to state unequivocally that Sabri al-Banna was born in Jaffa in 1937. By Arab tradition, one's father's name is also added to one's own, and this explains the confusion about his real name. Sabri al-Banna's father was Khalil, so it is not surprising that some publications list the son as Sabri Khalil al-Banna. Khalil was one of the richest Palestinian Arabs during the British mandate.

The name "al-Banna" simply means "the builder," and is a common one in the whole region. It can be found in Kuwait, Egypt (where a member of the family was one of the founders of the Muslim Brotherhood and its leader during Abdul Nasser's time), and in Iraq. Some of the members of the al-Banna family moved from Egypt to Palestine in the middle of the 19th century, and soon assumed important positions in Jaffa's commercial life.

Already at the end of the 19th century under the Turks, and increasingly after the British arrived in 1917, Sabri's father Khalil and Khalil's brother, Ibrahim, accumulated considerable wealth, primarily by dealing in property. "My father was a prominent businessman in the Palestinian economy," Sabri al-Banna admitted in a special interview he granted at the end of 1985 to a team from the West German weekly *Der Spiegel*. "My father, Hajj Khalil, was the richest man in Palestine," Muhammad al-Banna, Sabri's brother, proclaimed proudly. And if there are those who think he was exaggerating, his claim is substantiated by various old-timers still living in Jaffa who remember the al-Banna family well. "At the end of the 1920's they bought land from us and planted citrus orchards," stated Karman Abu Sayf, a fruit and vegetable merchant with a number of stands in the Jaffa market. "My father was involved in a number of other business deals with them. They were very respected people. The word of Hajj Khalil and his brother Ibrahim could be trusted completely."

Sabri al-Banna was born in May 1937, in a three-story house with a large porch which fronted onto the ocean. Khalil's legendary wealth had enabled him, in accordance with good Muslim tradition, to buy and marry a number of women. Khalil had no less than thirteen wives. Sabri al-Banna was the youngest child of his eighth wife, a Syrian. "My father had another sixteen sons and eight daughters from his thirteen wives. I am the uncle of more than three hundred children," Sabri al-Banna told the reporters of *Der Spiegel*. Thus Sabri al-Banna was born not with a silver but rather a gold spoon in his mouth. From his earliest childhood he never lacked anything.

His father's primary wealth lay in his orchards, of which he owned over six thousand acres, extending from south of Jaffa to Majdal (today's Israeli Ashkelon), bordering the Gaza Strip. All the al-Banna land was confiscated by the Israeli government in 1948 and was acquired by the Jewish state. Part of the land was used for building housing for the new immigrants. The home in which Sabri grew up now serves as a district court of the Israeli army.

Not only is the home of the terrorist most wanted by
Israel used by its army, but Sabri's brother is considered
one of the greatest "collaborators" with the Israeli occupation forces among the Palestinians on the West Bank.
Muhammad Khalil al-Banna is one of the largest fruit and
vegetable merchants in the West Bank. He buys fruit,
especially apples, from Jewish settlements in the north,
the Upper Galilee and the Golan Heights. He often leaves
his home in Nablus early in the morning and travels to
northern Israel, where he buys produce, returning home
late at night.

He has exceptionally strong ties with the military
administration. "We are not looking for trouble," his son,
Jihad, who works with him, said. Muhammad has refused
adamantly to speak to reporters unless he has prior permission from the authorities. "If I didn't request permission," he admitted, "Captain Abu Ghazal of the Shin Bet
[the Israeli secret service] would bother me." By military
administration regulations, Muhammad does not need to
receive permission to be interviewed, but his stubborn
insistence on receiving it shows how strongly he wishes
to maintain good relations with the authorities.

Once Muhammad received permission to be interviewed by me, he was all sweetness and light, even if he
was hesitant to answer all my questions. I sat in his small
office above his large warehouse in the wholesale produce
market in Nablus. The walls of the office were covered
with posters of the Israel Fruit Board. The air was almost
intoxicating with the pungent odor of apples, and below
I could see hundreds of crates marked "Apples of Galilee."

Muhammad, a large man with a receding hairline,
broke out into a smile whenever he mentioned his father.
"My father, Hajj Khalil, was the richest man in Palestine. He marketed about ten percent of all the citrus crops
sent from Palestine to Europe—especially to England and
Germany. He owned a summer house in Marseilles,
France, and another house in Iskenderun, then in Syria
and afterwards Turkey, and a number of houses in Palestine itself. Most of the time we lived in Jaffa. Our
house had about twenty rooms, and we children would go

down to swim in the sea. We also had stables with Arabian horses, and one of our homes in Ashkelon even had a large swimming pool. I think we must have been the only family in Palestine with a private swimming pool.''

Muhammad interrupts himself for a second, as if trying to recall the past, and then continues, ''Our family also had orchards in Majdal, Yavneh, Abu Kabir and near the village of Tirah, in the vicinity of Kfar Sava. The kibbutz named Ramat Hakovesh has to this day a tract of land known as 'the al-Banna orchard.' Of course this used to belong to us. My brothers and I still preserve the documents showing our ownership of the property,'' he continues, ''even though we know full well that we and our children have no chance of getting it back.''

Like his brothers, Sabri al-Banna spent most of his childhood in the large house in Jaffa. Their father tried to give his children the best education money could buy. Some brothers were sent to private schools in England. Only Muhammad, due to an eye disease which left him half blind, was not given a proper education. He cannot read or write.

Sabri al-Banna, the youngest child, was sent to a French mission school in Jaffa. This school in the Old Jaffa quarter still has records showing that ''Sabri al-Banna completed the first grade in our school.'' But the school keeper, under orders of the school administration, refuses to show the documents. The only thing he was willing to admit was that Sabri had only attended the school for a single year. That was 1945. That year his father Khalil died, but not before having earned the title of Hajj for having made the pilgrimage to the holy mosque of Mecca.

The burden of supporting the large family, maintaining its property, and managing its affairs fell on Sabri's older brothers. As they were more devout Muslims than their father, his brothers took him out of the Catholic school and enrolled him in a Muslim one instead. Their choice for this was the Jerusalem school now known as al-Umaria. While today it belongs to the city public school system, at that time it was considered one of the most prestigious private schools in the country. It was a school for children of the wealthy which tried to offer an excellent education to its pupils, including foreign languages, especially English and French. The family could afford to send Sabri from Jaffa to Jerusalem. Twice a week a car would drive to the school gates and pick up Sabri in the evening, drive him to Jaffa, and return him to school the following morning. This continued for about two years.

Two months after Sabri began the fourth grade, the United Nations General Assembly resolved to partition Palestine into two states—a Jewish and an Arab one. Immediately after the resolution of November 29, 1947, battles broke out, even though they were then sporadic and unorganized, between armed militias of the Palestinian Arab community and the semi-military organizations of the Jewish community. These battles soon spread to Jaffa. At first they consisted of no more than sniping in both directions between the southern suburbs of Tel Aviv and Jaffa.

The Arab suburb of Manshia was especially badly hit. Ibrahim, Khalil's brother, had a large house in that suburb. He and his family were forced to evacuate their home and to move into Khalil's home in the suburb of Ajami. But even there life was unbearable. There was a food shortage, and the shipment of citrus fruits, almost the only export of the country and primarily in Arab hands, was completely disrupted.

Booby-trapped cars were driven into the center of Jaffa by the Jewish fighting militias, and on a number of occasions caused great damage, killing or injuring scores of people. As with other cities with a mixed Arab-Jewish population, many Arab families decided to leave Jaffa until the fighting was over.

The al-Banna family had excellent relations with prominent personalities in the Jewish community. "My father was a close friend of Avraham Shapira, one of the founders of Hashomer, the Jewish self-defense organization," Muhammad al-Banna told me. "He would visit [Shapira] in his home in Petah Tikva, or Shapira riding his horse would visit our home in Jaffa. I also remember how we visited Dr. Weizmann in his home in Rehovot." All these ties, however, including those with Weizmann, who would later become the first president of Israel, did not help the al-Banna family.

When the fighting increased between the Jews and the Arabs, and even before Jaffa was conquered in April 1948 by the Jewish forces, the al-Banna family decided to flee the city. "At the beginning of 1948, due to the war, we abandoned our villa in Jaffa and moved to our house near Majdal. It was a large house in the midst of all our groves in the area. My mother ordered us to lock up all her jewelry in a closet. 'In any case,' she said, 'we will return in a few days.' " But the Jews conquered this area as well, and they were forced to leave their possessions and flee again.

This time, though, they had to live in tents set up to house the tens of thousands of fleeing refugees. They were in the al-Burj refugee camp in the Gaza District for nine straight months. It is possible that these experiences as part of a refugee family fleeing before the Israeli forces sowed the seeds of Sabri al-Banna's terrorism, and that the influence of that year, in which the family was forced to move four times and adjust to a new life-style, was decisive in the formation of young Sabri's character.

Instead of unlimited wealth, Sabri was suddenly forced into abject poverty. Rather than having large houses and rooms filled with toys, he had to adjust to nothing more than a tent. Instead of having servants at his beck and call, he saw how his mother and brothers had to make their way to the UNRWA (United Nations Relief and Welfare Agency) offices to receive their weekly food allowance—oil, rice, and potatoes. Those who knew him later were aware of how he tried to bottle up his feelings about those days and not express them. When, however, they were able to get him to talk of that time, they heard harsh criticism of Israel and Britain, which had brought tragedy on his family and himself.

After the family had been in the camp for nine months, including a severe winter, it was decided to move from the Gaza Strip, then under Egyptian military occupation, to Nablus, the largest of the West Bank cities, which was under the military occupation of King Abdallah, of the Hashemite Kingdom of Transjordan. This occurred in early 1949. The skill of the family members in commerce and the fact that, unlike the majority of Arab refugees who had fled with nothing, the al-Bannas had managed to take a small amount of money with them, enabled them to open up a business as merchants in Nablus.

They were aided in their move from Gaza to Nablus by the excellent connections their father had had. Many of his former workers had in fact come from Nablus. Now the al-Banna brothers asked for help in return for all their father had done.

Sabri al-Banna was twelve years old at the time, and after a break of more than a year, returned to school. This time, though, he was sent to a government school. His brothers were no longer able to afford a private education.

He was not considered an exceptionally bright student, even though he loved reading adventure stories and was considered very studious. He completed elementary school and continued to the city high school, graduating from it in 1955. Sabri applied to and was accepted by the engineering department of Cairo University. Two years later, though, he returned to Nablus without having graduated. Even though Sabri has no official engineering degree, he consistently portrays himself as having one. This is part of his constant effort at "embellishing" his past and creating facts to suit him.

After returning to Nablus, he taught in the local school for a short while, but soon decided that he did not like teaching and it did not pay well enough. His brother, Zakariya, who worked as an engineer for the Aramco oil company in Saudi Arabia, wrote him about the great employment opportunities in the oil fields which were being developed in Saudi Arabia and the Gulf Emirates.

Influenced by his brother, Sabri al-Banna travelled to Saudi Arabia in 1960. He soon found a job in a construction company near the city of Jedda, as an electrician's assistant. Those who remember him from that time describe him as an introvert, who refused to get involved in the stormy political debates of many of the members of the Palestinian community in exile there. The one trait that did stand out was his stubbornness.

This characteristic did not surprise his brother Muhammad. He remembers that when they lived in Nablus his mother bought Sabri a suit. "At the time we were very poor, and Mother saved every penny to be able to buy him a good suit which he would be able to use to attend school. One day Sabri returned home from school without the suit. 'Where is the suit?' Mother asked. 'I gave it away as a gift to another student poorer than I,' he answered. 'Go and get the suit back right now,' Mother ordered him. But Sabri refused to listen to her. He was adamant and was willing to be beaten by his brothers if that was the price he had to pay for doing what he felt was his right to do."

Muhammad al-Banna also praises his brother's family ties. "Sabri was very attached to the family and a devoted son. Each year he would return from Saudi Arabia to Nablus to visit his mother. He was very attached to her, and every few months would send money to support his mother."

On one of his visits, in 1962, Sabri al-Banna met a young woman whose family had also fled from Jaffa. He asked for her hand in marriage and after receiving her family's approval, they were married in Nablus and left for Saudi Arabia. During the twenty-four years of their marriage, they have had three children, two daughters—Bisan and Na'ifa—and a son, Nidal. Sabri has only one wife. When asked if he would follow in his father's footsteps, he replied, "One is definitely enough!"

Sabri al-Banna went back to working as an electrician, but under the influence of Palestinian friends began getting involved in politics. First he joined the ranks of the Ba'ath party, which operated illegally in Saudi Arabia. It was his work in the Ba'ath party at that time that enabled him at a later point to be on such good terms with the Iraqi regime.

Afterwards, but there is no clear evidence as to exactly when, he joined Fatah. There are very few details available on the circumstances surrounding his entry into that Palestinian organization. According to one version, he was one of the first in Saudi Arabia to join it. Another version claims that he joined it in the course of a visit to

Amman. In either event, his increased political involvement drew the attention of his employers in Aramco, and, later on, of the Saudi secret services. He was fired, and afterwards imprisoned, tortured, and finally expelled from the country. His bitter experiences in Saudi Arabia may explain his later hatred for that country and its regime.

As a terrorist, Sabri al-Banna displays a mixture of political and personal hatred for the country which tortured and expelled him. The late Palestinian heart surgeon, Dr. Issam Sartawi, who knew al-Banna well, gave a psychological explanation. Sartawi believed that al-Banna's psychological problems traced back to the time when he worked as a common laborer in Saudi Arabia. To be a common laborer in Saudi Arabia is to be at the bottom of the ladder in a wealthy country whose residents despise physical labor. According to Sartawi, this was the source of al-Banna's hatred of Saudi Arabia and its allies.

Sartawi also claimed that the experience of growing up as the son of the eighth wife of his father can also explain his perception of the entire world as an arena of plots and counterplots. This would explain his fierce desire to take revenge on the entire world establishment and, as shown obsessively in the few interviews he has given, to make his own personal imprint on the world—even if this is by acts of cruel and unbridled terrorism.

Sabri al-Banna returned to Nablus with his wife and small son. This was a few months before the 1967 Six Day War. He found himself odd jobs until the first days of June, when in the space of six days the Israeli forces captured the Sinai peninsula, the Golan Heights, the West Bank, and the Gaza Strip. As for many Nablus residents, the entrance of the Israel Defense Forces tanks into Nablus was a traumatic experience for him. The conquest aroused him to action. While he had been a member of Fatah for years, his had been a passive involvement. Now, after the conquest, he decided to become more involved in the underground.

His decision to become a professional terrorist was also influenced by a short visit he and his family paid to Jaffa. "A number of the members of the family decided to visit our home in Jaffa," said his brother, Muhammad. "Only my mother did not want to make the trip. She said that previously she had had eight servants, and was ashamed to visit her home as a refugee." The visit to the family house only increased Sabri's anger, even though at that time, only weeks after the occupation, he was not directly furious at the Zionists or the Jews.

When Israel's security services began uncovering the membership of Fatah on the West Bank, Sabri decided to leave Nablus and to join a number of his older brothers living in Amman. "It is very sad," concluded Muhammad al-Banna. "I am the only member of my family now living in Nablus. One brother lives in Florida. Two others died. The rest live in Jordan. There is almost no contact between us. I think that we have about a thousand to fifteen hundred members of the al-Banna clan. All love Abu Nidal. I also love him. After all, he is my brother. But I am also a friend of the Jews. I speak Hebrew and trade with them. Sometimes they say to me, your brother did this or that, but their hatred or anger at Abu Nidal is never directed at me. I would not like to be in his shoes."

There is very little available on Sabri al-Banna's work in Fatah while he was in Amman. Like other members of the organization, he was asked to select a *nom de guerre*, and chose Abu Nidal. The name translates as "father of Nidal," but also as "father of the struggle." It is known that he was close to Salah Khalaf ("Abu Iyad"), one of Yasser Arafat's aides, who is now the number two man in Fatah and the P.L.O. Due to Abu Iyad's patronage, Abu Nidal was given a number of important posts. Contrary, however, to the impression he has tried to create in recent years, he is not one of the "founding fathers" of Fatah. His name never appeared among the members of the Central Committee nor among the list of the much larger Palestinian National Council.

Abu Nidal's efforts to portray himself as being one of the founders of Fatah, as well as his attempts to claim that he completed his engineering studies, are all part of the syndrome of the modern terrorist. This is the adoption of a revolutionary "pose" which is meant to impress world public opinion and especially the international news media.

The fact that he was a simple laborer is not only likely to harm Sabri's stature, but also stands in stark contrast with the biography of many of the founders of Fatah and the other Palestinian terrorist organizations. Yasser Arafat, for example, studied engineering at Cairo University. Khalil al-Wazir (Abu Jihad), the head of the military wing of Fatah and the P.L.O., studied liberal arts at the University of Alexandria. Abu Iyad took philosophy and literature at the Dar al-Ulum College of Cairo. Dr. George Habash, founder of the Popular Front for the Liberation of Palestine, is a doctor of medicine, as was also his ex-aide and later opponent, Dr. Wadi Haddad, both having been students at the American University in Beirut. Issam Sartawi was a cardiologist.

But the fact that he lacked a university degree did not prevent Abu Nidal from trying to become a member of the leadership. Issam Sartawi believed that his relatively fast advancement, within a space of but two years, to key positions in Fatah and the P.L.O., stemmed from a number of basic qualities which impressed his superiors. The most prominent of these was his obedience—almost blind obedience—to his commanders, but he was also known for his great ambition, stubbornness, and initiative. Of course the fact that he knew Abu Iyad helped him to advance in the organizational hierarchy.

In 1969, Sabri al-Banna was sent by the Fatah command to set up a branch of the organization in Khartoum, the capital of Sudan. Immediately on arriving there, he energetically set about to recruit the local Palestinian students for the organization. By prior agreement with the Sudanese authorities, Fatah had agreed to coordinate its actions with them. The government secret services soon found out, however, that Sabri al-Banna was not honoring the agreement. His efforts at recruiting students, as well as his attempts to set up secret cells in the country, contradicted the spirit of the agreement.

After eight months of activity, during which al-Banna was warned to desist from his actions, the Sudanese government sent a secret letter to the Fatah leader, Yasser Arafat, in which it complained about al-Banna and asked that he be withdrawn from the country. Arafat agreed to

the request, and removed him from Khartoum. He was
returned to the Fatah headquarters in Amman, and after
a series of briefings and meetings with Arafat and others,
it was decided to appoint him as the organization's representative in Iraq. The fact that he had been a member
of the underground Ba'ath party in Saudi Arabia helped
him in his appointment. Arafat and the other leaders of
Fatah believed that the appointment of one who was a
member of the same party which rules Iraq might serve
to strengthen their ties with the Baghdad government.

For Sabri al-Banna, the move to Iraq was the turning
point in his life. He arrived in Baghdad in August 1970,
and immediately became totally involved in consolidating
the Fatah offices in the country. While he was officially
the P.L.O. delegate in Iraq, where the P.L.O. was the
umbrella organization for all Palestinian factions, in
actuality he worked only on behalf of Fatah, the largest,
but certainly not the only faction within it.

Since Arafat and the Fatah leadership had managed to
take over the P.L.O. in 1969, the identity between Fatah
and the P.L.O. had increased. Arafat made sure that the
key positions in the P.L.O. were filled by people personally loyal to him. While Abu Nidal had never been
thought of as one of Arafat's men, his close ties with Abu
Iyad, and especially his flattery, had enabled him to persuade Arafat's aides that he was the right person in the
right place.

In the first years of his work in Baghdad, Abu Nidal
indeed showed obedience and loyalty to the leadership, so
much so, in fact, that he was one of the first members of
Fatah sent for military training in North Korea and Communist China. There he studied guerrilla tactics and the
use of explosives, all of this accompanied by heavy doses
of Marxist-Maoist ideology. The four months he spent in
the two countries made a tremendous impact on him.
After returning from the training camps, he kept talking
in awe of the amazing order and organization of the
Communist Party in China. To this very day he claims
that ''of all modern politicians, I admire most the disci-
pline and organizational ability of Chou En-lai.''

Another member of the Fatah delegation was Muhammad Da'ud Awda ("Abu Da'ud"), later one of the Black September commanders who planned the murder of the eleven Israeli athletes at the 1972 Munich Olympics. During their visit, Sabri al-Banna was photographed wearing a military cap, dressed in civilian clothes, and smoking a cigarette, together with a North Korean instructor, evidently an army officer, also in civilian clothes. That picture was published in the Lebanese weekly *al-Di'ar*, and is the first ever to appear in print of the terrorist.

The fact that Abu Nidal and Abu Da'ud were together at this training course led some commentators to the conclusion that Sabri was a member of Black September. This is also implied by Helena Cobban.[1] It is indeed a reasonable possibility, and not only because of the friendship between the two terrorists, but also because Abu Iyad[2] was the patron of both men when they first entered Fatah. While Abu Iyad does not mention Sabri al-Banna in his autobiography, this absence is readily understandable. After all, why should he link his name to a person who was considered by Fatah to be a traitor, and who had been condemned to death? It is true, though, that at the beginning of the 1970's Abu Iyad was the contact between Fatah and the secret terrorist organization, Black September.

Abu Iyad claims that the creation of Black September was a spontaneous act following the attacks on the Palestinian organizations by Jordan in September 1970 and their subsequent expulsion from the country under King Hussein's direct orders. The Palestinians who had fled wanted to avenge the slaughter of their brothers. Israeli and Western intelligence experts, on the other hand, are convinced that Black September was established by a secret decision of the Fatah leadership to perform terrorist

[1] Helena Cobban, *The Palestinian Liberation Organisation: People, Power and Politics* (Cambridge: Cambridge University Press, 1984).
[2] Abu Iyad with Eric Rouleau, *My Home, My Land* (New York: Times Books, 1981).

acts against Israeli and Jordanian targets. This way Fatah would be able to claim its innocence and deny that it was involved in terror.

As in other cases, Sabri al-Banna was in no rush to contradict or acknowledge his membership in Black September, because the rumors surrounding him serve his purposes and add to the aura of mystery about the man and his past. In addition, as a matter of policy, Black September never listed its members and worked in total secrecy, so that there is little knowledge to be gained from that quarter.

From time to time Black September was aided by the official offices of Fatah and the P.L.O. in Western Europe as well as in the Arab states. It is thus quite possible that Sabri al-Banna, either in person or through his office in Baghdad, helped Black September by transporting arms or supplying false passports or funds to this or that branch of that group. But in the final analysis, most of al-Banna's time was spent working for Fatah in Baghdad.

5

The Ideological and Historical Background

Throughout the years the Iraqi regime, like the other Arab countries, used the Palestinian issue to advance what it saw as its own political interests. "The 1948 disaster," as the Arab defeat and the establishment of Israel were referred to in the Arab press and literature, increased even further the bickering among the Arab states. But the polarization of the Arab world reached its peak with the Egyptian revolution of 1952 and the emergence of Colonel Abdul Nasser as president there.

In March 1959, the term "Palestinian entity" was coined by Nasser's office, and evoked great enthusiasm among all the Palestinian communities. It was the hope of the Palestinians, and especially of the young generation, that the Egyptian leader would help them return to Palestine, and that his army would bring about the liquidation of the State of Israel and the establishment of a Palestinian state in its place. Nasser's call was one of the earliest attempts to bring about a Palestinian rebirth. He believed that he would be able to awaken Palestinian nationalism, and then utilize it in his own battles on the inter-Arab front, primarily in the political and personal struggle between himself and the Iraqi leader, General Qasim. The two leaders were both interested in using the "Palestinian question" to further their own ends and to undermine each other in an uncompromising struggle for hegemony in the Arab world.

General Qasim, who had led a bloody revolution on July 14, 1958, ending with the murder of the entire Hashemite royal family in Baghdad, now set his sights on the Hashemite Kingdom of Hussein in Jordan. He called openly for severing the West Bank from Jordan and the Gaza Strip from Egypt, and for setting up a Palestinian republic in these areas. His appeal was meant, of course, to enhance Iraq's prestige in the Arab world and to decrease that of its opponents. The Iraqi leader also became the patron of the Mufti of Jerusalem, Hajj Amin al-Husseini, and with his help established the first battalion of Palestinian soldiers within the Iraqi army. This battalion was involved, nine years later, in an attempt to undermine King Hussein, in which Na'if Rosan also took part.

In February 1963 there was a second revolution in Baghdad, led by the Arif brothers and the Ba'ath party. General Qasim was killed, and Abd al-Salam Arif became the titular president, but with very little authority. The real authority remained with the Ba'ath party. In July 1968, there was another *coup d'etat*, and General Ahmad Hasan al-Bakr became president of the republic. His assumption of power strengthened the Ba'ath party's influence even more.

In order to better understand the Abu Nidal organization and its aims, it is necessary to first analyze the ideology of the Ba'ath party. The Party of the Socialist Arab Revival, as it is officially named, was founded in Syria in 1953, unifying two bodies, the Arab Revival Party led by Michel Aflaq and Salah al-Bitar, and the Arab Socialist Party under Akram al-Hurani. The Arab Revival Party had started years earlier, primarily to protest against French rule in Syria. After the granting of Syrian independence and the departure of the French garrison in 1946 the party's emphasis shifted. Now the cry was concentrated more and more on social change and agrarian reform. This ideology, which is important for understanding modern-day Syria and Iraq (and the background to the Abu Nidal group's actions) was expressed clearly in the party's constitution, which states officially that it is "a popular and nationalist revolutionary party which is struggling for Arab unity, freedom and socialism.'' This combination of Arab nationalism and socialism, which might at first blush seem a glaring contradiction, is in reality the basis for the Ba'ath ideology.

The party platform sees the Arabs as ''a single eternal nation.''[1] The first of the founding principles of the constitution states that ''the Arabs are a single nation. This nation has the natural right to exist in a single state, to be free and to determine its own fate.'' Michel Aflaq, who was one of the drafters of the constitution, wrote in 1959 in an essay entitled ''Toward a Revival'' that ''the nationalism which we are calling for is first and foremost love. This is the feeling which binds an individual to his family. And the homeland is but an extended family house, and the nation an extended family. Nationalism, as any other type of love, fills the heart with joy and spreads hope in the soul.'' According to the Ba'ath party, the aim of this nationalism is to unite the entire Arab world, so that it can properly fulfill its historical role and contribute to human civilization. In the Ba'athist ideology, though, the unity of the Arab world can have meaning only through a social and spiritual revolution. Such a revolution, which will eliminate the imperialistic and feudal forces threatening it, will eventually bring about a free and just socialist society.

The Ba'ath party had already gained a prominent place in Syrian affairs by 1958, with its adherents assuming control over the country. But the unified ideology was not enough to prevent power struggles within the party and the development of various factions within it. In 1966 even the founders of the party were expelled from Damascus to Baghdad. The internal struggles in Syria increased after the 1967 war with Israel and the loss of the Golan Heights.

When General al-Bakr and his colleagues of the Iraqi Ba'ath party assumed power in Baghdad in July 1968, the Syrian leaders, who were also Ba'athists, should have been delighted. This, however was not the case. There

[1] Silvia Haim (ed.), *Arab Nationalism* (Berkeley: University of California Press, 1964).

were three reasons why the two regimes were antagonistic to one another.[2] First, Baghdad refused to acknowledge the predominance of the Syrian Ba'ath party. Second, the Syrians were disturbed that the Iraqis had granted asylum to Aflaq and al-Bitar. And finally, Iraq was furious at Syria's readiness to accept U.N. Security Council Resolution 242 for a peaceful solution to the Arab-Israeli conflict. Iraq declared that it would not forgive Syria's "treachery" in accepting that resolution.

The ninth Ba'ath party congress in 1968 adopted a resolution to the effect that the strategy of the armed struggle was the sole way to regain Palestine. This was meant as a clear warning to Syria not to follow the political path, and to expose its "treachery" should it indeed do so in the future.

According to the Iraqis, the fact that Syria had accepted a cease-fire with Israel in 1967 was in itself a concession and an omen of things to come. In fact, the Ba'ath regime in Iraq went further. Al-Bakr blamed Syria's "petit bourgeois" deviations, its political degeneration, and its "revolutionary prattle" without any corresponding action, for the 1967 loss of the war with Israel. All these, in al-Bakr's view, had brought about calamity and would bring further disasters upon the Palestinian people and the entire Arab nation.

The ideological battle between the two Ba'ath parties increased the involvement of al-Bakr, and his successor as Iraqi president, Saddam Hussein, in the Palestinian issue. The Iraqi leaders decided almost immediately to consolidate their position within the Palestinian movement by forming a terrorist organization which would receive their support. Such an organization would serve not only the Ba'ath in Iraq, but would act as a counterforce to al-Sa'iqa, a similar organization established earlier, in April 1968, by the Syrian Ba'ath party.

The pro-Syrian al-Sa'iqa was based on Ba'ath party members of Palestinian origin, and its doctrines and ideology were identical to those of the Syrian Ba'ath party.

---

[2] Based on a conversation with Professor Eli Kedourie of the London School of Economics.

Aryeh Yodfat and Yuval Arnon-Ohana[3] note that al-Sa'iqa was almost entirely dependent on Syria, which supplied it with funds, weapons, personnel, training courses, logistic support, and instructors.

Al-Sa'iqa regarded the "Palestinian revolution" as part of the "pan-Arab revolution," and saw no justification for the establishment of a separate Palestinian state. Instead, it strove for the unification of all the Arab states under the historical leadership of Syria. This explains why, unlike most of the other Palestinian organizations, the word "Palestine" doesn't even appear in its name. Al-Sa'iqa, which was the second largest Palestinian organization in terms of equipment and manpower, presented itself as an alternative to Fatah, and tried for years to usurp the military and political power that Fatah had achieved among the different Palestinian population centers.

In any event, the founding of al-Sa'iqa was meant to serve a number of functions for the Syrian Ba'ath party: it would free the party from the pressures of those extremist members who demanded that it act against Israel; it would enable the party to become involved, but by indirect means, in the Palestinian arena in Jordan and Lebanon; and most importantly, al-Sa'iqa could be used as a tool for solving internal Syrian problems.

When the Iraqis later set up their own Palestinian organization, its goals were wholly analogous to those of al-Sa'iqa. The name chosen for it was the Arab Liberation Front (ALF). This group, founded in mid-1969, was composed primarily of cadres of the Ba'ath party. Most members were from various Arab states, with only a minority of Palestinian origin. Its first leader was Abd al-Wahhab Kayyali, who was later replaced by Abd al-Rahim Ahmad. The Front stressed its Arab character, and just like the pro-Syrian al-Sa'iqa, was given the full backing of its host's army, and was controlled completely by the Iraqi regime.

[3] Aryeh Yodfat and Yuval Arnon-Ohana, *P.L.O. Strategy and Tactics* (London: Croom-Helm, 1983).

At the same time, Iraqi intelligence began expressing increased interest in the other Palestinian organizations which had sprouted in the Middle East, almost like mushrooms after the rain. It even took one of them, the Active Organization for the Liberation of Palestine, led by Dr. Issam Sartawi, under its wing.

In the last years before his assassination in Portugal in April 1983, Sartawi was known as the leader of the moderate wing of the P.L.O., and he openly proclaimed his belief in the right of Israel to exist as an independent state. Earlier, though, as he himself admitted, he had been involved in terrorism.

Up to 1971, Sartawi received funds, aid in training, and weapons from Iraqi intelligence agents in Jordan. His links with the Iraqi regime also brought him into contact with Sabri al-Banna, at the time the Fatah representative in Baghdad. The ties between the two lasted for nearly three years, and during that period they met in Baghdad a number of times. Only when Sartawi decided to abandon his link with Iraqi intelligence was the relationship broken off.

Sartawi realized that too close a relationship with specific Arab states would make it more difficult for the Palestinian organizations to maintain their independence, and would, in fact, eventually turn them into the lackeys of these states. He drew the necessary conclusions and decided to join an independent Palestinian group such as Fatah. There he became one of Yasser Arafat's closest confidants, and was eventually entrusted with the duty of P.L.O. contacts with Israelis.

Sabri al-Banna, on the other hand, took the opposite course. His position in Baghdad by its very nature required him to be in close contact with the various government departments, and especially with the Iraqi secret services. As long as al-Banna followed his instructions and maintained the correct distance from the Iraqi officials, the Fatah leadership encouraged him to meet with the local intelligence officers whenever necessary. When, however, disturbing reports began coming in to Fatah headquarters that the relationship between the sides had undergone a marked change, suspicion was aroused as to

al-Banna's motives. We should note here that Yasser
Arafat and the other "founding fathers" of Fatah
believed, like Issam Sartawi, that Fatah should depend on
the Arab states as little as possible, and certainly not on
any single state.

In his book,[4] Abu Iyad stressed that all the representatives of the P.L.O. throughout the world were given
clear orders along those lines, stating that they were not
to seek the excessive aid of any Arab government or
organization except where this was necessary. Al-Banna,
though, refused to follow these orders. Soon he was on
singularly close terms with Iraqi intelligence. In fact, from
the beginning of the 1970's, or just a few months after
al-Banna arrived in Baghdad, information reached the
Fatah command about the close ties its representative had
with Iraqi intelligence, and how he ignored the instructions sent to him.

Throughout the time he was in Baghdad, Sabri al-Banna
consolidated his position both with the Iraqi authorities
and with the Palestinian community. Soon he became the
"number one Palestinian in Iraq," a status which in a different context and at a later time would give him greater
power and influence.

Using the Iraqi intelligence services and exploiting his
position as the local Fatah representative, al-Banna grad-
ually built his own independent power base. When the
Fatah leaders learned of his disloyalty, they became infuriated. They were extremely concerned about any attempts
by individuals or groups to isolate themselves from the
mainstream. Yasser Arafat tried, and is still trying to this
day, to preserve the unity of his movement, almost at any
price. Emissaries were sent to al-Banna asking him to
return to the fold, but came back to Arafat empty-handed.

With the open backing of Iraqi intelligence, which was
seeking to restore for itself a power base among the
rejectionist Palestinians after the defection of Dr. Sartawi
and the failure of the pro-Iraqi Palestinian Liberation
Front, Sabri al-Banna began to set up the infrastructure
for an autonomous organization under his command dur-

[4] *My Home, My Land.*

ing the course of 1973. Al-Banna objected to Yasser Arafat's and the Fatah leadership's moderation; and this opposition meshed perfectly with the rejectionist ideology of the Iraqi regime concerning a political settlement.

It is worth stressing that at the time Sabri al-Banna isolated himself from the P.L.O. fold, the Iraqi government was in a similar process of isolating itself in the Arab world. This helped even more in solidifying the ties and the cooperation between them. In those years they sealed what may be referred to as "the treaty of the isolated," sharing a rejectionist ideology. Basing himself on the Ba'athist ideology which opposed all attempts to solve the Israeli-Arab conflict by political or diplomatic means, Sabri al-Banna attempted to formulate a doctrine and ideology of his own for his organization.

The political and ideological links between the different terrorist and guerrilla movements in the twentieth century have been a cause for confusion. Professor Walter Laqueur[5] stresses how much this confusion derives from these organizations' own ideologies and doctrines. This is certainly true for the Palestinian groups. Most of them cannot be pigeonholed as belonging to the "left" or "right," a fact equally true of al-Banna's group. That doesn't mean that this group doesn't have its own doctrines. As with all terrorist organizations, it must claim to have an ideology to justify its actions, even though in reality this consists of no more than a string of slogans.

If one does nevertheless attempt to reveal the principles underlying Abu Nidal's political doctrines and their ideological base, one must first understand the ideology of the Ba'ath party and of the organization from which Abu Nidal seceded, Fatah. After all, al-Banna constantly trumpets that he is the faithful proponent of Fatah's true ideology. He has consistently claimed that Arafat and the rest of the Fatah leadership betrayed the movement they had founded and its original goals.

[5] Walter Laqueur, *The Terrorism Reader: A Historical Anthology* (New York: New American Library, 1978).

As in the history of the Christian church, when one or another group proclaimed itself as representing the "true believers" and all those who disagreed with it as "heretics," so too Sabri al-Banna sees himself as carrying the torch of Fatah ideology, and all his opponents as betraying Fatah's aims. This was apparent not only in the way he founded his group, but in the very choice of its name and ideology. Therefore we must first briefly examine the history of Fatah and its ideology during the 1950's.

Generally, one can classify Fatah, as does Professor Laqueur, in the group of nationalist terrorist organizations with separatist tendencies, such as the Basque E.T.A., Irish I.R.A., and Armenian A.S.A.L.A. Just as these groups evinced a surge of development with the growth of the New Left and the student movements in the 1960's and 1970's, Fatah too owed its great success and the support which it garnered to leftist ideologues in Europe and the student protest organizations. Unlike the Western European terrorist movements, however, Fatah is the outgrowth of the totally autonomous Middle Eastern dispute. The aim it set for itself was maximalist in content: to free Palestine from what is referred to as "the Zionist occupation" or "the Zionist entity" and to replace it with a Palestinian state. This was Fatah's major goal when it was founded, and has remained its goal today, more than a quarter of a century later.

Abu Nidal's group preaches precisely the same goal. "Our program is based on Fatah's program," declared Sabri al-Banna in one of his interviews. "Total destruction of the Zionist entity. Participation in Arab unity. The path of Pan-Arabism. Building a democratic people's regime in which Palestine is a homeland. In other words, our struggle is for the liberation of Palestine, in which we wish to establish a secular democratic state."

From its founding, Fatah adopted the "armed struggle" as the central vehicle for freeing its homeland. This ideology underlies all its actions. Yasser Arafat has been quoted tens of times, especially in the years preceding the 1973 Yom Kippur War, as having stated that "Palestine fell in a storm of fire and lead, and it will be liberated in a storm of fire and lead, and as is known, lead has no ideology." "Our principles are the guns pointed at the enemy's chest." "We derive our ideas from our mines."

From its first terrorist acts against Israel in January 1965 (against the Israeli national water carrier), Fatah attempted to drag the Arab states into a war against Israel. In June 1967, Fatah was able to take the "credit" for just that. After the war, the organization attempted to force what it referred to as "the second stage" of the struggle. In other words, it tried to form an urban and rural guerrilla movement in the territories occupied by Israel, and especially in the West Bank, based on ideas imported from the Algerian F.L.N., and the Vietcong in Vietnam, as well as the liberation ideology of Franz Fanon.

In his book *My Home, My Land* Abu Iyad writes of other guerrilla theories which influenced the movement: "The visits made to military bases and training camps [in Communist China and North Vietnam] were of great aid to us, we could learn there the organizational and training methods of the guerrillas, in order to modify them afterwards for use by our fighters. . . . General Giap of Vietnam impressed us immensely. . . . Franz Fanon, who is one of my favorite authors, wrote in *The Wretched of the Earth*—a book I have read a number of times—that only a people which does not fear the cannons and tanks of the enemy is able to bring its revolution to a successful conclusion." In spite of this imported ideology, however, the Israeli secret services were able to crush the "second stage" in a few months. Sabri al-Banna was forced to leave Nablus and to move to Jordan immediately after the Israeli occupation, while Fatah and the other Palestinian organizations had to adopt new methods.

In the late 1960's and early 1970's, the Palestinian guerrilla movement attempted to continue its armed struggle against Israel, using three basic methods:

1. Shelling Israeli settlements across the border.
2. Hit-and-run attacks on Israeli settlements and vehicles, including attempts to take hostages.
3. Attacks on both Israeli and Jewish individuals and institutions in countries which were not directly involved in the conflict, as well as attempts to damage the interests of these other countries, both by hijacking their planes and

killing their diplomats. In other words, an attempt was made to internationalize the Israeli-Palestinian conflict. This idea of internationalizing the dispute originated primarily with the P.F.L.P. under Dr. George Habash. It reached its peak at the end of the 1960's and the beginning of the 1970's. From then on most of the Palestinian organizations abandoned the idea of internationalizing the struggle. Black September, which had been set up by the Fatah leadership specifically to undertake international terrorist acts, ceased functioning in 1973.

The P.F.L.P. has also ended its involvement in plane hijackings, especially as, according to intelligence reports of the Western states, Dr. George Habash is suffering from a severe heart condition, and Dr. Wadi Haddad, who was the operations officer of the organization and the ''brain'' behind the spectacular hijackings, died of cancer in an East German hospital. (According to another version, he was poisoned by the Iraqi intelligence service.) Thus, for all practical purposes, the only one who still preaches internationalizing the Palestinian conflict is Sabri al-Banna. He believes that the armed struggle in all its forms, and especially its internationalization, is the only way which can bring about the ultimate aim: the destruction of Israel and its replacement by a Palestinian state.

In its efforts to legitimize the idea of destroying Israel, the Abu Nidal organization has made a point of using the symbol of Deir Yasin, an Arab village where a Jewish underground is alleged to have slaughtered about 200 Arab civilians in the 1948 war, and more recently the massacre by Lebanese Christians in the Sabra and Shatilla refugee camps in September 1982, when the Israeli armed forces had approved the Christians' entry into these camps.

Abd al-Rahman Isa, spokesman of the group, stated in a March 8, 1983 interview with the London *Times* that ''Thousands of unarmed Palestinian citizens were killed in Lebanon in 1982, even though they were not involved in politics. They, the Zionists, killed men, women and children in Deir Yasin and in Sabra and Shatilla.''

The concept of the armed struggle is central to the organization's doctrine. Thus, it has proclaimed its support of any Palestinian group which is willing to continue with the armed struggle. "We identify with all the Palestinian operations carried out against Zionism," said Sabri al-Banna. This view was also echoed in the London court case, when Na'if Rosan was asked if he supported Palestinian terrorism. He answered, "I believe that all guerrilla groups are justified in their struggle, if they fight against their enemy, the Zionist movement."

Sabri al-Banna believes in, and acts in accordance with, the doctrine that "I shoot, therefore I am." He has therefore constantly rejected every attempt by the P.L.O., and the Fatah leadership to accept the political approach. According to Sabri al-Banna, the readiness of Fatah and the majority of the P.L.O. member organizations since the middle 1970's to act by political means, reaching its peak in the appearance of Yasser Arafat at the U.N. on November 22, 1974, is a betrayal of the pure idea of the armed struggle. Even the fact that the P.L.O. believes in utilizing both political and military means together does not, in his opinion, lessen the treachery.

After the idea of the armed struggle at any price, the next most important motif in the group's doctrine is opposition to "Arafat's and the P.L.O. leadership's progressive moderation." Their readiness to reach a political settlement is, according to Sabri al-Banna, "an international campaign led by Arafat and Sadat, with Saudi funds and Israeli cooperation." In the interview with the London *Times*, the group's spokesman stated: "Yasser Arafat and his men betrayed the Palestinian revolution. They are prepared to negotiate with the Zionists and therefore their fate will be the same as the traitor Sadat. We have announced clearly and sincerely that whoever betrays the Palestinian cause will not be permitted to implement his betrayal against the Palestinian and Arab masses."

The use of slogans about the Arab masses brings us to the third most important doctrine of the group. After stressing the need for the armed struggle and its determination to stamp out the "traitors," the group emphasizes the importance of freeing the Arab nation from various "reactionary" regimes. This principle was derived primarily from the influence of the Ba'ath party, the party under which Sabri al-Banna served for many years. Al-

Banna believes that objectively the Arabs are one people and have one homeland, which was divided up by imperialist plots into separate geographic, political, and economic entities, which are all artificial. "In the future, after its liberation, Palestine will be an integral part of Syria," states al-Banna. Israel, he continues, is supported by world imperialism, and represents a national danger for the entire Arab people. Therefore the entire Arab people must unite in the armed struggle against it.

Sabri al-Banna has admitted that his ideas of a struggle against the conservative Arab states stem from his ties with the Ba'ath party. He has stated that "we agree with the major idea of liberating Palestine and the Arab world. We trust the political leadership of Iraq and Syria, and this is based on long and joint experience. Our allies the Iraqis, the Syrians, and the Libyans are themselves involved in the struggle and are responsible for the fate of the masses. The first priority is the struggle against the Zionist enemy. The second priority is the destruction of the reactionary regimes in Egypt, Jordan, Lebanon, and Saudi Arabia."

Sabri al-Banna perceives himself as being the reviver of the Qarmatian movement, a marginal and fleeting episode in Muslim history that dates back a millennium. The Qarmatians took their name from an Aramaic word meaning "teaching the secret of an occult doctrine." For a few decades the group maintained an independent emirate along the Persian Gulf and preached communism to the masses and agnosticism to a select elite, along with hostile contempt for orthodox ethics. More to the point, the Qarmatians regarded indiscriminate terror as "the means to achieve happiness." Abu Nidal has assumed the role of the Qarmatian "master of purity," making him the modern heir to the old one, who dared to spirit away the sacred black stone from the Ka'aba mosque in Mecca and massacre countless pilgrims in an incident that makes pious Muslims shudder to this day. Abu Nidal is convinced that the Qarmatian creed is the best way to effect a true revolution in the Arab world. He regards terror, or "armed propaganda" in his phrase, as the most effective way to convey his message.

In the interview with *Der Spiegel*, he declared that "I want to tell you what I dream about: about a single Arab people, living in freedom, justice, and equality. My enemies are the Zionist occupation of my homeland. My enemies are imperialism in all its forms, and division and divisiveness of my Arab people, and the chaos in our Arab society."

To summarize Abu Nidal's doctrine and its ideological background, one may state that just as with Fatah in its early years, the group has no clear and formulated political direction. Aryeh Yodfat and Yuval Ohana-Arnon claim in their book that "the ideological basis of Fatah from its inception was deliberately weak in order to avoid the creation of factions and splinter groups. . . ." Similarly, Abu Nidal's group has no clear political line, and its opponents perceive him as nothing more than an agent of the Iraqi secret service, and thereafter of the Syrians and Libyans. And indeed, more than being a political theory, Abu Nidal's doctrine is a world view composed of a collection of shopworn slogans. The group has gathered together scraps of the most general concepts which revolve about three major axes: the armed struggle against Zionism, against Palestinian treachery, and against Arab reaction. Sabri al-Banna formed his organization and turned it into an underground terrorist group around these three lines. The organization is structured in such a way that its operational plans are meant to implement these three objectives.

6

The Structure

As mentioned earlier, the sources of the split which brought about the formation of the Abu Nidal group go back to the period before the 1973 Yom Kippur War. It was then that the Fatah branch in Baghdad, under Sabri al-Banna, began to act without the authorization of the movement leadership. Abu Nidal's first independent action took place on September 5, 1973, when five of his men occupied the Saudi Arabian embassy in Paris, and took eleven members of the staff hostage. The gunmen were eventually flown out to Kuwait, and later to Libya. The attack on the embassy apparently had a double motive: it was intended by Abu Nidal to embarrass Yasser Arafat and by the Iraqis to intimidate Saudi Arabia. Responsibility for the attack was taken by a group called "Al Iqab" (the Punishment), which was later revealed to be one of the names used by Abu Nidal.

The Western media and secret services tended to blame Black September, a Fatah front, for the incident. In reality, though, Sabri al-Banna had carried out the operation without the permission of Salah Khalaf, the contact between Black September and the P.L.O. leadership. The event infuriated Arafat, and deepened the rift between the central command and its Iraqi branch.

In his book, Salah Khalaf (Abu Iyad) has this to say about the events of the that time: "This weapon too [plane hijackings], to our chagrin, was shown to be valueless. Except for the hijacking of the first plane in 1969, which caught Israel by surprise, the Zionist leaders

refused as a matter of course to negotiate with the hijackers. . . . Thus we soon realized that hijacking planes did
not aid our cause at all. On the contrary, it caused us
serious damage in our attempts to have people understand
the significance of our struggle for liberation. It is for this
reason that Fatah has rejected totally various other operations, such as the illogical adventurism of those who
invaded the Saudi Arabian embassy in Paris and took diplomats as hostages.''

About two months later, immediately after the war,
while discussions were being held about the convening of
a peace conference in Geneva, Abu Nidal's men seized a
K.L.M. airliner in Iraqi airspace. Here too the blame was
laid on Black September. The organization which claimed
to have carried out the attack called itself the Arab
Nationalist Youth Organization. The Fatah leaders, however, were sure that this was the work of the rebellious
Abu Nidal, acting from Baghdad. He wanted to warn
Fatah not to send representatives to the peace conference.
In response, al-Banna was expelled from Fatah in March
1974, and a communique was issued that he had com-
pleted his term of duty in Iraq. He was summoned to the
Fatah headquarters in Damascus, but refused to appear.
The rift had become final.

Even prior to this, Abu Nidal had begun setting up the
infrastructure for his own personal organization. Encouraged by the Iraqi Ba'ath government, he recruited tens of
volunteers among the Palestinian community in Iraq. He
was also joined by some of the Fatah office workers and
members who had been ''unemployed'' since the dissolv-
ing of Black September. Over the next ten years a few
hundred supporters joined the movement, having been
recruited throughout the Arab world and in Western
Europe. Most of these were Palestinian students drawn
from the Palestinian centers in France, Spain, Italy, Austria, and Britain.

Israeli and Western intelligence services estimate that
in 1985 the group had no more than 150–200 active
members and another few hundred supporters and sym-
pathizers. The individual cells are frequently based on
family and clan ties. Thus, Marwan al-Banna in London

was a relative of the leader. A document was found in Marwan's room at the Y.M.C.A. hostel in Wimbledon giving the names of other relatives belonging to the group.

Terrorists are not born, they are made and nobody makes them better than the Palestinian refugee camps, especially those in Lebanon. Sabra and Shatilla, vast shantytowns near Beirut, where in September 1982 800 men, women, and children were killed by the Christian militias ostensibly under the jurisdiction of Israeli troops, produced Muhammad Sahran, the only terrorist who survived the attack on the El Al ticket counter in Rome airport. Sahran lost his father, a taxi driver, in the camp massacres. His brothers and sisters fled, and his mother died of an illness.

The great effort that the group makes in garnering support among the Palestinian students reminds one of the methods Fatah itself used just after it was founded. One of the primary goals of Fatah in those days, at the beginning of the 1960's, was to gain control of the General Union of Palestinian Students, which had been founded in 1959 and had tens of thousands of members. Sabri al-Banna, who sees himself as the authentic bearer of the original Fatah flame, also adopted the methods, recruitment system, and structure of the movement he left. Special emphasis is placed on propaganda, persuasion, and recruitment among the young and intellectual classes of the Palestinian communities.

According to one report, in the French *Le Monde*, between 1976 and 1978 the group managed to acquire a monopoly on the distribution of scholarships in Iraq to Palestinian students in Europe. In return, students receiving such scholarships had to agree to be "sleepers" for the organization. Then, when the day comes, they can be called upon to act and to pay their debt. It appears that it was this recruitment scheme which granted Marwan al-Banna his scholarship to study in Britain. In another case, a young Palestinian who was involved in the murder of the P.L.O. representative in Paris admitted that he had been blackmailed by Sabri al-Banna's group, and had become involved in the murder in return for an airplane ticket to Western Europe.

But Sabri al-Banna's efforts to imitate Fatah are not restricted to his recruitment procedures. They appear time and again in his other actions. Even the official title the group chose for itself is the Arabic equivalent of the Palestine Liberation Movement, the words being the exact ones from which the Arabic acronym Fatah was derived, but in reverse order ("Fatah" in its full Arabic form translates as the Movement for the Liberation of Palestine).

As an expression of his perception that Fatah had deviated from its original aims, Sabri al-Banna called in 1973 for a general conference of the organization, before finally leaving it. He also embarked on a propaganda campaign to foster his views and began to set up new institutions which used the exact names as those of Fatah, as if to emphasize that henceforth only his organization embodied the revolutionary principles of the original Fatah. For example, after establishing a radio station under the patronage of the Ba'ath party in Baghdad, he named it "the Voice of Palestine," the name used by the Fatah broadcasting station. His news agency was called Wafa, again identical to the name of the Fatah news agency.

The movement's publication was given the title *Felastine al-Thawra*. It is distributed by mail only to subscribers. At first it was printed in Baghdad, and thereafter in Damascus. At the end of 1985 it was put out in a small town in the Lebanese Biqa valley. Its circulation is so small that even Israeli intelligence finds it hard to obtain copies.

Nevertheless, in spite of the basic similarity in organizational structures, there are differences between Abu Nidal's faction and the original Fatah, which evidently decided at the end of 1968 when it took over the P.L.O. to cease being an underground movement. Al-Banna believes that was a fatal error. It was the beginning of what he terms the petrification of the movement and its forsaking of its revolutionary character. He therefore continues to insist on an organization based on clearly conspiratorial foundations. All of his group's cells are underground, in exactly the same format as that adopted by Fatah in its first ten years. "My success depends on total secrecy," Abu Nidal stated in one of his interviews. "Even my daughter Bisan doesn't know who I really am."

He attempts to preserve as much as possible the anonymity of the group and normally refrains from granting interviews to the media. Only five times has he broken this rule (three of these in 1985). The first time was in an interview with the Lebanese *al-Di'ar* in December 1974, and the second in July 1978, to a reporter of the pro-Arab British publication, *Middle East*. More than seven years later, in 1985, when rumors were circulating that he had died, he gave three more interviews. (In June 1984 *Newsweek* had carried a story that he was on his deathbed in Baghdad.) The two latest interviews were given in Tripoli, Libya, to journalists of the West German *Der Spiegel* and the Kuwaiti *Al Qabas*.[1]

Following their leader, the members of the group in Iraq, Syria, Lebanon, and Western Europe maintain a strict code of secrecy. They belong to underground cells, numbering three to seven members, and the organization is deliberately compartmentalized so that few of its operatives know comrades in other cells. Once a cell has been chosen for an operation, it is completely isolated from the others. That particular cell then normally spends several weeks being briefed on the target, including the method to be used in the attack and how to escape after it.

Each member must adopt an alias. As was ascertained in the British trial, even when members make contact with others in their own cell, they know, or should know, them only by their aliases. They are trained to maintain a high degree of secrecy, and they attempt to minimize the number of their meetings and phone conversations. When there is need for a cell to meet, this must be arranged in advance, and the meeting must be held in a public facility such as a railroad station, a hotel lobby, or a crowded restaurant.

Most messages are sent by "authorized couriers," as Marwan al-Banna told the police investigators in London.

[1] See Chapter 9.

These messages are generally coded and begin with the words, "Greetings in the Struggle" (*Nidali* in Arabic). They end with the message, "Revolution till Victory." When addressing each other, members use the term "Comrade."

The story of one alleged Abu Nidal agent, a seventeen-year-old Palestinian named Katas Hasan, is instructive. It is recounted by an Italian who has talked at length with Hasan, a suspect in the bombing of a British Airways office in Rome in September 1985.

In 1982 or 1983, Hasan says he was taken from a Palestinian refugee camp in Beirut and put through training in Syria, possibly in the Bekaa valley. One day in the summer of 1985 he was put on an airliner to Rome, with $500 cash and a fake Moroccan passport, which allowed him visa-free entry to Italy. He was told to stay at two specified small hotels in the Italian capital, and to wait in the Piazza Cavour each day at 7:00 A.M.

One morning, an Arabic-speaking Belgian approached him and gave him a bomb. Later he allegedly threw it into a British Airways office, wounding fourteen people.

The secretiveness of the Abu Nidal organization is a protective device. When an operation is over and done, the perpetrator has met only one or two people, so he cannot supply much intelligence even if caught.

This continuing code of secrecy emulates the tactics of Fatah in its earlier days, when each of the Fatah leaders chose an alias. Arafat became Abu Amar, Salah Khalaf used Abu Iyad, Khalil al-Wazir was known as Abu Jihad, and Sabri al-Banna chose Abu Nidal.

Another tactic adopted from Fatah is the use of numerous names for the group itself, in order to confuse the Israeli secret services as well as those of the Arab states and of Western Europe who are searching for it. Thus, the Abu Nidal group has used at least the following names when calling the international media after its attacks: Fatah—the Revolutionary Council; al-Asifa (the Storm); Black June; the Revolutionary Arab Brigades (see Appendix B); the Revolutionary Organization of Socialist Moslems. The leader of the London cell, Na'if Rosan, for example, told police investigators that the name of his group was The Democratic Nation for a Popular Revolution.

According to the group's policy in its early years, it did not assume responsibility for the murder of Palestinians. In one case, in fact, the murder of Sa'id Hamami, when both the Arabic and international press claimed that the Abu Nidal group was responsible, its spokesman actually made a point of denying the allegation. Recently, though, in his interview with *Der Spiegel*, Abu Nidal admitted that his members had killed Hamami, who was, incidentally, one of his relatives. ''We have committed almost a hundred such actions, without publicizing them. The reason was always the same: ties with the Mossad. Every Palestinian or Arab contacting the Mossad will end like them.''

On the other hand, in attacks on Israeli targets, the group has taken responsibility for its actions, even taking the ''credit'' for certain attacks in Jerusalem and on a bus travelling from Jaffa to Gaza in April 1984, even though these were perpetrated by other organizations using some of its many aliases.

When the group wishes to take responsibility for a particular action, the information is usually transmitted anonymously by phone or mail to a newspaper or international news agency. Thus, on June 9, 1982, three days after the Lebanese war broke out, a note arrived at the Reuters agency in Beirut, in which al-Asifa claimed that it was responsible for the attack on Ambassador Argov in London. The spokesman of Fatah, whose military arm is also known as al-Asifa, hastened to deny their responsibility for the act.

About nine months later, an anonymous caller dictated a telephoned message to the French news agency in Bucharest. The message demanded that the British government free the group's three members convicted of attacking Ambassador Argov, otherwise ''its judges will learn what revolutionary justice is.'' That message also threatened the *Guardian*, because of a feature story that its correspondent, Ian Blake, had published about the group. In another message transmitted to the Arabic paper *al-Arab* which appears in London, the organization blamed Uri Avnery (whom it called an agent of the Mossad), an Israeli journalist and former member of the Knesset who has had extensive contacts with different Palestian organizations, and Dr. Issam Sartawi for leaking materials to the British papers.

After the attempted assassination in June 1984 of Zvi Zedar, a bodyguard at the Israeli embassy in Cairo, an organization calling itself the Revolutionary Egypt sent the Cairo office of the Soviet news agency, *Tass*, a full-page communiqué stating that "the organization has begun the armed struggle against the spies of the Israeli Mossad who are in Cairo under the guise of diplomats." In Damascus, though, a group calling itself Al Iqab claimed that one of its special units, named "the Martyrs of Sabra and Shatilla," had carried out the operation.

A few hours after the murder of the Israeli diplomat Albert Atrakchi in Cairo in August 1985, Revolutionary Egypt sent a communiqué to a number of news agencies in the Egyptian capital stating that Atrakchi was "an agent of Israeli intelligence."

Despite the fact that the group is a small, underground one, it claims its decision-making process is quite democratic. This was the picture that Marwan al-Banna wished to present both to the police investigators and in his courtroom testimony.

The prosecutor, Roy Amlot, asked him: "The group you belonged to, the Palestinian National Liberation Movement, is known in Baghdad as Abu Nidal. Isn't that so?"

Al-Banna: "No sir. I know nothing about that."

"Do you at least know that it is known by that name in the Middle East?"

"No sir. I have no personal knowledge to that effect. Only from reading the newspapers. The papers refer to the group as Abu Nidal, but that is only the name of a person living in the Middle East."

"Is Abu Nidal or Sabri al-Banna the leader of the group?"

"No."

"Are you trying to protect him?"

"No sir. Why should I protect him? He can protect himself. I told the police and I repeat here as well that the Palestinian National Liberation Movement split off from the P.L.O. in 1974 because of the Palestinian situation."

"Who is the leader of the group?"

"It doesn't have a leader. There is only a general council."

"Who is the head of the general council?"

"There is no leader."

"Then how are decisions adopted?"

"There are general discussions among the senior members, until a consensus emerges."

"What then is Sabri al-Banna's position?"

"He is one of the senior members of the organization."

This testimony is another attempt to portray the Abu Nidal group as democratic, with a formal and collective leadership, just as is the case with Fatah. In fact, al-Banna himself has said that he was not the general secretary of his own group, but was no more than a member of the Revolutionary Council, and therefore part of the collective leadership.

It is true that in 1978 Abu Nidal seemed ready to share his authority with Naji Alush, who joined the leadership of the group, lending it prestige and an intellectual dimension which it had so sorely been lacking. Alush, who was appointed deputy chairman of the Revolutionary Council, is considered one of the most important Palestinian ideologues. His articles and essays, going back to the 1950's, are considered to be forerunners of the Palestinian concept. Back then, when the Palestinians tended to believe it was the duty of the Arab states to restore their homeland for them, Naji Alush called upon the Palestinians to take their fate into their own hands. Then he was a voice in the wilderness. After the Six Day War, though, when the Palestinian movement became the focus of the Middle East conflict, his message gained a vast following.

With his book, *The Road to Palestine*, Alush became the "theoretician" of the Palestinian guerrilla fighters. He attempted to learn from the experiences of the Cuban, Vietnamese, and other guerrillas throughout the world, and to apply these lessons to the struggle against Israel. In his book, he criticized the beliefs prevalent among the Palestinian organizations led by Ahmad Shuqayri, the first chairman of the P.L.O. (whom he referred to in the book as a comedian and clown), and advocated the adoption of other positions, primarily the merging of the Palestinian idea with pan-Arabism.

In 1969 Alush officially joined the P.L.O., and became a member of the Palestinian National Council as an independent not representing any organization.

For Alush, the dispute with Israel can serve to hasten the unification of the Arab nation and the finding of a solution to all the problems of the Arab world. In this, his views are similar to those of the Iraqi Ba'ath party, states Matti Steinberg, of the Truman Institute at the Hebrew University. And it was this closeness in viewpoints that brought Alush to join Abu Nidal. Prior to that, he had been the secretary general of the General Union of Palestinian Writers, one of the most important organizations in the Palestinian movement, and one with great prestige.

Alush's views, as expressed in the union's journal, *al-Katib* (*The Author*), angered Yasser Arafat. Due, however, to Alush's reputation, Arafat was powerless to do anything about it. Since 1975, though, Arafat has been trying to have Alush expelled from his position as secretary-general of the union, but in vain. Alush has continued attacking Fatah and the P.L.O. leadership in general and Arafat's work in particular.

The final break between Alush and the P.L.O. occurred in April 1978, following Israel's incursion into Lebanon in what was known then as Operation Litani. (The Litani is a river in southern Lebanon.) Many members of Fatah were incensed at Arafat's conduct during the battles against Israel in southern Lebanon. They were particularly angered by his willingness to accept U.N. Security Council Resolution 425, which established a cease-fire for southern Lebanon and permitted the sending of U.N. troops (UNIFIL) to the region. Arafat's readiness to allow

this and to agree to prevent his men from acting against
Israel in the future enraged many of the Fatah leadership.

The entire high command split into two camps. Those
who supported Arafat included Abu Jihad, Abu Walid
(who was killed in Syria in 1982) and others, while his
opponents included Naji Alush (even though he was not
an official member of the central committee), Abu Salah,
Abu Da'ud, and others. Alush and Abu Da'ud (who knew
Abu Nidal from the time they had been together in training camps in Communist China and North Korea) turned
to the rebel in Baghdad and secretly decided to undermine Arafat.

With strong support from the Iraqi secret service, Abu
Nidal infiltrated about 150 of his men into Lebanon.
There they met Abu Da'ud, who was appointed their
commander. The group took an intensive training course
meant to teach its members how to penetrate the Israel
Defense Forces lines in southern Lebanon. Once across
the lines, they were to create provocations against Israel
and thus sabotage the cease-fire. The Fatah command,
however, under the deputy commander of its military arm,
Khalil al-Wazir (Abu Jihad), exposed the link, imprisoned the members of the group, and accused Abu Da'ud
of organizing a revolt. Abu Da'ud denied the accusations,
but at the same time men loyal to him attacked some
Fatah positions at the Ubra camp in Beirut.

In the fierce fighting that broke out, sixteen people were
killed and many others injured. In response, Arafat's men
attacked the Nabatyya camp in southern Lebanon, where
Abu Da'ud's men were concentrated. Later in June, a
Fatah court executed two of Abu Da'ud's men.

The fighting, which continued for a number of days,
marked the third armed rebellion against the Fatah leadership, and especially against Yasser Arafat. The first
occurred in 1966, while the second in 1973 ended with
Abu Nidal's defection.

But the coalition of Abu Da'ud, Alush, and Abu Nidal
did not last long. Abu Da'ud changed his mind, expressed
regret for his actions, and was accepted back into Fatah
and the P.L.O. Naji Alush continued to support Abu
Nidal for a time, but disagreed with him in 1979 and

parted ways. Alush left Iraq and flew to Libya, where, aided by the Libyan leader, Colonel Mu'ammar al-Qaddafi, he set up his own organization in November 1979, which he named the Arab Popular Liberation Movement.

While the cooperation between Alush, Abu Da'ud and Abu Nidal lasted for a relatively short time, it is important because it was the first attempt by Abu Nidal to portray his organization as a clearly defined group with its own ideology, and thus to remove the impression that he was no more than a "hired gun" or agent of Iraqi intelligence. His failure to retain his two allies is of importance, because it proves that the Abu Nidal group is indeed a "one man operation," and that he personally cannot function as part of a leadership team.

Matti Steinberg believes that the most important reason for their break with Abu Nidal was that Naji Alush and Abu Da'ud challenged al-Banna's sole leadership of his group, while also criticizing his methods. His answer to Abu Da'ud's and Alush's disagreements with him was to terminate the partnership with them. But that was not enough. In August 1981 Abu Nidal's men tried to assassinate Abu Da'ud in Warsaw.

The 1978 break with Fatah is further evidence of al-Banna's wish for total power. All the claims about the democratic structure of the organization, as parroted by Marwan al-Banna in the London courtroom, therefore sound hollow, without any basis in reality. The aim of such statements is obvious: to camouflage the simple fact that, unlike Fatah, where Arafat does not exercise sole control, the Abu Nidal group has no collective leadership, and Abu Nidal's word is final.

It is nevertheless worth stressing that the group does have a general structure reminiscent of Fatah in its early days. For example, the group has two major wings. The political wing is responsible for information services, propaganda, and obtaining funds, and it is to this wing that Marwan al-Banna claimed to belong. It is also responsible for publishing the group's paper, and for the distribution of scholarship funds to Palestinian students. In the 1970's it also ran the radio station put at its disposal by the Iraqi regime.

The military wing, which is named al-Asifa (the Storm), is responsible for recruiting fighters, training them, and carrying out terrorist acts. It has three departments: training, operations (of which Na'if Rosan was evidently deputy commander), and a small division responsible for intelligence and for processing information received from throughout the world regarding possible targets for future operations. Most of the information gathered in London was sent to this division by the London cell.

As reported in *Newsweek* on April 7, 1986, the group's command structure consists of al-Banna and four top aides, all of whom, like the leader, are former members of Arafat's Fatah. The top lieutenant is Mustafa Merad, described by a defector as ''the killer; the one who plans all the operations.'' The others are Ghasan al-Ali, who had been married to an Englishwoman until forced by al-Banna to divorce her as a security risk, Muhammad Wasfi Hannon, and Abd al-Rahman Isa, the latter having been expelled from Fatah for stealing, according to Fatah officials.

In addition to the group command which was located in Baghdad until the early 1980's, moving from there to Damascus and later to Libya, the group has branches in Beirut and the European capitals.

In the last few years it has tried to make contact with other international terrorist groups, such as Action Direct in France and Italian terrorist groups, in order to internationalize the Middle East conflict and to export it beyond the borders of the region. These were perfunctory efforts, however, which were limited at most to logistic cooperation. Abu Nidal does not trust the European organizations, and therefore refuses to have any intensive ties with them. In spite of proclamations of ''solidarity with the freedom organizations in the world,'' he prefers to preserve the secrecy of his group and has no real links with any European terrorist organizations.

The group also claims it has cells in the occupied West Bank. ''Of course we fight on many fronts and believe that the armed struggle is more important than any other, but on our part there is also importance in mobilizing the masses in the occupied territories. The enemy has admitted frequently that we have a strong presence in the occupied territories,'' Sabri al-Banna boasted in 1978. He repeated that claim in a 1985 interview.

The reality, though, is different. The group has no infrastructure in the West Bank, and is not known to have been involved in any attacks there, even though many of its recruits abroad hail from West Bank families.

The organization enjoys the full support of the Iraqi, Syrian, and Libyan regimes and their intelligence services. These services have invested considerable resources in supplying weapons and explosives to the group, as well as in training its members and in allocating it operating funds. Most of the weapons and explosives used by the group were obtained from the Iraqi and Syrian armies, and were manufactured in the Soviet Union or Soviet bloc countries. In addition to the group's Kalachnikov rifles and R.P.G.'s, its members make frequent use of the Polish W.Z.63 submachine gun. The latter was used in attacks in Vienna, Brussels, London, and Paris.

The Iraqi regime also permitted Sabri to be the head of ''The Political Committee of the Palestinian Revolution in Iraq,'' an umbrella group which includes all the Palestinian organizations under Iraqi patronage. That position automatically made him the most important member of the Palestinian community in Iraq. Thanks to Sabri al-Banna's chairmanship of this umbrella group, his organization was able to take control of a radio station, a small news agency, the local Palestinian newspaper, and— above all—the grants and other aid made available for financing the umbrella organization's ongoing activities. The former head of Israeli intelligence, Brigadier-General Yehoshua Saguy, was quoted by the *Washington Post* in 1981 to the effect that the Iraqi regime had given Abu Nidal about fifty million dollars in aid.

In addition to gaining control of the scholarship funds made available to Palestinian students, Abu Nidal received financial support from a number of Arab states, primarily from his host country, Iraq, but also from Syria, which gave him a million dollars, and Libya, which granted him a few hundred thousand dollars. Later, when he moved his base to Syria, he received about six million dollars yearly from that country. Since al-Banna's move to Tripoli, Colonel Qaddafi has promised him twenty-five million dollars annually. Past experience, though, has shown that Qaddafi is not known for keeping his word.

Additional income is received by the organization as "protection" money and by simple blackmail. By threatening to kill senior officials and diplomats in the oil-rich Arab states such as Saudi Arabia and the United Arab Emirates, Abu Nidal obtained a few million dollars from them as well. For years, the organization has been demanding that Kuwait turn over to it part of the funds Kuwait collects annually for the P.L.O. It has been traditional for Palestinians living in Kuwait to donate up to 5 % of their income as a "voluntary" tax to the P.L.O. As Kuwait has refused to meet Abu Nidal's demands, he has periodically attacked it.

It is clear that the organization's financial independence has enabled its members a certain freedom of action, in spite of the fact that they have been subject to partial control by the intelligence services of whatever country has been their host.

Six years after the Palestinian organizations had begun extending their terrorism throughout the world, their leaders were suddenly faced with the need to make bold decisions. The new diplomatic era following the 1973 war demanded that they take action as statesmen. No longer could they plead their case by setting off million dollar fires in the refineries of Trieste or Rotterdam or by killing athletes at international games. Every proposal to export Palestinian terrorism came to be regarded by the P.L.O. leadership as being of dubious value. The last P.L.O. terrorist act was the occupation of the Saudi Arabian embassy in Sudan at the beginning of 1973, with the murder of three Western diplomats, including the American ambassador.

As far as Arafat was concerned, the war put an end to all this activity. Fatah would now have to retreat to its home court, and the Black September squads outside Israel would have to cease operations. Arafat thus decided to abandon international terrorism and to concentrate on political activity combined with an armed struggle against targets in the occupied territories and Israel itself. Furthermore, in a series of secret meetings with American representatives, he promised to refrain from any terrorist actions against American interests, and to warn the Americans of any such attempts by other organizations which refused to accept his authority. His contact with the C.I.A. was Hasan Salama, who had until then been operational commander of Black September in Western Europe, and who later became the commander of the internal security unit of Fatah, known as "Force 17."[2] (The name was derived from the unit's phone extension at Fatah headquarters.) In 1979 Salama was killed in an explosion in Beirut when he tried to start his booby-trapped car. In a book published in 1983,[3] the authors, Eitan Haber and Michael Bar-Zohar—the latter a member of the Knesset—claim that Salama was killed by the Mossad in revenge for his involvement in the murder of the Israeli athletes at the 1972 Munich Olympics.

In any event, a clear rift in both Fatah and the P.L.O. began to show primarily as a response to two things. The first was the very fact that Arafat had addressed the U.N. General Assembly in November 1974 and the second that he was now willing to pursue diplomatic and political means to achieve his aims. His opponents saw this as ideological deviation from the whole concept of the "armed struggle." But they were even more incensed at the content of Arafat's speech. The chairman of the P.L.O. stood at the General Assembly of the United Nations in New York, wearing the *kufiya* which had become his trademark, carrying a gun in a holster under his suit. In his speech, he stated that in one hand he held an olive branch as the symbol of peace, and in the other he had a gun. During the speech, Arafat tried to mini-

[2] In 1984, Arafat appointed Abu Tayeb as commander of Force 17, and reassigned the unit from its duties as a bodyguard to an attack force, involved mainly in naval operations against Israel.
[3] Eitan Haber and Michael Bar-Zohar, *The Red Prince* (London: Weidenfeld and Nicolson, 1983).

mize the importance of the Palestinian Charter, and especially to explain away the existence of Sections 4, 5, and
6 of that document, which deal with the definition of
"Who is a Palestinian."

To understand his opponents' response, we must look
at the background of the charter. It is important to
remember that the charter was composed a decade earlier,
at the end of May 1964, at the founding meeting in East
Jerusalem of the Palestine Liberation Organization.

The meeting at which the charter was formulated had
been called a number of months earlier, at the end of the
Arab summit conference convened in Cairo in January of
that year. The summit had been held after Israel
announced that it was setting up its national water pipe-
line from the Sea of Galilee to the Negev desert. The
Egyptian president, Gamal Abdul Nasser, had consistently counseled that the Arab states refrain from a military confrontation with Israel as long as they had not
achieved military superiority. His enemies in the Arab
camp accused him of cowardice and of ignoring the Palestinian problem. In order to counter his enemies, Nasser
initiated the summit conference, pushed for the acceptance of a resolution to divert the sources of the Jordan
River, and called for the founding of what became the
P.L.O.

The founding meeting of the P.L.O. was attended by
Palestinian representatives from most of the Palestinian
communities throughout the Middle East. For the most
part, these were leaders of the older, more traditional
generation, the one which Arabic literature dubbed "the
dispersal generation." The conference chose a Palestinian
activist, Ahmad Shuqayri, as the chairman of the executive committee of the organization and also decided to
establish the Palestine Liberation Army (P.L.A.).

It was here that the Palestinian National Charter was
approved, which has served since that time (with a few
minor changes) as the binding instrument of the Palestinian movement. Section 5 of the charter states that "the
Palestinians are those Arab nationals who, until 1947,
normally resided in Palestine regardless of whether they
were evicted from it or stayed there. Anyone born, after

that date, of a Palestinian father—whether inside Palestine or outside it—is also a Palestinian.'' Section 6 goes on to say that ''the Jews who had normally lived in Palestine until the beginning of the Zionist invasion will be considered Palestinians.'' When did the ''Zionist invasion'' begin? That leaves much room for interpretation. Some set the date at 1882, when a handful of Hovevei Zion groups—forerunners of modern-day Zionism—settled in the country. Others speak of 1917, when the Balfour Declaration was issued by the British cabinet. What is clear is that this section, as well as others that claim that Zionism is linked to ''international imperialism and [is] antagonistic to all action for liberation and to progressive movements in the world,'' and is ''racist and fanatic in its nature, aggressive, expansionist and colonialist in its aims, and fascist in its methods,'' justifies the armed struggle against this ''demonic'' movement, in order to liberate Palestine and ''cleanse'' the Zionist presence from it. The fact, though, is that even at that time these sections caused consternation among many of the Palestinian intellectuals.

This background may make it easier to understand the dismay among many members of the P.L.O. at Arafat's speech in the U.N. The P.L.O. chairman stated that the future Palestine would include all those Jews living in the country without discrimination, provided they would be willing to remain there in peace. Arafat's appearance at the U.N. was the culmination of a process that the P.L.O. had slowly embarked on, shifting its emphasis to the use of diplomatic means to achieve its ends. This change began to crystallize in early 1974, immediately after the October 1973 war and it soon provoked a militant response.

In October 1974, under the sponsorship of Iraq, Algeria, and South Yemen, a conference was held in Baghdad, with representatives of the P.F.L.P., Ahmad Jibril's organization; the Arab Liberation Front (A.L.F.); and Abu Nidal. It proclaimed its opposition to the currents prevalent in the P.L.O., and announced the formation of ''the Front of those Palestinians who Reject Solutions of Surrender,'' or, in short, the Rejectionist

Front. The changes to which the participants of the conference, and especially Abu Nidal, were opposed, were the P.L.O.'s decisions to forego international terror, to close down Black September, to cooperate secretly with the United States, to use political means together with the continuation of the armed struggle, and, above all, its secret decision to open up a dialogue with the Israelis.

The major aim of this new front was to prevent the convening of a peace conference on the lines of the first Geneva conference held in December 1973, in which Egypt, Israel, the Soviet Union, and the United States had participated. The Geneva conference, which ended inconclusively, called for the convening of a new conference with the participation of all the parties to the dispute, including Palestinian representatives. This call initiated the split in the P.L.O. leadership, and thrust it into a dilemma from which it has not freed itself to this day.

All these changes in the policies of the P.L.O. and Fatah incensed Sabri al-Banna. He decided, with the active assistance of the Iraqi secret service, to embark on a series of acts of revenge against the P.L.O. leadership. In his book, Abu Iyad notes that a group of young Palestinians decided to assassinate the Jordanian, Moroccan, and Saudi Arabian kings, and Numeiri, the Sudanese president. The time set for this was the end of October 1974, when there was to be an Arab summit conference in Rabat. (It was that conference which decided that the P.L.O., and not Jordan, was the sole legitimate representative of the Palestinian people.)

The Moroccan secret services uncovered the plot, and those involved were arrested, but this setback did not faze Abu Nidal. On the contrary, it only spurred him on to continue in his efforts, which were meant to make the Fatah despised throughout the world. A band of his followers hijacked a British airliner in November that year, and forced it to land in Tunis. They demanded the release of fifteen of their comrades in prison in Egypt. Abu Iyad reveals that they also had another demand: the return of the P.L.O. delegation headed by Yasser Arafat from the U.N. General Assembly in New York. By the Egyptian president's personal request, Salah Khalaf, who knew

Sabri al-Banna from their Fatah and Black September days, was asked to negotiate between the sides. According to Abu Iyad, there was a "happy end," with the hijackers withdrawing their demands and rejoining Fatah.

But this was not the way another terrorist attack by the Abu Nidal group ended. At the beginning of November 1974 the U.P.I. news agency reported from Beirut that a Fatah court had convicted Sabri al-Banna of an attempt to provoke "an armed rebellion against the Arafat organization."

Behind that conviction lay a drama whose details would only become known years later. At this point it is important to note that three months before that time al-Banna had already been officially removed from all his positions in Fatah. In a July 26, 1974 announcement by the Palestinian news agency, it was stated that Sabri al-Banna, "known by his alias as Abu Nidal, has been removed from all his positions as representative of the organization (Fatah) in Baghdad because he accused the Syrian authorities of arresting 32 Fatah people." The announcement noted that this accusation was groundless and that the Voice of the Palestinian Revolution, which broadcast from Baghdad and which was under Abu Nidal's control, no longer reflected the P.L.O.'s position.

It is clear that the P.L.O. and Fatah leadership used Abu Nidal's accusations as an excuse for expelling him from the movement. The real reason, of course, was the fact that he was no longer willing to be subservient to the central command or to accept its authority.

In October of that year, a number of armed men were caught near an elegant villa on the outskirts of Damascus. This was the home of Muhammad Abbas, who at the time was the treasurer of Fatah. The group was caught by Abbas's bodyguards. After a short interrogation the members of the band admitted that they belonged to the Abu Nidal group, and that they had been sent from Baghdad to assassinate not only Abbas, but Yasser Arafat as well.

In the resulting trial by a Fatah court, al-Banna was sentenced to death *in absentia*. The three members of the attack group were given prison sentences of from one to seven years with hard labor. The Fatah leaders demanded

Abu Nidal's extradition so that the sentence could be carried out, but the Baghdad government refused point-blank to even consider such a step.

Sabri al-Banna's action caused tremors among the P.L.O. leadership. While the annals of the Palestinian organizations are filled with stories of bitter fighting between factions, they had always been governed by one unwritten rule, that leaders were never to be attacked. Battles and bloodshed between factions were permissible, but they never involved any of the leaders. It was a tacit agreement, one which surprisingly enough had been kept throughout the years—until Sabri al-Banna arrived on the scene. His action was considered so serious that even his new colleagues in the Rejectionist Front condemned him and refused to cooperate with him.

Al-Banna proposed that the Rejectionist Front embark on a campaign meant to eliminate the "traitors" of Fatah and the P.L.O. When the rest of the front refused to even consider this, he decided to leave the front. But even though the vast majority of members of the Palestinian camp, including his closest allies in the Rejectionist Front, had rejected his plans, al-Banna still enjoyed the full support of the Iraqi regime. As far as Saddam Hussein was concerned, Abu Nidal had become too valuable to be turned over to those in Fatah who wished to kill him. He had become so useful, in fact, that Baghdad was willing to continue to assist him in his efforts to eliminate his opponents in the Palestinian movement (including an unsuccessful attempt in April 1980 to assassinate Abu Iyad in Belgrade), even if this meant having Iraq branded as an enemy of the Palestinian people—as long as it could continue to make use of his services.

The ideological struggle between the two Ba'ath regimes in Syria and Iraq began to heat up at that time. Baghdad decided to use Sabri al-Banna to further its interests at the inter-Arab struggle. The time was right in June 1976. For three years Iraqi intelligence had trained and closely supervised the development of the Abu Nidal organization. The group's men had been trained by the Iraqis in combat and guerrilla tactics. And in June of that year the Iraqi intelligence decided that the time was ripe to reap the dividends of its investment.

This was the period following Syria's invasion of Lebanon. The Syrians came to the defense of the Christian community, which was on the verge of collapse in the civil war between it and the combined Muslim, Druse, and Palestinian forces of the left. The Syrian president, Hafiz al-Assad, who believed, as had his predecessors, in eventually incorporating both Lebanon and Palestine into a ''Greater Syria,'' was not willing to allow a change in the status quo of his neighbor. Therefore, contrary to what one might have expected from a regime whose rhetoric called for ''the liberation of Palestine,'' rather than helping the Muslims it came to the aid of the Christians. The Syrian incursion into Lebanon gave Abu Nidal and his Iraqi backers a perfect excuse for attacking Syrian targets. It is clear that the initiative, the planning, and the motivation behind these attacks all originated with the Baghdad regime. The Syrian action had supplied the ideological justification for Abu Nidal's actions.

As far as Abu Nidal was concerned, just as Jordan had betrayed the Palestinians in September 1970, Syria was now doing the same by supporting the Christians. Using the same logic, just as Fatah had established Black September to deal with Arab traitors after Jordan's betrayal, so too did al-Banna set up an equivalent ''new'' organization named Black June, to take care of the contemporary ''traitors to the cause.'' In reality, it was simply Abu Nidal's organization under a new name. All the infrastructure, resources, and personnel which al-Banna had built up in Baghdad since 1973 were now directed to attacking Syria.

Thus, in September 1976 four armed men attacked the Semiramis Hotel in the heart of Damascus. In return for freeing the hostages they had taken, the terrorists demanded that the Syrian authorities free a number of political prisoners who had opposed the regime, most of them evidently agents of Iraqi intelligence. The al-Assad government refused to acquiesce, and instead ordered a military force to attack the hotel and free the hostages. In the raid which followed, one terrorist was killed, as were three hostages. About a month later, the Syrian embassies in Pakistan and Italy were attacked.

In December 1976, Abu Nidal's men tried to assassinate the Syrian foreign minister, Abd al-Halim Khaddam. An armed motorbike rider shot at Khaddam's car as it was travelling on the highway between Damascus and the local airport. A bodyguard was killed and the minister was lightly wounded. Almost exactly a year later there was another attempt to kill Khaddam.

The second attempt on Khaddam's life by Abu Nidal's men took place in the Abu Dhabi airport terminal. Sa'if bin Sa'id al-Ghubash, the foreign minister of the United Arab Emirates, was accidentally killed. Abd al-Halim Khaddam himself was again miraculously saved, and the attackers finally turned themselves in to the authorities, but not before having taken hostages.

Meanwhile, Syria decided not to take this lying down. According to one version, it obtained the services of Carlos, the Venezuelan terrorist, to counterbalance Iraq's attacks using Abu Nidal. Carlos was placed under the direct orders of Brigadier-General Ali Khadar, who was responsible for Syria's security services, and was directed to inflict harm on Iraq.

While engaged in attacking Syria, the Abu Nidal group continued to maintain its "normal" functions, namely its struggle against what it considered the "reactionary" Arabs. Thus, in November 1976, four terrorists took over the Intercontinental Hotel in Amman, Jordan. Five hours later, the Jordanian security forces freed the hostages. During the attack, which the Jordanians believe to have been planned by Na'if Rosan, two Jordanian soldiers were killed, as were three hotel guests and three terrorists. The fourth terrorist was captured alive but wounded, and was executed about a month later by the verdict of a military court.

Then came the dramatic trip by President Sadat to Jerusalem in November 1977. That made him "enemy number one" among all the radicals of the Arab world. Mu'ammar Qaddafi placed a price on Sadat's head, and tried to organize "hit teams" to kill him. Stewart Steven claims that it was only the information that the Mossad sent to the Egyptian security services which prevented Sadat's assassination at that time.

Of course Abu Nidal's organization was among those attempting to kill Sadat. His command in Baghdad, with the active involvement of Iraqi intelligence, came up with a number of assassination plans. They all failed, though, because the security surrounding President Sadat was so tight as to make such a step impossible. The fear of an assassination attempt was so great that even when Sadat was at Camp David in 1978, Presdient Carter ordered the U.S. Secret Service to redouble its efforts and to keep an eye even on Sadat's closest advisors.

When al-Banna was unable to execute this plan, he decided to attack a more accessible target. The whole country of Egypt became his greatest enemy. The Egyptians saw him as a deadly threat to their political existence, and fought back. "The Egyptians tried to infiltrate our organization," al-Banna announced. "Colonel Hani Abd al-Aziz, head of one of Sadat's secret departments, was given the assignment to infiltrate our organization. Abd al-Aziz was under the direct orders of Vice-president Mubarak. He was given two assignments: to liquidate one of the strongest centers of opposition to Sadat's plans for a solution to the Middle East conflict, and to find a scapegoat for Egypt's woes. In the first months of 1978 Abd al-Aziz managed to set up a number of spy centers in the Arab world. The two most important were in Kuwait and Beirut. Within three months, however, our fighters were able to liquidate these spy centers totally, sometimes physically, and to expose their links. This resulted in a decisive blow to Sadat, and his reaction, as we saw in Cyprus, was irrational."

What happened in Cyprus, that made Abu Nidal mention it in his interview with *Middle East* as the scene of one of his greatest victories? The fact is that this was al-Banna's only success in attacking an important figure in the Egyptian leadership. In February 1978, three months after Sadat's trip to Jerusalem, Abu Nidal's men attacked Yusuf Siba'i, chairman of the Egyptian newspapers syndicate, and a friend of President Sadat. He was shot to death at the entrance to the Hilton Hotel in Nicosia. This action was similar to previous ones in Damascus, Amman, and Abu Dhabi.

Rather than arranging an escape route in the event that the attack failed, the band involved preferred the so-called "successful" method of taking hostages. After killing Siba'i, they grabbed a number of hotel guests and took them as hostages. After lengthy negotiations, the Cypriot government gave in and agreed to provide the terrorists with a plane to fly them to any destination they wished, in return for releasing the hostages. The agreement was observed scrupulously. The hostages were freed and the terrorists flew to an unknown destination in the Middle East. A few hours later, though, they returned to the Larnaca airport, for it appeared that no Arab country was willing to grant them sanctuary. Not even Iraq.

When the Egyptian authorities discovered that the plane had been forced to return to Cyprus, they sent in a military transport with a commando unit. The Egyptians demanded that the Cypriot government allow their military force to attack the terrorists, so that they could be captured and brought to trial in Cairo. The Cypriot cabinet, however, refused to permit this, and ordered its national guard to protect Abu Nidal's men. The result was a bloody clash between the Cypriot army and the Egyptian commando unit, during which fifteen Egyptian soldiers were killed and seventeen wounded.

The blow suffered by the Egyptian regime in Cyprus and the continued threats on Sadat's life did not sway him from his peace strategy. He continued to negotiate with Israel, in spite of the threats and difficulties. The more the contacts between the two countries increased, the greater became the rift between the Egyptians and the Palestinian camp.

In practice, all the Palestinian organizations, including those which did not belong to the Rejectionist Front, repudiated Sadat's trip to Jerusalem and his readiness to sign a peace treaty with Israel. This stand was endorsed at the highest levels, at a summit meeting in Tripoli, Libya, in December 1977, when the P.L.O. leadership unanimously decided to join the Rejectionist Front, which included Libya, Iraq, Syria, South Yemen, and Algeria.

At the conference, which was sponsored by Colonel Qaddafi, the participants agreed on a common program, which included, inter alia, the establishment of the "Steadfastness and Confrontation Front," which opposed "submission to Zionism, imperialism and the Arabs serving them"; the rejection of U.N. Security Council Resolutions 242 and 338; the rejection of international conferences; the imposition of a political boycott of the Sadat regime; and the adoption of "actions to realize the right of the Palestinian people to return to Palestine and its right for self-determination on every part of the soil of Palestine which will be liberated, without granting recognition or involvement in negotiations in return." Yasser Arafat himself participated in this conference, and the P.L.O. took part in two further ones in 1978—in Algiers and Baghdad—which endorsed in general terms the Tripoli resolutions.

The most important results of the conference were not only the total rejection of the political settlement between Egypt and Israel under American patronage, but also the reconciliation between Arafat and his opponents in the Rejectionist Front. The "lost children," Habash, Jibril, and Hawatmah, all returned to the fold. There was an attempt, with Iraq as the intermediary, to bring about a reconciliation between Arafat and Sabri al-Banna as well. Iraqi diplomats tried to have the Fatah leaders repeal the death sentence against al-Banna and to arrange a meeting between Arafat and Abu Nidal. But right then another major dispute broke out between Fatah, on the one hand, and the Iraqi regime, on the other, thus terminating the short honeymoon between Fatah and the Rejectionist Front.

The "rehabilitation" which Arafat had granted the radical groups evidently led them, including Abu Nidal, to believe that the chairman of the P.L.O. would permit them to embark on a major terrorist campaign and a continuation of the "armed struggle" against Israel. At a certain stage the Fatah leadership even considered going underground again and reverting to the secret structure which had marked it in its earliest beginnings. Arafat, however, soon decided to continue with diplomatic means coupled with the armed struggle. At his express orders and without the knowledge of Faruq al-Qadumi, head of the P.L.O. Political Department, representatives of the P.L.O. became involved in secret contacts with the Egyptian and American governments. These contacts, which were meant to enable the Palestinians to join the peace process, included high-level figures in the American administration, such as Rosalyn Carter, wife of President Carter.[4] The P.L.O. was represented by Sa'id Hamami, a close friend of Arafat, and the organization's representative in London since 1973. But Hamami was also one of the most controversial members of the Palestinian camp, for in an article he had published in the London *Times*, he had called on the Palestinians to take part in the peace talks and had supported the establishment of a "mini" Palestinian state on the West Bank and the Gaza Strip.

At that time, most Palestinian organizations, including Fatah, interpreted his declared readiness to settle for less than all of Palestine as heresy, contradicting their most sacrosanct principles. Hamami's statement was greeted by them with unprecedented anger. But he was not dissuaded by their opposition. About five months later, in April 1974, he gave a special interview to the London *Jewish Chronicle*, which is known for its strong support for the State of Israel. In that article, Hamami repeated his previous positions and even suggested the establishment of a binational Israeli-Palestinian state.

Following Hamami's interviews, Faruq al-Qaddumi, who is considered to be one of the extremists within Fatah, demanded Hamami's ouster, while Naji Alush insisted that he be expelled from the union and be tried for treason. Hamami, though, was completely unfazed by these reactions. As soon became apparent, he enjoyed Arafat's full confidence, and continued his contacts with various high level politicians in Europe, on the chairman's direct orders, in order to arrange channels of communication with Israeli left-wingers.

[4] See Zbigniev Brzezinski, *Power and Principle* (New York: Farrar, Straus and Giroux, 1983), Chapter 7.

The fact is that since 1974 rumors had been circulating about secret contacts between various Israeli and Palestinian leaders. These rumors were always denied by both sides. Today this is no longer a secret. The first meeting was initiated by Uri Avnery, an Israeli journalist and a member of the Knesset at the time. "Hamami and I met for the first time in 1974," revealed Avnery, "in a London hotel, and from then until 1978 we had numerous meetings, most of them in London or in other Western Europe capitals. After every such meeting, Hamami would report back directly to Arafat, and at my own initiative I reported to Prime Minister Yitzhak Rabin."

The number of those involved in these secret talks soon grew. They began to gain momentum when prominent people, such as the former premier of France, Pierre Mendes-France, and the Austrian prime minister, Bruno Kreisky, lent their support. Mendes-France, for example, put his country house at the participants' disposal. Among the Israelis involved were Aryeh (Lyova) Eliav, General Matti Peled, Yaakov Arnon, Ran Cohen, and others who were involved in establishing the Israel-Palestine Friendship League.

The Palestinian side was represented by Dr. Issam Sartawi; Ibrahim Sus (who was the president of the General Union of Palestinian Students and the P.L.O. representative to UNESCO in Paris); Izz al-Din Qalaq, the P.L.O. representative in Paris; Da'ud Barakat, its representative in Geneva; Dr. Sabri Jiras; Abdallah Faranji, the P.L.O. representative in Bonn; and others. The meetings were aimed at exploring ways to find an agreed solution that could be acceptable to Israel and the Palestinians. In the end, in spite of the cloak of secrecy which had been imposed on the contacts, reports of the meetings began appearing in the press, and of course drew the attention of the radical groups.

These meetings spurred Abu Nidal on in his struggle with Arafat and the P.L.O. leadership. Sabri al-Banna rejected what he regarded as a total deviation from the path of the pure armed struggle. He wanted to kill Arafat, but knowing how much the Rejectionist Front was against this, and especially as Arafat had increased the security surrounding him, he decided to hit at easier targets. This meant attempting to liquidate all the P.L.O. representatives who had participated in or had been involved, either directly or indirectly, in contacts with Israel.[5]

This was the first stage in Abu Nidal's strategy, which was meant to harm Fatah and to undermine Arafat's credibility. Another factor involved was Iraq's attitude to events at the time. The P.L.O.'s increased dependence on Syria (following the civil war in Lebanon) and Sadat's peace initiative made Baghdad conclude that it needed to increase its influence in the Palestinian camp. It attempted to do so by organizations such as the Arab Liberation Front, which was a member of the P.L.O., but primarily through Abu Nidal. The method adapted to increase its influence was a world-wide campaign to murder the P.L.O. representatives (primarily Fatah members who were close to Yasser Arafat).

[5] One of those killed was Izz al-Din Qalaq. His two assassins, Asad Khayid and Husni Hatim, were sentenced in 1978 to a 15-year prison term by a French court, but were freed in February 1986, at a time when there were mysterious explosions in a number of major stores in the French capital. The French weekly, V.S.D., believed that the release was part of a secret deal between French intelligence and Abu Nidal. Under this agreement, Abu Nidal promised, in return for the two terrorists, to desist from taking any further hostile actions on French soil. While the agreement was signed in Vienna in October 1982 by Abu Nidal's representative, Walid Awadah, and the French president's adviser on national security, Francois de Grossouvre, the French evidently did not honor their commitment for another three years. Thus Abu Nidal resorted to violent means. It is interesting to note that the responsibility for these explosions was taken by an unknown organization calling itself the Committee for the Freeing of Arab Prisoners. The bombs that were used were described by the French police as primitive and simple. It is just because of this that the police believe that they were prepared by professionals, who were intent only on providing a warning to the government, but did not wish to inflict extensive damage and injury.

In a matter of months, the P.L.O. offices in London, Kuwait, and Pakistan were attacked. The first victim was killed in January 1978, when a lone gunman walked into the London offices of the P.L.O., entered the room of its representative, Sa'id Hamami, and shot him in the head at close range. Even those who find it hard to identify the killer have no difficulty in guessing the reason for the murder. This was meant as an ''object lesson'' for the Palestinian moderates not to dare to have any further contacts with the ''Zionist enemy.''

Hamami's murder was but the prologue. Within three years five more P.L.O. representatives or people closely associated with Arafat would be killed. The logic behind these attacks on the P.L.O. ''traitors'' was quite clear. It was the product of a consistent and well-planned policy meant to impart an atmosphere of terror and fear among the ranks, so that others might learn their lesson.

Did these threats affect the P.L.O.? There are those who believe that this is indeed the case. Uri Avnery believes from long conversations with P.L.O. members that ''the murders of the past have frightened the moderate representatives of the P.L.O.'' Abu Nidal's men feel the same way. They are convinced that their assassinations served their purpose and frightened off P.L.O. members from further contacts with Israelis. In an interview given to the Austrian journalist Renate Posaring[6] in July 1981, three members of the Abu Nidal, using the names Abu Elias, Abu Rahman, and Abu Mariam, told her, ''If we had not killed a number of people, Yasser

---

[6] Renate Posaring has written a number of cover stories for the Austrian newsweekly *Profil* but her reliability, as opposed to her tenacity, is not considered of the highest caliber. In February 1984 the magazine admitted that in return for an exclusive interview with Mu'ammar Qaddafi, she went beyond the call of duty, offering him sexual favors and even converting to the Muslim faith. She has also claimed to have received exclusive interviews with Arafat, Habash, and according to the magazine, with Abu Nidal himself. But it is doubtful whether she met al-Banna in person.

Arafat would have come to Jerusalem a long time ago, as did Sadat.''

In response to these attacks, Fatah blamed Iraq for Abu Nidal's deeds, and attacked the Iraqi embassies in London, Beirut, Paris, and Tripoli, as well as the offices of the Palestine Liberation Front (PLF) in Beirut. That explosion on July 13, 1978, killed about 200 people. Arafat claimed that the PLF had pro-Iraqi tendencies.

At a certain point, Sabri al-Banna decided that the attacks should not be limited only to those who had had contacts with the enemy, but should be extended to those who had helped to organize them as well. Thus the decision was reached to assassinate the various intermediaries involved. Heinz Nittal was chosen to be the first one. He was a prominent public figure, a member of the Vienna city council, and his sin consisted in having been the head of the Israel-Austria Friendship League.

He was murdered in May 1981. About two days later, the Austrian embassy in Damascus received an official notice in writing from the Abu Nidal organization. In its announcement, the organization took responsibility for the action, claiming that Nittal had been killed because ''he made the contacts between the P.L.O. leaders and Zionist leaders.''

Following Nittal's death, the Austrian secret service undertook a comprehensive investigation, and was aided by information supplied by Yasser Arafat himself through Dr. Issam Sartawi, who lived in Vienna and was a close friend of the Austrian chancellor. The investigation was very thorough, and found a broad-scale conspiracy. The Austrian foreign minister, who had previously flown to both Baghdad and Damascus to obtain an undertaking from both countries to no longer assist the Abu Nidal group in conducting any attacks in Austria, told the weekly *Profil*: ''An Iraqi-Palestinian terror squad numbering eight people infiltrated Austria with the aim of assassinating Chancellor Bruno Kreisky. We have reliable information that we cannot prove in court. We also know that the hit squad that arrived in Vienna belongs to the Abu Nidal group, and is threatening to kill Kreisky.''

Bruno Kreisky could indeed be considered an important target. Since the 1973 Yom Kippur War, the Austrian chancellor had been one of the initiators of Israeli-Palestinian dialogue. As deputy chairman of the Socialist International, he was in constant touch with the Israel Labor Party. On the other hand, his pronouncements in favor of Palestinian rights gained him the confidence of the P.L.O. Through Dr. Issam Sartawi, Kreisky became fast friends with Yasser Arafat. Kreisky was also involved in organizing a number of secret meetings between Israelis and Arab leaders, and attempted to arrange such a meeting between Prime Minister Rabin and President Sadat. It is thus not surprising that Kreisky's actions had aroused the wrath of the Abu Nidal group. The group's spokesmen in fact announced, "the killing of Nittal was a warning to Kreisky not to get involved in our matters. It isn't his business. We will liquidate him if he doesn't stop his mediating efforts between Israel and the P.L.O."

When the Austrian connection was exposed, additional protection was given Chancellor Kreisky, and the special police anti-terror squad was put at his disposal around the clock. The extra security did indeed stop Abu Nidal's men from assassinating him, but did not prevent the attack on the Vienna synagogue. The importance of that event is not merely the fact that two people were killed, but that it marked another milestone in the group's organizational methods.

7

The International Stage

After starting off by attacking Syrian interests and targets in moderate Arab countries, Abu Nidal's group had moved on to attacking P.L.O. members. Now it entered the third stage: attacks on Israeli and Jewish targets. As with Fatah and other Palestinian organizations, Abu Nidal's group had also "graduated," after a number of years, to the internationalization of its tactics. Even though, as will be seen, there were still attacks against Palestinian and Arab targets, Abu Nidal stressed Israeli and Jewish targets in Western Europe during the period beginning in 1980.

The first sign of this change in tactics by the group is normally taken to have been the midday attack, on July 29, 1981, on the Vienna synagogue[1], at a time when the congregants were celebrating a Bar Mitzvah. A man and a woman were killed, but the attackers were shot by the personal bodyguard of a Jewish businessman attending the reception. Two of the "hit men," Hasan Marwan and Hisham Hijah, were arrested and admitted under interrogation that they belonged to the Abu Nidal group.

[1] While there had already been an attempt in November 1979 by the Abu Nidal group to kill the Israeli ambassador in Lisbon, Efraim Eldar, the attack in Vienna is considered to have been the first of its indiscriminate terror attacks against civilians, be they Israeli targets, synagogues, embassies, or schools, continuing through the December 1985 attacks on the El Al counters in Vienna and Rome.

Their imprisonment was followed by the discovery of a large arms cache in Salzburg. This included more than fifty Spanish revolvers, Polish W.Z.63 submachine guns, Soviet hand grenades, explosives, and detonators, all in the possession of a young Palestinian who was acting as the "quartermaster" of the squad. Ballistic tests at the police laboratories showed clearly that one of the weapons seized had been used in the murder of Heinz Nittal.

The apprehension of the squad in Austria also helped solve the murder of Na'im Khadir, the P.L.O. representative in Brussels. He was shot and killed on June 1, 1981, less than two months before the attack on the Vienna synagogue, as he walked out his front door in the morning. Following a strategy it had often pursued on other occasions, the P.L.O. accused the Israeli security services of attempting to liquidate the P.L.O. representatives in Europe. Especially after the Liliehammer affair in Norway, where Israeli agents had gunned down an innocent person in a case of mistaken identity, it was easy for the Palestinians to make such an accusation, and to persuade large parts of world public opinion of its veracity. (At Liliehammer, a Moroccan waiter was killed on July 21, 1973, when Mossad agents mistook him for Hasan Salama, the operations commander of Black September in Western Europe.)

By direct orders of the then Israeli prime minister, Golda Meir, the Mossad had been carrying out a series of reprisals against the members of Black September who were responsible for the murder of eleven Israeli athletes at the 1972 Munich Olympics. After the Liliehammer affair, though, Israel stopped attacking leading Palestinians, but that, of course, did not prevent the P.L.O. from claiming that Israel was responsible any time a Palestinian was killed. The Lilihammer affair thus caused Israel's interests great damage, and enabled the P.L.O. to claim that every Palestinian killed by violence in Western Europe had been a victim of Israel's security services.

However, at heart (as they admitted in private conversations), the Palestinians knew that Na'im Khadir, like his colleagues in London, Paris, and Kuwait, had been killed on the cold-blooded orders of Abu Nidal. In addition, the evidence supplied by the Austrian authorities to their Belgian counterparts was very convincing. A photograph of Hisham Hijah was sent to the Brussels police, and eyewitnesses there identified him as the killer of Na'im Khadir.

The exposure of the Austrian-Belgian connection shed new light on the Baghdad faction. The apprehension of those responsible for the attack on the Vienna synagogue supplied a great deal of valuable information to the Western security services, which have been cooperating in the struggle against international terrorism. At least once a year the heads of the different security services of Western Europe and North America or their representatives meet and share information.[2] The data their services had accumulated about this pro-Iraqi organization was not something to be dismissed lightly.

This information supplied a first-hand account of the Abu Nidal group's methods, and allowed an evaluation of its capabilities. The picture that emerged was one of a completely professional terrorist organization, whose members were well-trained and familiar with all the rules of conspiracy. A small amount of this information, as we saw before, was exposed in the London trial, primarily about the organizational structure of the group. The West European security services were even more interested in finding material on its links with other international terrorist groups. And this too was now forthcoming. It was found that, contrary to its practices in the past, the Abu Nidal group had shifted its operations from the Middle East to Western Europe. In order to strike at Israeli and Jewish targets in Western Europe, it had begun cooperating with other terrorist groups. Of course, attempts to link up with other international terrorist groups were not something new for Palestinian organizations.

In fact, it was in 1968 that Palestinian terrorism reached European shores. The first person to "export" this terrorism from the Middle East was Dr. George Habash,

---

[2] The information is shared at a secret meeting of what is known as "the Kilowatt Group." This group includes representatives of the secret services of fourteen Western states, including Israel.

leader of the Popular Front for the Liberation of Palestine (P.F.L.P.). Supported by leftists such as the Italian publisher Giacomo Feltrinelli, who encouraged him to internationalize the Israeli-Palestinian conflict, Dr. Habash decided to force the entire world to pay attention, by bringing the conflict onto the television screen in everyone's living room. Apparently, there was very little ideology involved in the cooperation between the Palestinian and European terrorists. As far as Habash was concerned, both the far right and the far left were equally fertile fields for recruiting "fighters for the cause."

When Habash sent his first commando unit to Rome to hijack an El Al plane in 1968, he seemed to be a proponent of Marxism-Leninism. (His adversary, Na'if Hawatmah, who split off from Habash and established his own group, would later claim that Habash had never shaken off his "fascist" mentality.) Yet, in spite of his so-called leftist orientation, he had no compunctions about using volunteers from neo-Nazi and pro-fascist organizations. To him, all was permissible in his war against the Zionists.

Sabri al-Banna has always wanted to emulate Habash. In spite of his alleged belief in the original Fatah ideology, he prefers the spectacular, world-shaking terrorist acts of the P.F.L.P. He has also learned to appreciate the "profits" that can accrue from ties with international terrorist organizations. He proclaimed in 1978: "We have a principle that we don't get involved in the armed struggled of each state or of any other organization. . . . We nevertheless, of course, support any action aimed against American imperialism." At that time he had already laid the ideological foundations for a shaky alliance, based on the lowest possible common denominator, of international cooperation among the various terrorist groups.

As mentioned earlier, even while a member in good standing of Fatah, Sabri al-Banna had attended courses in North Korea and Communist China, where he learned to appreciate the importance of international contacts with sympathetic governments, movements, and organizations. After establishing his own organization, he waited for the first opportunity to try to actualize this cooperation. Indeed, soon after establishing his group, he reached the conclusion (at the end of 1979 or the beginning of 1980) that the time was ripe to enter a new phase of the internationalization of the struggle. To embark on this phase, he sent special recruitment officers to Europe to enlist volunteers and supporters from the European left, as well as from the anti-Semitic and neo-Nazi movements. At the same time, though, he was very cautious about such contacts. He wanted to exploit his ties with these organizations, but was afraid that too-close ties with them would expose his own group to infiltration by foreign and hostile security services.

Another duty of his recruitment officers was to try to form ties with local terrorist organizations. They were especially successful in France, the country chosen as the bridgehead to internationalization. The socialist government of Francois Mitterand, in spite of its good relations with Israel, was supportive of the Palestinian cause. It was symbolic that one of Mitterand's close advisors had himself once been a terrorist. Régis Debray had worked closely with Che Guevara in the 1960's, and had been sentenced to a thirty-year prison term in Bolivia. After his release due to political pressure, Debray ceased being an active terrorist, but his sentiments for national liberation movements were still strong.

It is obviously difficult to show any direct link between the attainment of power by Mitterand's socialists and the fact that many terrorists from Spain, Armenia, and the Middle East began to find France an easy place to carry out attacks. But that was a fact. In this easy-going atmosphere, Abu Nidal's members began to form ties with a number of French guerrilla groups, primarily with Action Direct, the leftist-oriented organization which believes in urban guerrilla tactics, and which in the 1970's declared a war of destruction against ''American imperialism and the capitalist order in France.'' In those years, Action Direct's members attacked hotels, department stores, and even the French Military Academy in Paris, all of these representing in its eyes "the bourgeois establishment regime."

Was it only coincidental that Na'if Rosan visited France in 1981? His Iraqi passport shows that in March he flew from Baghdad to Paris, where he remained for four consecutive months. What exactly did he do there? In answering the prosecutor's questions, Rosan answered: "It is true that I spent a lot of money in France, but that was my vacation." West European security sources believed, and the information was passed on to the French security services, that he had other reasons for being there. He was sent by the group, and his true aim was to supervise the establishment of new cells in Paris and the initiation of ties with Action Direct. Details about these contacts and their true nature were brought to the attention of the public only about a year after Rosan left the French capital.

In the summer of 1982, Israel's invasion of Lebanon brought with it a wave of anger and protest throughout the world. Governments deplored the invasion and called for Israel's withdrawal. The British government went even further and imposed an arms embargo on Israel. During the war, the number of anti-Semitic occurrences in Western Europe increased. In Britain these grew three-fold. In France, rather than being limited primarily, as previously, to verbal anti-Semitic outbursts, they became full-fledged terrorist attacks. During July and August of that year, there were at least fifteen attacks on Israeli or Jewish targets in Paris alone. Bombs exploded near the Discount Bank, which is a member of the Rothschild group; near a Jewish store in the eastern part of the city; and under the parked car of an Israeli diplomat. On August 9, 1982, "hit men" opened fire on the restaurant of Jo Goldenberg, in the Jewish Pletzel quarter. An anonymous caller, identifying himself as a spokesman for Action Direct, took the responsibility for the attack.

The attack on the restaurant, in which six people were killed, caused a world-wide protest. The French government was blamed, and not only by the Jews and the Israeli prime minister, Menahem Begin, for being powerless to deal with the terror. Local French politicians and the French media echoed the argument, accusing the government of displaying weakness, cowardice, and a failure of will to act against terror.

Given the strong impact of the murder and the increasing criticism directed against it, the Mitterand government decided to ban Action Direct as an illegal organization. At the same time, police detectives began to look for members of the group and to search their homes.

On October 13, the police arrested the two leaders of the group, Friedrich Oriash, 29, and Christien Goudan, 25. They were apprehended in a subway station, while examining documents that had been left in a private locker. As far as the police were concerned, the documents they seized were more important than the leaders themselves. They proved the ties between Action Direct and other terrorist organizations, and especially supplied evidence of the links with the Abu Nidal group. Even though the police investigators did not think that Action Direct was responsible for the attack on the restaurant (in spite of the anonymous phone call), the documents it had found exposed the group's involvement in other terrorist incidents against Israeli targets. It was clear from the documents that members of Action Direct were planning to fly to Baghdad for military training.

The minister for public safety affairs, Joseph Franchesi, held a dramatic news conference, in which he stated, ''We have in our possession proof that the terrorist acts of Action Direct were part of an anti-Israeli and pro-Palestinian international terror campaign.'' This discovery corroborated the findings in Vienna that the Abu Nidal group cooperates with European terrorist groups.

Interrogation of the Action Direct members who had been arrested, and the evidence produced at their trial, showed that the Abu Nidal group had been involved in some of the attacks of Action Direct, although, contrary to public opinion, no convincing evidence links the two groups to the murder of the Israeli diplomat, Yaakov Bar-

Simantov, in April 1982,[3] or to the murder of the six people in Jo Goldenberg's restaurant.

When the French organization was banned, it also destroyed, at least temporarily, Abu Nidal's base in France—or at least that was the opinion of the police. But that did not stop Abu Nidal from maintaining ties with other terrorist organizations, such as those in Italy or an Armenian organization.

In September 1982 two armed terrorists attacked the international airport in Ankara, Turkey. In this suicide raid, which was reminiscent of the Japanese attack in July 1972 on Ben Gurion airport in Israel, ten people were killed and eighty wounded. At the end of a short battle with the terrorists, the security forces were able to kill one of them and to capture the second. Livian Akmakian, aged 24, was tried by a military court. Before being sentenced to death, he revealed that he was a member of A.S.A.L.A., the Armenian Secret Army for the Liberation of Armenia. This the largest of a number of Armenian organizations which are struggling to gain independence, and to take revenge on the Turks for the genocide of one and a half million Armenians in 1915.

The Armenian terrorist told the court in Ankara that the weapons used in the attack were supplied by the Abu Nidal group. In his testimony, he mentioned that he had heard this personally from Agip Agipian, one of the leaders of A.S.A.L.A.

This cooperation between the Abu Nidal group and the Armenian organization was given even greater expression about ten months later, at Orly airport in Paris. A booby-trapped suitcase, which exploded prematurely on July 17,

[3] The murder was committed by a strange terrorist group known as L.A.R.F. (Lebanese Armed Revolutionary Factions). This is a Lebanese-Palestinian group, whose leader, George Ibrahim, was captured in 1985 by the French authorities. L.A.R.F. is suspected of murdering Leaman Hunt, Director General of the Multinational Force in Sinai, in a Rome suburb, in February 1984. This group had strong ties with Action Direct, and is considered to be an offshoot of the original P.F.L.P.-S.C. led by Dr. Wadi Haddad.

1983 near the Turkish national airline counter, caused the death of 7 people and the injury of 65. A.S.A.L.A., in a message sent to the French news agency, claimed responsibility for the deed, and announced that this was another act of revenge for the slaughter of the Armenians. The Paris police engaged in a massive manhunt to find the perpetrators, laying particular emphasis on the Armenian community in France. The houses of hundreds of Armenians known to be hostile to Turkey were searched, a number of people were detained, and others were expelled from the country. This investigation yielded much valuable information on the structure of A.S.A.L.A. and its methods. The D.S.T., the French internal security service, tends to believe that the Armenian organization had been in contact with Syrian intelligence since the beginning of the 1980's. As evidence, the French secret service notes that tens of young Armenians arrived in France at the beginning of 1983, most of them carrying Syrian passports.

According to the French, Syria is operating the Armenian organization, under instructions from Moscow. The Soviets are interested in destabilizing the Turkish regime as part of their strategy to weaken the southeastern wing of NATO. Since Iran collapsed as a pro-Western stronghold, Turkey is even more important to the NATO alliance. On its soil are secret military facilities, including stations for monitoring Soviet nuclear missile bases. The fact that many of these facilities are located in what used to be Armenia only increased the Soviet interest in the Armenian movement. The Soviet's motives are clear: to exploit the Armenian terror group for the Soviet Union's political and strategic interests against Turkey and the West. Of course it must be very cautious when doing so, lest Armenian nationalism spread from Turkish Armenia to Soviet Armenia. Thus, rather than being directly involved, the Soviet Union has been using Syria as its surrogate.

A.S.A.L.A. was founded by a group of young, radical Armenians at the beginning of the 1970's. Its primary aim is to force Turkey to admit its guilt for the massacre of the Armenians. Using terror tactics, the group hopes to free its ancient homeland in Anatolia and to establish an independent Armenian republic. Its first terrorist act took place in 1973, when the consul general of Turkey in Los Angeles was killed. Since then, the Armenian terrorists have murdered 28 Turkish diplomats throughout America, Europe, and Asia, and have carried out brazen acts of terror in Turkey itself, including a grenade attack on the Istanbul market (in June 1983) and the attack on the Ankara airport.

Since its founding, the organization has had the support of the Palestinian organizations, and its members have been trained in Palestinian camps in Lebanon. The clearest proof of this was given in April 1980, when George Habash's P.F.L.P. organized a special news conference in the market of Sidon, Lebanon. A number of masked men portrayed themselves as ''Armenian guerrilla fighters and Kurdish rebels,'' who had set themselves the common goal of fighting the Turkish government (at that time led by the conservative premier Suleyman Demirel).

A year later, according to assessments by the French secret service, A.S.A.L.A.'s ties with the Palestinian organizations in Lebanon began weakening, and the group decided to move its headquarters to Damascus. It was there that an indirect link was formed between the Armenian group and Abu Nidal. Finally, when Abu Nidal also moved his headquarters to Damascus, the ties between the two groups were strengthened. This was supported by Akmakian's evidence that Abu Nidal supplied them with weapons.

It should nevertheless be stressed once again that the links between Abu Nidal and other terrorist groups were primarily indirect and limited to logistic support. They involved supplying explosives and weapons, and in no way included recruitment of new members or direct meetings between the sides. In general, Abu Nidal's group would rather limit its membership than impair the secrecy of the group, and prefers Palestinian recruits over foreigners.

Even if Abu Nidal wanted to recruit foreigners, this would now present a problem, for what appealed to the student protestors of the 1970's does not interest the gen-

THE al-BANNA FAMILY HOUSE IN JAFFA.
IT IS USED TODAY AS THE TEL AVIV ISRAELI MILITARY COURT.

FIRST KNOWN PHOTO OF SABRI AL-BANNA (RIGHT),
SEEN HERE WITH A NORTH KOREAN OFFICER. IT IS PRESUMED THAT
THE PHOTO WAS TAKEN IN 1972, WHEN ABU NIDAL
SPENT TIME IN A NORTH KOREAN MILITARY TRAINING CAMP.

THE PHOTO ON THE LEFT, TAKEN IN 1978, WAS MISTAKENLY
IDENTIFIED AS ABU NIDAL AND DISTRIBUTED IN EARLY 1986
BY NEWS AGENCIES. ABDEL QADER YASSINE (RIGHT), A
PALESTINIAN AUTHOR, SAYS THE PICTURE WAS REALLY OF HIM.
IT IS ASSUMED THAT THE PHOTO WAS RELEASED AS PART OF A
MISLEADING CAMPAIGN OF PSYCHOLOGICAL WARFARE
CONDUCTED BY THE ABU NIDAL GROUP.

THE TWO TERRORISTS INVOLVED IN THE ATTACK
ON VIENNA'S SCHWECHAT AIRPORT, DECEMBER 1985.

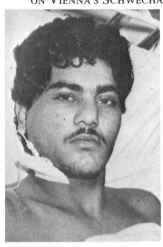
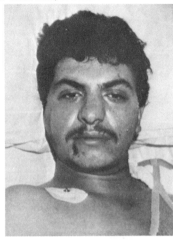

VIENNA AIRPORT—
POLICE EXAMINATION AFTER THE ATTACK
ON THE EL AL CHECK-IN COUNTER, DECEMBER 1985.

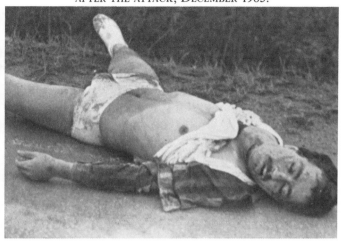

VIENNA AIRPORT—
A TERRORIST KILLED WHILE ATTEMPTING TO ESCAPE
AFTER THE ATTACK, DECEMBER 1985.

VIENNA INTERNATIONAL AIRPORT—
GUARDED AFTER THE DECEMBER 1985 TERRORIST ATTACK.

The "real Abu Nidal," Sabri al-Banna,
as shown in a photo released by the Israeli army, 1976.

eration of the 1980's. The reservoirs from which volunteers and cadres for international terrorist acts can be
drawn have diminished, and as a result Sabri al-Banna has
had to rely on his two old allies: Syria and Iraq.

This brings us to a delicate and controversial question.
The mere juxtaposition of Damascus and Baghdad seems
more than passingly strange, for the two countries are
mortal enemies. Even Salah Khalaf, of the P.L.O., who
is well acquainted with all the intrigues of inter-Arab politics, finds it hard to comprehend. How then is it that
Syria and Iraq, who agree about absolutely nothing else,
are both willing to enthusiastically support the terrorist
actions of Abu Nidal and to assist him? How can this be
explained?

It is obviously difficult to truly understand the roots of
the unusual, even bizarre, links between both Syria and
Iraq, which detest one another, and the Abu Nidal organization, but the fact is that Abu Nidal has managed to
serve both while also serving himself and the specific
interests of his group. Possibly the best way to describe
him is as a double agent, one who serves two masters,
both of whom know of the existence of the other but are
unable or unwilling to forego the services the agent ren-
ders them.

The opinion of intelligence officers in both Israel and
Western Europe is that in 1979 the leaders in Baghdad
decided Sabri al-Banna was more a burden than an asset.
This was particularly true as the regime was interested in
improving its relations with the West, and especially with
the United States. The effort to free itself from its military, economic, and political dependence on Moscow
gained greater urgency when Iraq declared war on Iran.
The more mired down it became in the war, the more all
its efforts seemed to be leading to a dead end, and the
more dire its position, the more it became dependent on
the financial and military aid of moderate Arab states such
as Jordan, Saudi Arabia, and Kuwait.

Iraq needed help from any possible quarter, including
the P.L.O. Saddam Hussein, the Iraqi ruler, sought ways
to communicate with Yasser Arafat, and was willing, in
return, to sacrifice the special ties that Iraq had had with

Abu Nidal. In addition, Abu Nidal's very presence in Baghdad undermined Hussein's efforts to gain the support of the West. Iraq was interested in acquiring military and economic aid, and the loss of Abu Nidal was considered a relatively cheap price to pay for these. Washington sent clear signals to Iraq that as long as Abu Nidal was on its soil, it would continue to be considered a state which offered support and refuge to terrorists.

At first, the Iraqi intelligence services tried to restrict al-Banna's freedom of movement, but when the pressure on these services increased, they decided, either at the end of 1979 or the beginning of 1980, to ask him to leave his headquarters in Baghdad. This was not an expulsion order. Sabri al-Banna left Iraq without any hard feelings. He understood the position the Iraqis were in, and acceded to their request.

Al-Banna decided to move to Damascus. Since his entire organization was so small, the transfer to the Syrian capital took very little time and was relatively easy. What is not too clear is how Syria reacted to its new guest. Why was Syria's president Hafiz al-Assad willing to admit an Iraqi intelligence agent? How could the leaders of Damascus, including its foreign minister, Abd al-Halim Khaddam, forgive a terrorist "hired gun," who had been responsible for major attacks against Syrian targets, including two attempts on Khaddam's life?

The answers to these questions are complex. First, this was not the first time that the Syrian regime had adopted a hostile organization and then proceeded to forgive its past sins against the regime. Syria's ties to Arafat's Fatah could certainly serve as a precedent. The inter-Arab political scene had over the years brought together the most unlikely of bedfellows. Yesterday's sworn enemies had become today's close allies.

We must also remember that the condition of Syria's rulers, and of its intelligence services, was extremely shaky at the time. The murder in 1979 on the French Riviera of Zuhir Muhsin, head of al-Sa'iqa, had dealt an almost fatal blow to that organization. Al-Sa'iqa had originally been established by the Syrian Ba'ath party to increase its influence over the Palestinian movement, and

had developed over the years into an efficient tool for liquidating opponents of the regime and for staging terrorist
attacks against targets determined by Syrian intelligence.
The organization had not recovered since the assassination, and had in reality ceased operating. The Syrian
intelligence services, and especially Ali Duba, director of
military intelligence, and Muhammad al-Khuli, director
of Air Force Intelligence (considered to be one of the
strong men in the regime), had looked in vain for an
acceptable substitute.

What they were seeking was a new "contractor," who
would be able to perform their dirty work for them. They
were primarily interested in taking out "contracts" against
the Muslim Brotherhood, which had been increasing its
assaults against the atheistic regime of Hafiz al-Assad.
Sabri al-Banna, known for his open hatred of religion and
its leaders, was more than willing to accept the task.

And thus the bond was formed between the terrorist and
the Syrian regime. In return for refuge, logistic support,
and financial aid, Abu Nidal moved his command from
Baghdad to Damascus. He settled into a small, three-story
building in one of the Damascus suburbs. The payment
he had to make for Syrian "hospitality" was not excessive. Syrian intelligence used his "contracting services"
primarily in attacks against Jordan and its institutions.
Continuing the history of mutual hatred between the Syrian Ba'ath regime and the Hashemite Kingdom, relations
between the two had deteriorated even further in the early
1980's when King Hussein had offered assistance to the
Muslim Brotherhood. Its members found sanctuary in Jordan, and set out from there for attacks across the Syrian
border. In retaliation, Khuli and Ali Duba used Abu
Nidal's men to attack Hashemite targets in both Jordan
and Europe.

This terrorist war continued for about five years. It was
only toward the end of 1985 that Damascus and Amman
undertook a policy of reconciliation, in the wake of the
peace process in the Middle East (the zenith of this reconciliation process being Hussein's visit to Damascus in
November 1985), culminating in a "cease-fire." Even
though there was no pressing need to do so, the Syrians,

like the Iraqis before them, began to disassociate themselves from Abu Nidal's organization. Sabri al-Banna and his central command were asked to pack their bags and move elsewhere. Al-Banna chose Libya. Colonel Mu'ammar Qaddafi was a familiar face, and even while al-Banna was serving first the Iraqis and then the Syrians, he had continued to maintain excellent ties with the Libyan intelligence services.

The first link between Abu Nidal and Qaddafi was made through Naji Alush, who lived in Libya. Even though Alush had had his differences with al-Banna and had left the organization, the good relationship between the two had continued. Abu Nidal appointed one of his trusted aides, Shafiq al-Arida, as go-between with the Libyan government. Shafiq al-Arida is a building contractor of Palestinian descent who left Fatah, joined Abu Nidal's organization, and enjoyed the special confidence of the three lieutenant-colonels in command of Libyan intelligence, Abdallah Hijazi, Abdallah Sanusi, and Salim abu Sharukai.

In mid-1985, when Sabri al-Banna was asked to leave Damascus, he moved his headquarters to Libya. His organization immediately began strengthening its ties with the regime, and he has made no attempt to hide them. There is a great deal that al-Banna and Colonel Qaddafi have in common as regards the Arab-Israeli conflict and inter-Arab relations. An office of the organization works openly in Tripoli, and al-Banna himself manages the group's organizational and political activities (including attempts to strengthen his ties with other organizations), and plans terrorist attacks from that base.

Abu Nidal has given interviews to the media from his headquarters in Tripoli. He is so confident of Libyan support that when the Kuwaiti foreign minister visited Tripoli in October 1985, al-Banna did not hesitate to warn him that unless Kuwait changed its policies to his group, freed his men in Kuwaiti prisons, and allowed him to open an office in the country, he would continue to attack Kuwaiti interests. Prior to that, on September 8, 1985, Abd al-Salam Jallud, a member of the revolutionary command and prime minister of Libya, who is considered the number two man in the country, met with Abu Nidal. At this meeting they discussed ways to intensify the links between Libya and the organization. About three weeks later, on September 28, Qaddafi met personally with Sabri al-Banna. The official Libyan news agency gave a short report of the fact that a meeting had taken place, but not of its contents. All these meetings indicate a close cooperation between Libyan intelligence and the terrorist organization.

Libya's involvement in attacks initiated by Abu Nidal has been exposed on numerous occasions. The United States government transmitted to both Israel and Egypt satellite photographs of training camps in Libya, which Abu Nidal used to train not only members of his own group, but also terrorists of other Palestinian organizations. The ties between his host state and Abu Nidal are so close that when Egypt deployed its troops along the Libyan border, Sabri al-Banna announced that he was placing his forces at Libya's disposal.

In return for the shelter and logistic and financial aid that he receives from Libya, Abu Nidal offers his "contracting services" to Colonel Qaddafi. In November 1985, when he sent some of his men to hijack an Egyptair plane on a flight from Athens to Cairo, agents of Libyan intelligence and Ahmad Qaddafi, the Libyan leader's nephew, directed the actions of the four hijackers. The plane was brought down in Valletta, the capital of Malta, and was freed in a commando raid by a special force of the Egyptian army. The commando raid ended in tragedy, with about sixty passengers and crew members killed, as were three of the four hijackers. The hijack was carried out on behalf of Libya, which is interested in destabilizing Hosni Mubarak's government.

Clearly Abu Nidal does not need any special incentives to act against the Egyptian regime. After all, in all his interviews, he has stressed that "in the entire world there are no solutions by peaceful means. If you read Arabic history, you will see that no peaceful method has ever brought about a solution to our problems. I admit that the presence of the Zionists in Palestine will continue for a long time, but we are not dreaming. The Camp David peace treaty was signed by Sadat and died with him. It is only a question of time until his successor, Hosni Mubarak, will pay dearly for his treason to Arab history.''

The responsibility for the hijacking was taken by an organization calling itself Revolutionary Egypt, the same organization that was responsible for the murder of the Israeli diplomat Albert Atrakchi, killed in August 1985 while driving in Cairo. It is the opinion of intelligence sources that Libya was behind both actions, and it is Libya which aids Egyptian extremists opposed to Mubarak's rule and the peace treaty with Israel, and which provides the links between them and Abu Nidal's group.

The ties to Libya were even more fully exposed after the attacks on the El Al counters in Vienna and Rome in December 1985. The two terrorists who survived the attacks handed over their passports to the investigators. These were the same Tunisian passports which Libya had confiscated from Tunisian workers sent back to Tunis during 1985. When the workers arrived home, they reported their loss to the local police. The latter sent the information, including passport numbers, to Interpol. Thus, the apprehension of those responsible for the El Al attacks provided the missing link tying the Abu Nidal terrorist group to Libya. Previously, the intelligence services could only analyze, evaluate, and speculate who was behind Abu Nidal. Now they were able to pinpoint Libyan responsibility.

Israel's and the United States' accusations of Libya, with implied threats to launch military actions against it, displeased Colonel Qaddafi. At the beginning of 1986 he offered a ''deal'': in return for ceasing his support of terror, the West, including the United States, would obligate itself not to use force against him. The ''deal'' was not consummated, but the Tripoli colonel has still acted to cover his ties with Abu Nidal. Indeed, he ordered the execution of Hasan Ashkal, a colonel in the Libyan army, who was involved in planning the hijacking of the Egyptian plane, and who personally handed Abu Nidal five million pounds sterling as a down payment.

Qaddafi was also furious at *Der Spiegel* for revealing that the interview with Sabri al-Banna had taken place at an isolated villa near Tripoli. (The weekly's reporters had mentioned that a flag of the organization, named "Fatah—the Revolutionary Council," flew over the villa where the interview was held.) In January 1986, to punish the newspaper, Qaddafi refused to grant other reporters of the West German weekly permission to enter his country.

Syria's leaders also began to panic at the accusations in the West that they too aid Abu Nidal. (The Syrian foreign minister, Faruq Share'a, admitted during a stay in London in March 1986 that Abu Nidal did indeed have an office in Damascus, but tried to justify this by adding, "but this is only a press liaison office.") Ahmad Jibril, the head of the Popular Front for the Liberation of Palestine—the General Command, considered one of the most devoted lackeys of Syria and Libya, rushed to have himself interviewed by papers in the West (the New York *Times* and *Corriere della Sera*), so he could try to obscure the ties between Abu Nidal and both Damascus and Tripoli. "Sabri al-Banna moved to Teheran recently," announced Jibril. "He doesn't spend any time in Syria or Libya. And he even forces conservative countries such as Kuwait to support him by blackmail."

But this was too transparent an attempt to shift the blame and pin it on others. Intelligence sources are highly skeptical of this account, not only because Sabri al-Banna is a radical secularist who is opposed to the extremist Muslim politics of the imams in Teheran, but also because there is an absence of common interests that could link them. It is nevertheless possible that there have been extremely indirect links between the radical Iranian Shi'ite organizations, acting under the weak unbrella of the Hizballah (God Party), and Abu Nidal's men grouped in Ba'albak in the Lebanese Bekaa valley.

Yet the rumors about Abu Nidal's ties with Iran have continued to spread in 1986. A report by Jack Anderson at the end of March 1986, for example, claimed that some of al-Banna's men had trained in a camp named Manzaria Park in Iran. According to this report, the leader himself also spent some time at that camp, where he was accompanied by Ahmad, son of Ayatollah Khomeini. It is not beyond the realm of possibility for Abu Nidal to have some type of link with Iran. He certainly will not hesitate to form such ties if he feels that Syria and Libya are withdrawing their support from him. If circumstances warrant, he, the proclaimed secularist, will even be ready to accept the aid of Teheran's clerics.

After the accusatory American and Western finger was pointed at Libya, Sabri al-Banna was asked to leave the country, even though it is clear that he would have done so without being officially requested. The fact that he is wanted by the secret services of Israel, Egypt, Fatah, the United States, and a number of Western European states, made him come to the conclusion that the ground was burning beneath him, and that it was time to find a new refuge.

Where has al-Banna moved to? Since he began acting independently in 1973 or 1974, he has gotten around with the help of six forged passports, of Morocco (whose passports are favored not only by the Abu Nidal group but also by other Palestinian terror organizations—possibly because holders of Moroccan passports have not needed visas to enter most European countries, but this is changing), Iraq, South Yemen, Syria, Libya, and Egypt, moving from one country to another that has been willing to grant him temporary shelter. Contrary to rumors circulating in Italy, Sabri al-Banna has not visited Europe since the end of the 1970's. Abu Nidal loves to brag about the fact that he has visited the United States, Britain, and Germany. "I know every single city and region in Germany," he boasted in an interview.

Hunted, but nevertheless confident in himself, al-Banna continues to move about under forged passports. He is wanted, but has not undergone plastic surgery (as claimed by a number of sources in the media), and travels between Iraq, Syria, Libya, and South Yemen, all of which continue to secretly grant him aid. Contrary to the accepted impression, he continues to keep in contact with the intelligence services of these countries. And even when he has acted or acts as a "terror contractor" for this or that Arab intelligence service, Sabri al-Banna has continued, together with his group, to enjoy a certain freedom of action. In other words, he does not need Syrian encouragement or any Iraqi incentives to act against Israeli, Jordanian, P.L.O., Egyptian, or Kuwaiti objectives. It is true that on occasion he does so under instruction of this or that intelligence service, but in many other cases he acts entirely on his own initiative. The attack on the Israeli ambassador to Great Britain, Shlomo Argov, is a case in point.

8

Who Gave the Orders?

In the shooting of Ambassador Argov, there are at least three important questions which have not been answered.

1. How were the weapons smuggled into the United Kingdom and gotten to the group?

2. How did the terrorists find out that Argov would be at the Dorchester?

3. And finally, the most important question, which deals with motivation: why did the Abu Nidal group decide to shoot an Israeli ambassador? Who sent it? What was its aim?

We will try to analyze and answer these three questions.

First, the entry of the arms into the U.K.

There are two possibilities, both of which are quite reasonable. First, the guns might have been brought into Britain by a messenger, who hid them in his baggage or car, and British customs missed them. Alternatively, the London police offered the hypothesis that they were sent in the diplomatic mail of one of the Arab embassies. The police investigators tend to think the latter is the more likely of the two alternatives. The head of the anti-terrorist squad, Commander William Hucklesby, stated, "We know, and it's no secret, that the diplomatic mail of a number of embassies is used as a cover for smuggling, including weapons and explosives, into the country. But as signatories of international treaties on the immunity of diplomats and their mail, we are prevented from acting as we in the police force would wish to."

Douglas Hurd, at that time a junior minister in the Foreign Office, confirmed that his office had sent a note to all the foreign embassies in London asking them to observe the rules of diplomatic immunity. It is not surprising that there was need for a reminder. The British police have been informed by intelligence sources on scores of occasions in the past years of the abuse by foreign diplomats and employees in foreign embassies of their immunity. Even though the London police do not know exactly how the weapons were brought in, they have certain clues about the method. Rosan was in constant contact, throughout his eight months in Britain, with the office of the military attaché of the Iraqi embassy. That embassy has, in its cellar and safes, a sizable cache of arms. Various sources in Israel believe that it was the Iraqi embassy that supplied the weapons, and especially Polish submachine guns, one of which was used in the attack. These guns are standard issue in the Iraqi army, and are issued to its tank commanders. The same exact type of weapon was used in the terrorist attack, in May 1980, on the Iranian embassy staff in Princess Gate, London. A number of members of the Iraqi embassy staff were involved in planning the attack, which was carried out at the initiative of Iraqi intelligence, using Iranian terrorists trained in Baghdad. After the hostages were released unharmed, the British Foreign Office decided to overlook the Iraqi involvement revealed by British intelligence.

A few months after the siege of the Iranian embassy, the Iraqi embassy was involved in another incident. At the beginning of 1981 there was a massive explosion at the embassy, which terrified the area's residents and smashed windows throughout the district. The uniformed policeman assigned to guard the building, who offered his aid, was asked by the Iraqi security men guarding the embassy not to stick his nose into areas of no concern to him.

Given the clear access that the Iraqis have to considerable stores of arms, it is quite possible that one of the embassy staff, or a fourth man who managed to escape after the assault on Argov, transferred the gun to Na'if

Rosan and Marwan al-Banna. It is possible that this same person is still employed in London by Iraqi intelligence, under the guise of an embassy staff member, for the Iraqi embassy has a larger staff than any other in London, even including the Soviet embassy.

In summarizing the event, the *Guardian* quoted a senior Palestinian official who claimed adamantly that the guns used in the attack on the Israeli ambassador came from the Iraqi embassy. The paper also went on to state that that was also the assessment of the Israeli Mossad.

The answer to the second question, as to how the terrorists were aware of Argov's presence at the Dorchester, on the other hand, is very simple. According to London police investigators, scores of people were involved, either directly or indirectly, in organizing the dinner, including employees of the De La Rue company and of the hotel. It is thus possible that one of these people, either deliberately or accidentally, informed an unauthorized person of those on the guest list.

We also cannot forget that this was an annual dinner for the diplomatic corps. Shlomo Argov was an active member of the corps, and used to attend most of its functions. The possibility was raised that one of the drivers of the diplomats involved heard that Argov would attend, and was paid by one of the members of the organization or its supporters for passing on that information. This is also the opinion of the police, as proposed by Superintendent John Paul and Commander Hucklesby.

It is interesting to note that all the Arab diplomats cancelled at the last moment. One cannot, of course, conclude from this that they had received prior warning of the attempted assassination. It is quite possible that they cancelled because they had heard that the Israeli ambassador would be attending. It is possible that one of the Arab ambassadors made a point of informing the others that the Israeli ambassador was due to be present at the hotel, and that information made its way back to Abu Nidal's people.

These explanations lead us to the major question, the motivation behind the assault, or, in other words, who gave the orders? It is clear to everyone involved in investigating the case, and certainly to the British security services, that those who carried out the action belonged to Abu Nidal's group. But what is not clear is why they did it, and above all, why they chose that particular timing. I think that there are three reasonable hypotheses in this case.

1. The attack was an Iraqi initiative.
2. It was a personal initiative by Abu Nidal without Iraqi involvement.
3. It was initiated by another party.

This time, we will start with the third possibility.

The fact is that the Syrian regime was interested in weakening the P.L.O., and it might therefore have planned the attack as a provocation which would arouse the Israelis against the P.L.O. On the other hand, we must remember that Damascus was not interested in war with Israel at that time, as it did not yet feel itself ready for a war.

There are a goodly number of P.L.O. members who believe that the Israeli government, through its security services, was behind the act. The person probably most responsible for propagating this version was Dr. Issam Sartawi. In the middle of the Lebanon War, or to be more exact, in August 1982, Sartawi participated in a joint news conference in Paris, together with General Matti Peled. In answer to one of the questions, the P.L.O. representative stated that in his opinion the Abu Nidal group works for Israeli intelligence, or—at the least—Mossad agents have managed to infiltrate it. Sartawi and many other P.L.O. members truly believed that Israel was seeking an excuse to invade Lebanon. The pro-Arab weekly *Middle East* claimed that the attack on the ambassador was the sign which Israel was awaiting to invade Lebanon.

Those who advocate this theory note that from July 1981 on the P.L.O. had observed the cease-fire on the Israeli-Lebanese border, as arranged by the American diplomat, Phillip Habib. The P.L.O. members knew that given any good opportunity Israel would not hestitate to attack their bases in Lebanon. Knowing their inferiority, they tried to prevent giving Israel any excuses for engag-

ing in battle. Those who believe this version of events
feel that it is supported by the haste in which the attack
in London was executed.

The Israeli journalist Uri Avnery stressed that the Abu
Nidal faction is normally very professional in its actions
and uses revolvers which can be smuggled into a country
for its assassination attempts, and that its people flee
immediately after the completion of the action. In the
London episode, Abu Nidal's group acted very differ-
ently. It used "sleeper" agents who had been planted in
Britain for an extended period of time.

The fact that Marwan al-Banna—a relative of Sabri al-
Banna—was used, would tend to show that the order to
attack the ambassador was given literally at the last minute. With no alternatives at that late time, it was decided
to use whoever was available, even if it meant endanger-
ing the life of one of the leader's relatives. Support for
this can be found in the letter to Thabit which informed
him to prepare for an action against the Arab Emirates,
with no mention of Israel.

On the other hand, one cannot ignore the possibility
that the haste with which the decision was made was due
to the fact that the final confirmation that Ambassador
Argov would be attending the dinner only came through
a few hours before the attack. In addition, as we have
seen, the Abu Nidal group has no great respect for human life, neither that of its victims nor that of its own
members. In almost all its previous actions, its members
had been caught, because the rescue plan was impossible
to execute or simply did not exist. Whoever examines the
London attack and other attacks carried out by Abu
Nidal's group can wonder if there was even a rescue
plan for Sa'id. It follows that the organization has no
compunctions in abandoning its members, even sending
them on suicide missions, if their leader decides that the
venture is worthwhile and will serve his purposes.

It is true that the P.L.O. members had no interest in
granting Israel the excuse it needed. Abu Nidal, on the
other hand, had all the interest in the world to carry out
the attack. This leads us back to our first two hypotheses.

The first begins with the assumption that Abu Nidal carried out the attack by Iraqi order. As we have seen in previous chapters, the organization has on many occasions acted as a tool or paid agent of Iraqi intelligence. But why would Iraq be interested in attacking the Israeli ambassador? At the beginning of the summer of 1982, Iraq was in the midst of a bloody war with its neighbor Iran, a war which still continues. The dead end which seemed to result from all the inconclusive battles made Saddam Hussein search for a possible excuse to end the war honorably, without diminishing his prestige. When the Iraqi forces crossed the Shatt al-Arab in September 1979, everyone thought—and this was the reason the Iraqi president launched the war—that Iran, under the reign of Shi'ite priests led by Khomeini and isolated from the outer world, would fall as a ripe fruit into Saddam Hussein's lap. But the Iraqi leader had misjudged badly. The Muslim fanatics of Teheran managed to mobilize their army in spite of the lack of spare parts for their weaponry, and opposed the invader vigorously. Since then, the war had reached an impasse. Iraq had lost the initiative in battle, and with that, the chances of emerging victorious. Its economy, and primarily its oil industry, was affected very badly, and was in danger of collapsing. Only Saudi, Kuwaiti, and United Arab Emirate aid enabled Iraq to continue fighting.

At the same time, there were internal political threats to the regime. The Kurdish minority in the north, the Shi'ites influenced by Khomeini's propaganda, and the underground Communist Party, began, from 1982 on, to attempt more and more to undermine Hussein's regime. An Israeli incursion into Lebanon, which many of the media in both Israel and the rest of the world would cover in the greatest of detail, might give Iraq an excuse for honorably ending the war in the gulf. If the Israelis would indeed invade, Iraq could request a cease-fire or declare one unilaterally, while appealing to the need for Muslim and Arab solidarity against the Zionist enemy. Iraq could even kill two birds with one stone. It could terminate its fruitless war and involve its enemy, Syria, which had been aiding Iran throughout the war, in a war with Israel.

And if we examine the actual course of events, it certainly appears to have followed this scenario.

As soon as Israel invaded Lebanon, Iraq announced a unilateral cease-fire in its war with Iran and its readiness to pull its troops back from Iranian soil. An announcement by the Revolutionary Command Council explained the reasons for this proposal: "We believe in the urgent need to direct all our energy and resources to a confrontation with the Zionist aggression against the Arab world, the Palestinian people, and Lebanon." The Iraqi scenario is therefore extremely credible. The Syrians did indeed become involved in the war in Lebanon and began to move troops from their common border with Iraq, but the Iraqis either did not take into account or ignored the way the winds were blowing in Teheran.

The Iranians simply ignored the Iraqi proposal. Their official news agency announced that the war in Lebanon was "an evil plot by the reactionaries in the region to rescue President Saddam Hussein and his Zionist-Ba'athist (sic) regime, and the Israeli attack was only meant to keep alive the dictatorial regime of Baghdad, which is toppling." In other words, if we strain out the rhetoric, the Iranian statement asserts that the assassination attempt was planned by Iraq in order to extricate itself from the mess it had gotten into by invading Iran. This was essentially the same view as that of the Western security services, who claimed that the only Arab state that could possibly benefit from an Israeli invasion of Lebanon was Iraq. The fact remains, though, that the Gulf war did not end, simply because Iran refused to play by the Iraqi rules.

We can now return to the second hypothesis, that Abu Nidal acted on his own initiative. Al-Banna's blind hatred for Arafat and the P.L.O. can easily explain why he would want to target Argov. Like his Iraqi masters, Abu Nidal could also assume that an attack on Argov would mean Israeli retaliation against the P.L.O. bases in Lebanon. It is thus quite possible that he decided to furnish Israel with the excuse for doing so. He wanted to supply the provocation which would cause the Israeli government to react. He could envision an Israeli invasion of Lebanon as destroying the P.L.O. power infrastructure in Lebanon—which was indeed what happened.

Such an action by Abu Nidal would be perfectly in line with his doctrine, which dated from the early days of Fatah. In 1966–1967, the Fatah leaders developed the "entanglement" theory. This defined the role of the organization as acting as a "primer" which would touch off the general war against Israel, and would so entangle the Arab states in the process that they would be forced, willy-nilly, to enter the fray against the Zionist enemy. The "entanglement theory" fits in well with the ideology of the Ba'ath party.

Thus according to this scenario, Sabri al-Banna either believed or hoped that an attack in London would bring about a chain reaction of the liquidation of the P.L.O., and a war between Syria and other Arab states against Israel. At the least, the destruction of his opponents in the Palestinian movement would make his own organization the leading and most important one in the struggle against Israel.

On Saturday, June 5, 1982, in the investigation room of the police station in Paddington Green, Sergeant Michael Howells and Superintendent John Paul continued their examination of Na'if Rosan. The sergeant's knowledge of the Middle East was, to say the least, very weak. But possibly out of curiosity he decided to question the suspect. "Do you know that as a result of what happened on Thursday night in Park Lane, there has been a chain reaction? Was that what your group wanted?"

"We didn't want that," answered Na'if Rosan. "I didn't want that. But I don't know. Maybe that's what our leaders wanted."

The leader of the organization, Sabri al-Banna, was asked the same thing by the *Der Spiegel* interviewer. "You gave the Israelis an excuse for invading Lebanon. Why did you carry out an action that had such drastic consequences for the Palestinians?" His answer highlighted once again his and his men's obsession with the Mossad and other security services of the Western states. He answered, "The Zionist ambassador in London was one of the heads and founders of the Israeli secret service, the Mossad. We attacked the ambassador when he had just been assigned a major role by the Mossad in Europe. Our fighters acted scrupulously in terms of my strict orders not to harm any other ambassador." (This fear of the Mossad is almost pathological, to the extent that in discussing charitable organizations and schools, Abu Nidal once stated that "many of these institutions, which appear on the surface to be innocent, secretly serve the Zionist secret service, the Mossad.")

"But you should have known that the Israelis had their army deployed on the northern border and were only waiting for an excuse to launch a war. Didn't you give them that excuse when you carried out the attack?"

"Let us say you are right. What were the results of the invasion? The Zionist forces suffered a terrible setback in Lebanon. The same was true of the so-called multinational force composed of Americans, Frenchmen, British, and Italians."

"Did you know Israel had plans to invade Lebanon?"

"Any blind man could see the Zionist plans to invade Lebanon. But in my eyes, it has not been proven and it is not true that the attack on the life of the ambassador was the spark that ignited the war."

"Arafat asserted to me that the attack which caused the war proved that you are actually an Israeli agent."

"What Arafat says about me doesn't bother me. Not only he, but also a whole list of Arab and world politicians claim that I am an agent of the Zionists or the C.I.A. Others state that I am a mercenary of the French secret service and of the Soviet K.G.B. The latest rumor is that I am an agent of Khomeini. During a certain period they said we were spies for the Iraqi regime. Now they say that we are Syrian agents. Maybe they will yet say that we receive money from the German secret service and King Fahd?"

"Whose service do you work for?"

"I will tell you something. Many psychologists and sociologists in the Soviet bloc tried to investigate this man Abu Nidal. They wanted to find a weak point in his character. The result was zero. Now they have given up on that.''

These last words of Abu Nidal are more than passing strange. Without even being asked to do so, Abu Nidal confesses to his interviewers that there has been some kind of attempt, without clarifying more than that, by some parties in the Soviet bloc to influence the organization. Is he referring to an attempt by an Eastern bloc country or its secret service to try to recruit him for its purposes? To operate him for its goals? There is no easy answer.

At the same time, though, the Israeli intelligence community has evidence, some of it circumstantial, of a certain link between the Abu Nidal group and the security services of the Soviet bloc. Amiram Nir, advisor on counter-terrorism to the Israeli prime minister, stated at a closed session that ''we suspect Abu Nidal has worked for Eastern European countries.''

The following episode would certainly tend to confirm this. In 1980, two members of the Abu Nidal group left by car from Baghdad, heading toward Western Europe. They had partitioned off the gas tank, and used the secret storage space created for weapons and explosives. There was no problem crossing the Turkish border, but they were stopped in Bulgaria. Carrying out a comprehensive search, the Bulgarian border police found the hidden arms cache. The two terrorists were held and their car confiscated. They remained in jail for two weeks until—out of the blue—they were freed. Evidently Abu Nidal had managed, by means of the Iraqi intelligence service, to reach the highest authorities in Sofia. What is more remarkable is that these same terrorists were then lodged in a luxury hotel in the capital, and were given first-class treatment during the rest of their stay. Technical experts of the Bulgarian security service worked a number of days at reconstructing the fake gas tank. The arms and explosives were placed back inside, and they were allowed to continue on their journey through Yugoslavia and into Italy. The arms were hidden there, and one of the weapons was evidently used in the attack on the Rome synagogue in October 1982.

The Vitosha-New Otani Hotel in Sofia, where the freed terrorists of Abu Nidal stayed, symbolizes the mixture of greed, capitalism, and political opportunism so apparent in the Communist world's attitude to international terrorism. The hotel's marble halls are a meeting place for a cross section of the criminal elite and politically motivated. Arabs from George Habash's P.F.L.P. meet with Turkish drug smugglers, Bulgarian currency dealers, and arms manufacturers.[1] Deals made here invariably bring much-needed foreign currency to the Eastern bloc while spreading the illegal flow of arms and drugs to the West.

Turkish officials believe that as many as six rings smuggling heroin from Turkey to West Germany and the United States operate from the Hotel Vitosha.

Bulgaria's association with the major criminal movement in Europe and the Middle East is of considerable importance to its intelligence network and to the K.G.B. This association carries with it certain obligations, among them a willingness to give sanctuary to terrorists and occasionally to help out with documents and arms. Little doubt remains that the Bulgarians were heavily involved in the plot to assassinate Pope John Paul II in May 1981. Mehmet Ali Agca, the assassin, has confessed that some members of the Bulgarian secret service helped him and that for a time he stayed in the comfort of the Hotel Vitosha. The Bulgarians supplied Agca with a gun and money, as well as putting him in touch with their agents in Rome.

If the Bulgarians knew the purpose of Agca's visit and therefore condoned and encouraged it, the K.G.B. most likely did, too. While there may have been a reason why the Bulgarians and the Soviets wanted the pope killed, this incident is not a convincing argument to suggest that either country is orchestrating the terrorist acts perpetuated by the large number of independent groups operating all over the world.

[1] See James Adams' new book, *Financing Terrorism*, to be published by Simon and Schuster in 1986.

Bulgaria has a long history of giving sanctuary to terrorists on the run and of supplying guns to different groups. Israeli intelligence believes that more than 80% of the P.L.O.'s arms come from the Bulgarian port of Varna, but this is hardly surprising, when the illegal trade in guns and drugs in Bulgaria reaches an estimated $1 billion annually.

General Ehud Barak, the former head of Israeli military intelligence, believes that Abu Nidal has used Bulgaria as the departure point for other operations. Except for this one documented incident, Israel has no additional solid proof of the ties between Abu Nidal and the Eastern European countries, except for certain facts which arouse suspicion. Abu Nidal's organization is the only one which is able to maintain a secret infrastructure in Eastern Europe. It is also the only one which has dared to carry out attacks in that area. In April 1980, its members tried to murder Abu Iyad, one of the heads of Fatah and the P.L.O., in Belgrade. In August 1981, Abu Nidal attempted to kill his former friend Abu Da'ud in Warsaw. Three members of the Abu Nidal group tried to assassinate the P.L.O. representative in Bucharest in September 1984, and about three months later another member of the group wounded two Jordanian diplomats in that same city. On various occasions, the group has sent announcements to the media via one or another of the international news agencies, generally Reuters, through its Bucharest office. Sabri al-Banna himself underwent a serious open-heart operation in East Germany in June 1984.

The circumstantial evidence of links between Abu Nidal and the Soviet bloc is more useful, however, in showing the characteristics of the organization than in conclusively proving the links between the two. This evidence certainly shows a certain boldness by the group. It has no fear in attacking the other Palestinian groups on East European soil. Sabri al-Banna himself said that "the Soviets are the true friends of the Arabs. But of course they too worry about their own interests. For example, they approve of the existence of the Zionist entity in Palestine. We cannot agree to that."

This possible link between Abu Nidal and the Soviet bloc also illustrates another of his characteristics: independence. As opposed to the popular impression, Abu Nidal's group, in spite of its bonds with Iraq, Syria, and Libya, is able to maintain a degree of autonomy, leaving itself some maneuvering room. And even when it accepts a "job" from one of its Middle Eastern "employers," it reserves the right to set the target. The "employer" specifies the general goal, but no more. For example, the Syrian intelligence service asked Abu Nidal to "hit" Jordanian interests, and the terrorist and his officers decided whether this should mean a Jordanian diplomat or the Jordanian Alia airlines. It is this independence of the group that enabled Abu Nidal to attack Ambassador Argov in London, without this necessarily having been by the specific orders of Iraq. In other words, it is possible that the conspiratorial theory doesn't apply to this group. It does not need any encouragement or incentives to act against Israel or against Jews.

9

Dead or Alive?

In the last few years, speculation has been rife as to whether Sabri al-Banna is still alive. The first time that a rumor to the contrary surfaced was in November 1984, when the British Independent Television network (ITV) announced that "Sabri al-Banna died of various diseases and was buried in Baghdad." Since then, there have been a number of news reports to the effect that he is no longer alive, and that his group has made deliberate efforts to conceal this fact. This is not, of course, the first time that rumors have swept the Middle East and the West of the death of terrorist leaders. This occurred with Dr. Wadi Haddad, the "operations officer" of the P.F.L.P. under Dr. George Habash.

When George Habash's P.F.L.P. decided to abandon its course of spectacular hijackings, Dr. Haddad split off from him in 1974 and launched his own group. He regarded Habash as "too soft." Haddad's group received support from the secret services of Iraq and South Yemen, and continued to specialize in plane hijackings. It was this group which was responsible for the hijacking of an Air France plane en route from Tel Aviv to Paris via Athens, with the plane being forced to land instead in Entebbe, Uganda, in June 1976; and for the hijacking of a Lufthansa plane to Mogadishu, Somalia, in 1977. After both groups of passengers had been freed in bold rescue operations by elite units of the Israeli and German armed forces respectively, Haddad continued to plan other such attacks, with the assistance of European terrorists with whom he had formed strong ties. He died on March 28, 1978 of leukemia. About a week later, on April 4, 1978, a large funeral was held for him in Baghdad. Some Arab papers claimed he had died in an East German hospital. A number of years prior to that, however, the media had carried stories of his "death."

The same was the case with "Carlos," to whom we have already referred. No single terrorist has managed to generate such a legend as Carlos. All types of myths and legends were woven about him. Young Palestinians and terrorists throughout the world regarded him as a hero to be emulated. He was born in Venezuela, to middle-class Communist parents. His real name was Ilich Ramirez Sanchez, Ilich being the middle name of the Soviet revolutionary Vladimir Lenin. In the 1960's Sanchez studied at the Patrice Lumumba International University in Moscow, which was then a hotbed of political radicalism for young students of the Third World. There he was persuaded by Palestinian students to join their cause. The Marxist doctrines of the P.F.L.P. suited Sanchez's ideological outlook perfectly, so he went next to P.F.L.P. training camps in Jordan.

After the 1967 war, when the P.F.L.P. began exporting its brand of terrorism to Western Europe, the Venezuelan terrorist became one of its most talented operations officers. Carlos, who took that *nom de guerre* from one of his many false passports, soon started to show his ability as a terrorist. He became a legend after killing three policemen in Paris, sparking an international manhunt.

He next emerged in London's St. John's Wood neighborhood to shoot Joseph Sieff, of the founding family of the Marks and Spencer store chain. In 1970, he threw hand grenades at the Israeli-owned Bank Hapoalim branch in the City of London. About five years later, under direct orders of Colonel Qaddafi of Libya, he led the astonishing kidnapping of the OPEC oil ministers from the cartel's headquarters in Vienna. The ministers were held as hostages until the Austrian government put at Carlos' disposal a plane which flew him and his comrades to Algeria, from where they made their way to Libya.

His ability to escape from his pursuers and to operate as a lone wolf added to the many legends about him. Since then, his whereabouts and involvement in terrorism have been a matter of speculation. In February 1986, however, the Israeli daily *Davar* carried a report to the effect that Carlos was believed dead and buried in Libya. According to *Davar*, he was probably killed by Libyan agents, because he knew too much about the Arab intelligence networks. As General Yehoshua Saguy, a former head of Israeli military intelligence put it, "He knew too much, and his intimate knowledge of the involvement of Arab leaders and their security services in international terrorism posed a danger to them, so they got rid of him." The *Davar* article has not received any official confirmation.

The fate of Carlos, with all the question marks surrounding it, is characteristic of the leaders of international terrorism. The fact that they live underground, are always on the run, try deliberately to falsify their background, and make a point of concealing their intentions, provides a fertile breeding ground for rumors, speculation, and false alarms.

This is the background for the rumors which began circulating on the fate of Sabri al-Banna. Already in June 1984, when he was hospitalized in East Germany for an open-heart operation, *Newsweek* reported that he was on his deathbed in Baghdad. Five months later the British ITV network carried reports of his death. A day later, on November 7, 1984, the French news agency reported from Jordan that "Abu Nidal died in Baghdad around October 20, after earlier paralysis, a source close to the family said." The French agency did not reveal the "source close to the family" to whom the report was attributed, but the news spread like wildfire. Israeli television repeated the report that very night. Abu Nidal's relatives in Nablus—Mahmud, Yusuf and their families—heard about it from the media. The next day they tried to confirm the information with their relatives in Amman, but when they were unable to contact them, they went into mourning. Only 48 hours later, on November 10, they received new information which contradicted the

first. "Sabri al-Banna is alive," they were told by a
Nablus resident returning to the West Bank from Amman,
who had heard this from relatives in that city.

But the rumors still persisted in the West. Different
versions of how he had "died" were circulated. Finally,
they reached Abu Nidal himself. In order to put an end
to them, and after consulting with the group's spokesman, Rahman Abu Issa, and other commanders, he
decided to invite a Western correspondent for a special
interview. The correspondent was chosen extremely carefully, after an intensive investigation as to whether he
could be trusted.

Lucien Bitterlin is not exactly a journalist by the cus-
tomary standards of the free press in the West. He is the
head of an organization named *France Pays Arabes*,
which periodically publishes a magazine. The organization and its magazine are considered to be supporters of
the Arab cause in general and the Palestinian cause in
particular, and are known for their close ties with the Palestinian terrorist organizations and the Syrian and Libyan
establishments. Through intermediaries, Abu Nidal's men
approached Bitterlin and invited him to interview their
leader. Bitterlin on his part agreed to fulfill all the conditions imposed on him by the Abu Nidal group.

The interview was neither photographed nor recorded.
The questions were submitted in advance and were not
permitted to deal with al-Banna's health. The interview
was published in Paris at the end of February 1985. Bitterlin later claimed that it had taken place in the Lebanese
Bekaa valley, but the Israeli intelligence experts doubt
this. They believe that this claim was part of the agreement between the two, and was meant to obscure facts
and spread incorrect information. In their estimation, the
interview was evidently held in Damascus—if it took
place at all. The Israelis are doubtful whether Bitterlin
even met Sabri al-Banna, and believe that he might have
interviewed one of al-Banna's assistants.

On March 6, 1985, a few days after the interview was
published, the Paris-based review, *Afrique-Asie*, stated
that "a purported interview with the Palestinian extremist
Abu Nidal published in a French magazine last month was

a fake." But the review added to the controversy by asserting that Abu Nidal was not dead, as had been widely reported, but had been in an Eastern country "for several months," where he was "receiving treatment."

The rumors continued to circulate and the guessing game persisted, and may even have intensified after al-Banna moved to Tripoli from Damascus in mid-1985. Again he tried to still the reports by granting two interviews. The first was with the Kuwaiti *al-Qabas* in September 1985, and this was reprinted in full in *Felastine al-Thawra*, Abu Nidal's organ. This was followed by an act which entailed a certain degree of danger to himself: al-Banna agreed to be interviewed by a well-known Western paper. Using a Lebanese "intermediary," a freelancer living in West Germany who occasionally works for *Der Spiegel*, a meeting was set up with al-Banna. The correspondent of *Der Spiegel*, Ditter Steinbauer, and the Lebanese intermediary travelled to Tripoli, and after biding their time there for a few days, were invited to meet Abu Nidal. He sat at a desk opposite his interviewers, but refused to allow himself to be photographed or to allow the interview to be recorded.

The journalists, suspicious about the identity of the person they were meeting, asked if he was indeed Abu Nidal, or just someone pretending to be the terrorist leader.

"You can trust that you see before you Abu Nidal."

"How can we be sure?"

"The information I will give you will convince you I am Abu Nidal."

"British television carried a report in November 1984 that Abu Nidal had died."

"That information comes from a number of security services that have tried to entice me into surfacing. The notice of my death was invented by the secret services of Jordan, Britain, and the Gulf Emirates, and is evidence of how helpless they feel. As you can see, I am not an evil spirit and I am Abu Nidal."

"Give us proof."

"Look at this." He slowly unbuttoned his shirt and showed surgery scars. "These are scars of my surgery."

"Open-heart surgery?"

"Yes."

In this interview, he claimed that the surgery had been done in the United States. Intelligence officers who follow Abu Nidal state that the operation certainly did not take place there, and that his comments to that effect in the interview were part of his normal operating procedure of obscuring the facts.

It is true, though, that he has a heart condition, and that he has had at least two—if not three—open-heart operations. The first was in 1977. According to one version, this took place at a hospital in Baghdad, even though an unsubstantiated rumor placed the venue as the Wellington Hospital in the St. John's Wood neighborhood of London. The latter is a private hospital many of whose patients are wealthy Arabs from Saudi Arabia and the United Arab Emirates. According to this version, al-Banna entered Britain with a forged passport.

The possibility of al-Banna's having travelled to various countries on forged passports is somewhat supported by his comments. He told *Der Spiegel* that "I entered the United States with a passport issued to a Saudi businessman." In any event, whether the operation took place in Baghdad or London—or even the United States—his health did not improve substantially, and seven years later he needed a second operation in a private hospital in East Germany. His constant ill-health has fueled the different rumors about his death.

In January 1986, after the attacks on the El Al counters in Vienna and Rome, the London *Sunday Times* repeated the allegation that Abu Nidal had died. A month later, in February 1986, the West German *Die Welt* reported that "the terrorist Abu Nidal is now in East Berlin, to receive treatment at an East German government hospital." Quoting diplomats in Vienna who attributed the information to an East German government source, the paper claimed that "Abu Nidal moves with difficulty and is evidently suffering from cancer of the liver." According to the paper, it was the disease that had brought him for treatment by Professor Helga Mukka-Wietbrodt. On the next day, February 13, 1986, East Germany denied the allegation.

Now, after all the news, the reports, the rumors, and the speculation, the question still remains: Is Abu Nidal alive or dead? "I believe he is alive," was the evaluation by General Ehud Barak, head of Israeli military intelligence, in February 1986. According to the data available to him, the following picture emerges: Sabri al-Banna is five feet seven inches tall. "He is well-built, but he is not chunky. He has scars on his face, and because of problems with his eyes does not see well." General Barak, as well as other experts, such as Dr. Ariel Merari of the Center for Strategic Studies of Tel Aviv University, know full well that "his condition is not good, but he is alive and is functioning." They are aware that there are many sources that would like to spread rumors of his death. First of all, there are his enemies. Yasser Arafat's Fatah has a clear interest in sowing demoralization in the ranks of the Abu Nidal group. News of his death can cause nervousness and uncertainty and can shake the loyalty members of the organization have to their leader. Even those regimes that have used him, the Iraqis, Syrians, and Libyans, have on occasion had their reasons for spreading such rumors, especially when they were accused of aiding terror. On other occasions, certain Western secret services have spread rumors about his death, in order to force him to surface. This too is a common technique employed by the intelligence community. But Sabri al-Banna himself has also had reason to spread similar rumors. Israel's intelligence experts are aware that most of the leaders of the Palestinian terrorist organizations are acquainted with the importance of psychological warfare. By disseminating disinformation and false rumors they try to cover their tracks, and gain a breathing spell from their pursuers.

When Dr. Wadi Haddad became ill, his people tried to hide this, and were even able, by planting certain news stories, to keep that fact secret for a number of months. In another case, the aides of Agip Agipian, the head of the Armenian terrorist group, A.S.A.L.A., indicated that he had been killed in Beirut in July 1982, during an Is-

raeli artillery bombardment. The group was interested in
having its leader "disappear" for a time. But a few
months later it became clear that he was still alive. After
all this, it is imperative for one to react with a great deal
of skepticism to the news of the "death" of this or that
terrorist. General Barak and Dr. Merari are of the opinion
that all indicators point to Sabri al-Banna still being alive.
Their opinion is based on:

1. The interviews he gave to the news media. Com-
paring the different interviews, one is struck by the use
of similar slogans and catch phrases, as well as the entire
spirit of the interviews. A comparative study shows
marked similarities between the recent interviews and the
earlier ones known to have been given by Abu Nidal
himself.

2. A long programmatic article in his periodical about
"terrorist politics" and the relationships between the different Palestinian terrorist organizations appears to be an
authentic and recent product of his pen.

3. If he were dead, it is logical to assume that his
family in Nablus and Jordan would have heard of his
death sooner or later.

4. The Israeli intelligence community, possessing the
greatest expertise on the Palestinian terrorist organizations, would know what had happened to him. It is true
that the fate of any particular terrorist leader is not the
Israeli intelligence community's highest priority, because
its first priority must always be preventive intelligence,
aimed at forestalling terrorist and other attacks by the
Palestinian organizations, but eventually this information
would have had to seep down to it as well. Israeli intelligence has not received any concrete information about
Abu Nidal's death, and one should therefore assume that,
until proven otherwise, he is still alive.

5. Perhaps the most important indication is that the
organization was most active just at those times that
rumors were circulating of his death, and carried out about
sixty attacks in the years 1984 and 1985. As a general
rule, when a leader dies, the group ceases functioning, at
least for a time ranging from a number of months to a
year. Only after a reorganization does the group come to

life again, choosing a new leader, using the ''hospitality'' of this or that Arab state's security services, and reactivating its infrastructure to carry out new terrorist attacks. That was what happened when Wadi Haddad died. His group remained dormant for some time thereafter, eventually splitting into two groups, and finally ''reawakening'' again. And when Zuhir Muhsin, the leader of al-Sa'iqa was murdered, his group entered a period of inactivity which, for all practical purposes, continues to this day.

The clear conclusion from all this is that Sabri al-Banna is still alive.

10

Developments and Prospects

At close to nine A.M. on Sunday, April 10, 1983, in the Montcoro Hotel in the resort town of Albufeira, Portugal, a lone man, of dark complexion, with curly hair and of medium height, who had been seen earlier in the hotel restaurant, quickly crossed the few yards of the lobby. He purposefully approached a gray-haired gentleman who was deeply engrossed in conversation and fired five shots at him from a distance of a few inches. Dr. Issam Sartawi collapsed in front of the horrified onlookers. A few seconds earlier, the Palestinian heart surgeon, who was attending a meeting of the Socialist International, had been speaking to Jean Bernard Cureil, of the French delegation. Cureil now tried to prop up Dr. Sartawi, who was bleeding badly. Sartawi's aide and escort, Anwar Abu Hisham, who was also wounded in the hail of bullets, threw himself with uncontrollable grief on the body, and it was hard to separate the two.

The gunman fled through the open door still holding his gun in his hand. Shocked police and plainclothes detectives did not try to stop him. Only after he had run some distance did they take off after him, firing shots in his direction. But it was too late. The gunman scaled a nearby wall and disappeared.

Dr. Issam Sartawi had been attending the meeting in the hotel, but because of Israel's opposition he had only been given the status of an observer, without any voting rights.

Immediately after the murder, the Portuguese prime minister, Francisco Pinto Balasmo, announced a full alert of all the police and intelligence services of the country. And a few hours later the police caught a 26-year-old Palestinian who was travelling by car from Lisbon. He was carrying a forged Moroccan passport, issued to Yusuf al-Awad.[1] Soon after "Yusuf" was arrested, a spokesman of the Abu Nidal group took the responsibility for the act. An announcement by the organization, which was released to journalists in Damascus, stated that "We are honored to announce our success in carrying out the death sentence against an evil man and traitor. The bullets which liquidated the life of Issam Sartawi are the bullets of Palestine." The communiqué which was later issued on white paper carrying the symbol of the Revolutionary Council of the movement referred to Sartawi as "a cheap lackey of the C.I.A., the Israeli Mossad, and British intelligence."

There was nothing surprising in this announcement, because the Abu Nidal group regarded Dr. Sartawi—who had been a central conduit between Fatah and the Israeli left—as a major target for murder. Dr. Sartawi was also well aware of that fact. He spent his last years believing that he was doomed to be killed. "Abu Nidal's people are the most dangerous murderers. They kill in cold blood! They are capable of anything," he told the author about six weeks before he was killed.

I first met him in August 1982, in the middle of the Lebanon war. He was lecturing in London at the Council for Arab-British Understanding (CABU), which includes members of the British parliament. Before an audience of a thousand people, Dr. Sartawi, carried away by his own

---

[1] After he had been sentenced, he admitted that his real name was Muhammad Hussein Rashid, but denied any involvement in the case. The Portuguese police claimed that he had indeed been involved, but were not able to prove this contention. The court sentenced him to three years imprisonment for illegal entry, but acquitted him of the actual murder. In February 1986, he was released, after having served about half his sentence, for "good behavior."

rhetoric, accused Israel of all the evil that was ever done and will ever be done in the Arab world, beginning with an attempt to commit genocide of the Palestinian people, and including a desire to take control of all the oil fields in the Gulf States.

It was hard at that time to be convinced of his moderation, and to see him as a sophisticated P.L.O. diplomat in Western Europe. On the contrary, he appeared as a radical Palestinian nationalist who, like the rest of the members of his organization, wanted to replace Israel with a ''democratic and secular Palestine.'' But when I met him the second time on February 28, 1983, he was a different person. He sat on an old and wobbly chair, in a dark corner, in the large and freezing hall of the Greater London Council, and waited for the beginning of a joint meeting with the Israeli journalist Uri Avnery. Sartawi sat on the stage behind a heavy curtain, hidden from the audience. He had a small chain of beads in his hand. Just as on the day he was murdered, he was not accompanied by bodyguards.

I went over to him and introduced myself—an Israeli journalist sent to cover the meeting. Sartawi smiled—and he had a winning smile—and asked ironically, ''Are you allowed to interview me? Won't they arrest you in Israel?'' He handled the beads in his hands nervously. Outside the window, the lights of Westminster Palace, the house of the British parliament, shone. One could sense the weariness in his voice. He said that most Palestinians wanted peace, no less, and even possibly more, than the Israelis. According to him, most leaders of the P.L.O. were also willing to recognize Israel. But he warned, raising his voice, that the leadership's patience was wearing thin, and that the sand in the Palestinian peace camp's hourglass was running out. The Palestinian people and its leadership, he added, were ready for an honorable peace, but not at any price, and they would certainly not hesitate to continue the armed struggle if they decided that was the only way to achieve their aims.

When the talk turned to the Abu Nidal movement, Dr. Sartawi became visibly more agitated. He rocked back and forth restlessly on his chair, and I could sense his unwillingness to discuss the entire topic, possibly because he was too upset to discuss this with a stranger, and certainly all the more so with a journalist from the "enemy camp." He felt better in the company of Western European journalists, and more than once opened up to them, even speaking openly of how he detested Sabri al-Banna. In an interview with a *Reuters* correspondent, Sartawi stated, regarding the damage to the Palestinian cause resulting from the attempted assassination of Ambassador Argov, that "I will put Abu Nidal on trial as soon as there is a Palestinian state. He gave Israel the excuse for opening an offensive, which brought about a catastrophe for the Palestinian movement in Lebanon." Speaking to Israeli journalists, though, he was more circumspect.

Only when I promised him that our talk would be off the record,[2] was he willing to tell me a little of what he knew about Sabri al-Banna and his organization. The organizers of the meeting began to look at their watches impatiently, and asked him to finish talking to me. His last words were in answer to my question as to whether he was not afraid of the death sentence passed on him by the Abu Nidal group. "Afraid? I am not afraid of them. I know they are trying to kill me. Perhaps they will succeed to do so one day, but anyway everything is in the hands of God, and that is probably my fate." I think that his words were more fatalistic than pious. After all, Dr. Sartawi knew from the moment that he agreed to become a roving ambassador for the P.L.O., and the one responsible for contacts with Israel, that he himself had signed his own death warrant.

In his joint meeting with Avnery in London, Sartawi stated that "in battles against Israel I acquired my military education and I can proudly assert that I see myself as having been a general of the Palestinian revolution, as I am now a fighter for peace." He emphasized the word "fighter" in his speech, and indeed in the last few months before his death he was forced to fight harder and harder for peace.

[2] Now that he is dead, I have taken the liberty of publishing this.

The Lebanon war completely dissolved the principles of the dialogue with Israel on which he had been working for years. In the last few weeks before his death, he found himself isolated, not only within the divided P.L.O., but even within his own organization, Fatah. But there is no doubt that his greatest disappointment came in February 1983, when the P.N.C.—the Palestinian "parliament"—refused to allow him to address it. Sartawi had wanted to urge the P.N.C. to unequivocally adopt the peace program of President Reagan (of September 1982), and to have King Hussein lead a joint Jordanian-Palestinian delegation in peace talks with Israel. But he was refused permission to speak, and found himself again isolated, both ideologically and physically. Even Yasser Arafat, upon whose direct orders he had been acting, turned his back on him. Faced with these facts, Sartawi called a press conference outside the conference hall, and distributed copies of the speech he had not delivered.

His actions angered not only his opponents, but even his close friends. According to various reports, Arafat was furious. With this as the background, along with a number of prior disagreements between the two, what had been an argument between them on tactics became one of strategy. While all of Sartawi's contacts with Israelis had enjoyed Arafat's tacit endorsement, the P.L.O. leader, as was his custom, refused to take a clear stand. Contrary to Sartawi's advice, he refused to endorse the Reagan peace plan. He preferred instead to preserve the unity within the movement. Preventing internal conflict became Arafat's most important goal.

Sartawi, on the other hand, did not hesitate to criticize Arafat's policy of following the path of consensus rather than that of the majority; Sartawi believed with all his heart that the majority agreed with him. His great mistake was his inability to correctly read the alignment of forces within the Palestinian camp. As it later became apparent, the voices of reason and moderation of Dr. Sartawi and his friends became weaker and weaker following the Lebanon war. The deep divisions between Sartawi and his leader led to rumors that he no longer enjoyed Arafat's support, and that the P.L.O. leader indirectly if not directly endorsed the death sentence against him. This rumor, which was also printed in the West German paper *Die Welt* in 1983, could not, of course, be confirmed. Whether or not it is true, it is clear that Sartawi's star waned while that of Sabri al-Banna shone all the more brightly, and Sabri al-Banna's audacity grew even greater.

Sabri al-Banna began moving slowly from the periphery of the Palestinian camp to the center of the political map, or, to be more exact, the center moved closer to the fringe. In any event, it is clear that the beginnings of this process—whereby the archterrorist sought by police forces throughout the world and even by Arafat himself received a certain degree of legitimization—are to be found in the Lebanon war. Not only the near-assassination of Ambassador Argov, which was directly responsible for the outbreak of war, but also the radicalization that followed it throughout the Middle East, aided this process. As the chances of renewed talks between Israelis and Palestinians, and especially their moderate wing, decreased, Abu Nidal's influence and his chance of becoming a prominent figure in the Palestinian movement increased. Uri Avnery and his friends in the Israel-Palestine Friendship League continued to claim, even after Sartawi's death, that they were still meeting with moderate leaders of the P.L.O., but the fact is that these contacts were almost totally broken off, and the channels of communication were disrupted.

In December 1982, after the P.L.O. forces were evacuated from Beirut, Abu Nidal set up his headquarters in Damascus. He still continued to commute between Baghdad and Damascus, as was confirmed by the Iraqi minister of information, who stated at the end of 1982 to a group of Italian journalists, "Abu Nidal is a member of the Arab nation, a valiant Palestinian, and he can move freely, to come and go from Baghdad. We do not interfere in his affairs." But even earlier he had begun to move his headquarters to Syria. This was a milestone in his journey from the political isolation of Baghdad to his return into the ranks of the mainstream Palestinian camp.

Robert Fisk, the London *Times* correspondent in Beirut, was the first Western newsman to be invited to the small three story house in one of the northern suburbs of Damascus that had become Abu Nidal's headquarters. At that meeting, which took place in March 1983, the spokesman of the group, Abd al-Rahman Isa, warned Britain to free the three terrorists convicted of attempting to kill Ambassador Argov. Similar warnings were later issued to the government of Portugal and France, who were also holding members of the group.

Another scrap of intelligence reached the Italian and French police. According to this unconfirmed information, the same squad that was responsible for the terrorist attack in Paris had also led the assault on the synagogue in Rome. In the latter, a Jewish infant was killed and forty people were wounded. The information, which also tied the group to the attack on the synagogue in Vienna in August 1981, was endorsed by Luigi di Gennaro, the investigating magistrate in Italy, who compared the weapons used in each case, and concluded that in all three cases the ammunition and weapons were Polish, Soviet, and Czechoslovakian, and had come from the same Austrian arms cache.

During the investigations by the West European police forces, there was a theory linking the suspect in custody in Portugal with involvement in planning the attack on Ambassador Argov. Additional bits of information, together with what had been pieced together at the "Kilowatt" meetings, made the Western intelligence experts believe that while the Abu Nidal group had enjoyed Iraqi support until the summer of 1982, thereafter the Syrian intelligence services had begun playing an ever-increasing role in working with the group.

Just then, the West European police received aid from an unexpected source—the security department of Fatah itself, Force 17. From time to time this department made a point of transmitting information on Abu Nidal's plans to the Western intelligence services. Its motives were clear. Arafat and his deputies Salah Khalaf and Khalil al-Wazir realized immediately after their defeat in Beirut in September 1982, when they were forced to abandon the Lebanese capital, that the welcome that Abu Nidal had received from the Syrian government did not bode well for them. The Abu Nidal group not only threatened the physical destruction of Arafat and his men, its actions were sullying the entire Palestinian cause among world public opinion. And there was another factor that contributed to the willingness of Force 17 to communicate with the West Europeans: in their obsessive fear of the Israeli Mossad, the Fatah leaders considered it possible that the Abu Nidal group had been infiltrated by Mossad agents, and that its *agents provocateurs* might be responsible for either planning or advocating some of Abu Nidal's attacks.

In any event, it was announced in April 1983 in Paris that the French minister for public safety had met four months earlier with Salah Khalaf. Most newspapers in France claimed that their government had received secret information about Abu Nidal's intention to attack targets in the United States, Italy, and France, as well as the multi-national force in Lebanon. This was corroborated from Damascus, where the French news agency quoted a P.L.O. source as saying that the organization "is cooperating with many states in the East and West to inform them of the possibility of a wave of attacks by the Abu Nidal movement."

Fatah's readiness to impart secret material to the Western nations must be understood against the background of events that had transpired since the summer of 1982. The defeat suffered by Fatah in Lebanon, the expulsion of its men from Beirut, and the revolt against Arafat in Tripoli and its expulsion from there also, caused the already poor relations between Syria and Fatah to deteriorate even further. Both sides had their reasons: on the one hand, Fatah believed that the Syrian president Assad had abandoned it when the Israeli forces attacked, and had refused to come to its aid, while Syria, on the other hand, was interested in exploiting the declining fortunes of the P.L.O. and Fatah so as to bring them back under its own control. In other words, Syria was interested in reverting to the days before the 1967 war, when Fatah was totally subservient to it.

The biggest obstacle to Syria's plan was Arafat himself, for one of the first lessons he had learned—and learned well—was not to be dependent on any single Arab state. Thus, if Syria wished to regain control of Fatah, it first had to neutralize Arafat.

And there was another factor that also helped to sour the relationship between Fatah and Syria. Assad objected strenuously to the negotiations between King Hussein of Jordan and Arafat for the formation of a joint Jordanian-Palestinian delegation for peace talks with Israel. Taken together, these facts help to explain the aid that Damascus offered those members of Fatah in the Bekaa valley who revolted against the P.L.O. chairman.

On a cold night in May 1983, four military vehicles crossed the border from Syria and turned southward into the Bekaa valley in Lebanon, toward the front lines with Israel. Each truck carried fifteen tons of weapons and explosives. Accompanying the small convoy was a Syrian guard unit, its men all dressed in civilian clothes. In an open field which marked their final destination, they met Palestinian fighters who had expressed their disillusionment with Yasser Arafat.

Twenty-four hours after receiving the arms, the Fatah fighters announced openly that they were revolting against the leadership of their movement. They proclaimed Arafat a ''traitor to the Palestinian cause,'' and announced they had no confidence in him as a leader. The central figure in the revolt was Sa'ad Musa, a colonel in the P.L.O., who had been an officer in the Jordanian army until 1970, and who is better known as Abu Musa.

A few months earlier, in January 1983, Abu Musa had been appointed deputy head of the operations wing of Fatah, and this was his rank when he embarked on his revolt. On Thursday, June 2, 1983, about a month after the revolt had officially broken out, Musa Awad (Abu Akbar) and Lieutenant Colonel Ziyad Sughayar (Abu Khazm) declared that they too had joined Abu Musa, in what the Western press was referring to as ''the revolt of the colonels.'' A short time later, they were joined by Salah Nimr (Abu Salah), who had already criticized Arafat's leadership before the revolt, and had as a result been removed from the central committee of Fatah; and by Samih Abu Qawiq, who was still a member of the central committee. The latter two were both members of the political department of the organization.

The reason for the revolt was ostensibly simple: opposition to Arafat's new appointments to Fatah. But there were deeper motives under the surface. Abu Musa and his fellow rebels were expressing a feeling shared by many in Fatah, about the luxurious and extravagant, if not downright corrupt, life-style of Arafat and his colleagues. This included trips throughout the world, staying at the most luxurious hotels, meetings at the fanciest restaurants, and all the other appurtenances of "the good life," which were so detested by the rank and file and aroused their opposition. "We are opposed to '*la dolce vita*' of the corrupt and rotten leadership," was the way Abu Musa put it.

But above all, the rift was due to the old disagreement over which Sabri al-Banna had left Fatah, over which Abu Da'ud and Naji Alush had tried to rebel in 1978, and which had led to the murders of Hamami, Sartawi, and the other moderates in the Palestinian camp. In other words, this was a struggle over the direction and the policy of the organization, surfacing once again. Was it to continue walking the tightrope of its "dual approach," of combining terrorist acts with diplomacy, as Arafat and his colleagues believed, or should the movement revert exclusively to the armed struggle? Abu Musa's "rejectionism" was close to Sabri al-Banna's position, and it was clear that Syria was the force behind this revolt.

Damascus exploited the authentic opposition in Fatah against Arafat for its own ends. Its aim was to topple Arafat as leader of the P.L.O. and Fatah. It is therefore not surprising that immediately after the revolt broke out, the pro-Syrian organizations of al-Sa'iqa and the P.F.L.P.-General Command announced their support for it in principle. Throughout the rebellion, the Syrians continued sending arms, food, and supplies to the rebels and Syrian tanks surrounded those units still loyal to Arafat in the Bekaa valley and in Tripoli. The Syrians also added Libyan leader Mu'ammar Qaddafi to the conspiracy. Sources close to Arafat have hinted that Libya sent Abu Musa no less than $34,000,000 as a contribution. When

Sabri al-Banna's men appeared in the Bekaa valley to aid
the rebels, there was no longer any doubt about Syrian
involvement.

Even before the rebellion broke out, a number of
French newspapers had reported that Sabri al-Banna himself was now in the area. Members of his group
announced smugly to *Le Figaro*, *Le Matin*, and *Le Quo-
tidien de Paris* who visited Abu Nidal's headquarters in
Baghdad that ''Abu Nidal is personally preparing
unpleasant surprises for Israel and its ally, Yasser Arafat.'' Before the revolt broke out, it was hard to relate to
these assertions as anything more than the arrogant slogans frequently voiced by the group. In retrospect, however, one should examine critically whether at that time
there had not already been coordination between Syrian
intelligence, Abu Nidal, Abu Musa, and the other pro-
Syrian Palestinian organizations. Be the truth as it may,
there is no doubt that Arafat and his aides see Abu Nidal,
from the time that he moved to Damascus, as Syria's
puppet. They are certain that at the end of 1983 and the
beginning of 1984 al-Banna was given orders directly by
Muhammad al-Khuli, one of the heads of Syrian intelligence.

At the time, the Syrian Ba'ath party planned to remove
Arafat and his supporters and to set up a new coalition
within the Palestinian movement, composed of Abu
Musa's group (presuming it would conquer Fatah), Abu
Nidal's group, and possibly even George Habash and
Na'if Hawatmah—who were both equivocating—which
would take control of the entire movement. This new
coalition would be subservient to Damascus.

At the beginning of 1985, Abu Nidal's group did in
fact carry on negotiations with Abu Musa's rebels. The
Syrian intelligence services encouraged the talks, and proposed that the two groups unite. But the negotiations
broke down. Sabri al-Banna refused to bring his group
under Abu Musa's leadership, and demanded that he
maintain his group's independence within the framework
of the unification. In spite of the failure of the talks, the
two groups agreed on tactical cooperation and on coordination of positions.

In March 1985, a new front was established under Syria and Libya, which was meant to strengthen the coalition of those organizations opposed to Arafat and his policies. Abu Nidal soon joined it. It was known as the Palestinian National Salvation Front (P.N.S.F.), and included George Habash's group, Na'if Hawatmah, Ahmad Jibril, Abu Musa, and the small splinter faction of Tal'at Yaqub, which had broken away from the P.L.F. and joined Habash's P.F.L.P.

The establishment of the Front and the readiness of its members to have Abu Nidal join it was an extremely important achievement for Sabri al-Banna. After long years of isolation and a lonely existence outside the Palestinian camp, he had won legitimacy and recognition as part of the radical organizations which opposed Yasser Arafat's leadership of the P.L.O. Even more, this new front included leaders such as Habash, Hawatmah, and Jibril, who but a few years earlier had refused to have anything to do with him, and had regarded him as "a bloodthirsty madman." His involvement in the P.N.S.F., unlike his experience with earlier "fronts," which broke up almost immediately after their formation, has lasted relatively long, and has even become stronger with time. The cooperation among the groups includes not only the coordination of strategic positions and the formulation of common policies, but even thinking in terms of planning common ventures.

In February 1986 the leaders of the Front met over a weekend in Tripoli, Libya, for what was defined as a "summit meeting" of the radical terrorist organizations and states. The official sponsor was the Allied Leadership of the Arab Nations Revolutionary Forces, and it involved twenty-two bodies, most of which are supported by Colonel Qaddafi. The participants included Habash, Jibril, Hawatmah, Samir Ghusha, the leader of a small terrorist group known as the Palestinian People's Struggle Front (P.P.S.F.), and Abd al-Ghanim, head of a pro-Syrian group which had broken away from the Palestinian Liberation Front (P.L.F.). Abu Nidal's group was represented by Shafiq al-Arida and other members of his Revolutionary Council. Among others, the conference adopted a resolution to unify all the radical organizations, including those of the P.N.S.F., within a framework which would include Arab organizations in Lebanon, Syria, Libya, Iraq, and South Yemen. This framework is to be known as "the National Command of the Revolutionary Arab Forces." Its goal is to establish a "revolutionary strike force and suicide squads" to retaliate against American interests, should the United States attack Libya or any other Arab country. After two days of deliberations, the Tripoli summit also adopted a resolution "to explore ways to intensify the struggle against the plots of Zionism and imperialism." Thus both the Syrians and Libyans have made Abu Nidal an important element in their intensive effort to depose Arafat and take over the Palestinian organizations.

The meeting would probably not have been publicized, and its decisions would have remained secret, had the Israeli security services not tried to bring down the plane carrying what it thought was all or a number of the participants in that meeting. Thus, on February 4, 1986, four Israeli F-16 planes forced an executive Gulfstream plane belonging to the Libyan Arab Airlines to land in a military airport in the north of Israel. To Israel's consternation, none of the leaders of the terrorist organizations were on the plane. Israel was especially disappointed that Ahmad Jibril, who was evidently its prime target, was not one of the passengers. From an interrogation of the passengers, it was found that Jibril had indeed been scheduled to be on that flight, but changed to a different flight at the last minute for security reasons. The only ones present on the plane were a number of politicians of radical parties in Lebanon, such as the Communist organization. The most important person present was Abdallah al-Ahmer, deputy chairman of the Syrian Ba'ath party, and one of the closest confidantes of President Assad. Al-Ahmer is known as being violently anti-Israeli, and is also a friend of Colonel Qaddafi. He is a strong supporter of international terrorism.

After a short investigation, Israel was forced to free the plane and its passengers, but the aims of the summit conference were exposed, so that the Israeli security forces did reap some benefit from the episode.

If the Syrian and Libyan scenario succeeds, this will bring the Palestinian organizations back to the 1960's, when they first started out. It is difficult, though, to see whether the revolt against Arafat will ultimately succeed, and above all what political and military effects it will have upon the Middle East stage.

Of course, Arafat has not taken all of these attempts against him lying down. Earlier, he had appealed to Nicolae Ceausescu, the Rumanian president, Prime Minister Indira Ghandi of India, and, first and foremost, to the leaders of the Soviet Union to help him restrain the Syrians. As before, Arafat, the world symbol of the Palestinian cause, has been called upon to prove his ability to survive. In the past, he showed an uncanny knack to rise anew, like the legendary phoenix, from the ashes. That was what happened in Jordan in September 1970, and again in Beirut in September 1982.

In a private conversation with the then Austrian Chancellor Kreisky, Arafat was quoted as saying that he was aware he still faced "another *Altalena*."[3] In other words, the Palestinian movement would still have to make its own crucial decision at some point in the future, one which might involve a civil war among the different factions. In the past, Arafat has always been willing to compromise with his opponents and to rule the Palestinian movement by consensus. He ignored calls by people like Dr. Sartawi to demonstrate his leadership and at the

---

[3] A reference to a ship brought in by the Jewish underground of the Irgun Tzvai Leumi to the newly-proclaimed State of Israel in May 1948. The Irgun insisted that a certain quantity of the arms on board the ship be reserved for its own men's use, while the new prime minister, Ben Gurion, saw this as an attempt at delegitimizing the government. When the Irgun refused to budge, Ben Gurion ordered that the *Altalena* be sunk off the Tel Aviv coast, and that the Irgun's men be disarmed. Ben Gurion went so far as to refer to the cannon firing on the *Altalena* as "the holy gun." This event marked a watershed in Israel's development as a democracy.

moment of truth to come out in favor of a moderate approach toward Israel. Arafat never tried to impose the majority's will on the minority, and it is doubtful if he will do so in the future. It is quite possible that he is simply constitutionally not able to do so. What is clear, though, is that "the holy gun" of the Palestinian camp has not yet been fired, and all the signs show that Arafat has preferred dealing with his opponents with moderation and compromise, both in the revolt of the summer of 1983 as well as in the subsequent attempts by the radical organizations to form a coalition against him. And then again, he may not have any other choice. His defeats in Beirut, the Bekaa valley, and Tripoli have seriously undermined his leadership as the uncontested head and most prominent figure of the Palestinian movement for fourteen years—from the 1967 Six Day War to the 1982 Lebanon War. Whatever will happen in the future, all agree about one thing: Fatah has been destroyed as Arafat's power base. If previously he had been the "first among equals," now he can at most be an equal among equals, and even that is not sure.

The relative strengths within the Palestinian camp remind one of a "zero sum game," where the loss of one participant (Arafat) is the automatic gain of the other (his opponents).

It is possible that Sabri al-Banna himself, in spite of his move from Baghdad to Damascus and then Tripoli, will continue to be at the fringes of the Palestinian camp, with his organization continuing to be considered as an irritant, dangerous and harmful, but without any influence. But one should not forget that one of Sabri al-Banna's aims is to become one of the main forces within the Palestinian camp, one which will have to be reckoned with.

The downfall of Fatah, and the dead end reached by the moderates in the Palestinian movement, has strengthened the belief among many within its ranks that they can only achieve their goals by an armed struggle. There have been signs of this tendency from the end of 1983 and through the beginning of 1986. More and more, most of the Palestinian organizations, including Fatah, have reverted to the patterns of the 1970's, in other words, to indiscriminate attacks against Israel, its institutions outside the country, and Jews throughout the world. And that is exactly Abu Nidal's desire. He wants to drag the Palestinian organizations away from the political course some had begun to adopt, which he sees as "ideological deviation" and as "treason to the revolution," and to return them to the armed struggle, as the only legitimate way which may be used for their goal: the establishment of a Palestinian state instead of Israel.

The change in the perception of these organizations and their adoption of the old-new tactics of terror have also forced Israel to find new patterns of response. At the beginning of 1986, Israel received information to the effect that a number of the leaders of the terrorist groups were in poor health. As we have said, Abu Nidal himself has undergone two open heart operations. One of Abu Musa's commanders suffered a heart attack in January 1986, and was hospitalized in Damascus. Dr. Samir Ghusha, P.P.S.F. leader, was sent to the Soviet Union for treatment of an ulcer. Tal'at Yaqub (who took his splinter group and joined Dr. Habash) was seriously injured in a car crash in Lebanon. The military commander of the P.F.L.P.-G.C. was wounded in an attempt on his life, and has stopped planning further terrorist attacks. George Habash is also not well.

But Israeli security services do not wait for nature alone to take its course. "The best way to deal with the new tendencies of Palestinian terrorism is by liquidating its leaders," was the last advice of the late General Gideon Mahanaymi, an intelligence officer and the deputy advisor on counter-terrorism to the Israeli prime minister. For obvious reasons, General Mahanaymi declined to elaborate, but one can sometimes deduce future events from what has happened in the past. In the year that followed the murder of the eleven Israeli athletes at the Munich Olympics, the Mossad pursued and eliminated the Palestinian terrorists involved in the planning and execution of the massacre. Israel does not make public commitments to renew a policy of eliminating terrorists, but the bringing down of the Libyan plane, the actions in the past, and the warning of Defense Minister Yitzhak Rabin that "Israel will use all the means at its disposal, including unconventional ones," can serve as a guide to what may be expected in the future. In fact, in February 1986 Foreign Minister Yitzhak Shamir went even further, and stated clearly, "Israel will get Abu Nidal."

Terrorist violence, clothed in revolutionary ideology and doctrine, has travelled a long road since it first made its appearance, but has always reached dead ends. Individual terror has never achieved its aims. It has killed rulers, liquidated symbols of power, executed innocents, disturbed peace and tranquility, but has never succeeded in realizing its aims. One should look at Abu Nidal in that light. He cannot undermine Israel's foundations, but can disturb it, and damage its vital interests.

Sabri al-Banna can certainly be considered as an authentic phenomenon within the Palestinian movement. His ability to recruit young Arab students indicates his charismatic character and attraction. His stubbornness, his readiness to continue with the armed struggle under all circumstances and at any price have made him a legendary figure among many of the young Palestinians. It is not impossible that if the political dead end continues in the Middle East, his way and doctrines will become dominant within the Palestinian movement in the second half of the 1980's and the early 1990's. At the same time, it must be remembered that during most of his career as a terrorist al-Banna has been an outspoken enemy of the Palestinian movement's leadership. His appeal has been to the radical fringe. His enemy has been anyone—Middle Eastern or Western, Arab or Jew—who has moved towards a policy of mutual understanding and accommodation among the conflicting interests of the region.

Mrs. Khalida Hamami, the wife of the moderate Fatah and P.L.O. representative in London, Sa'id Hamami, feels the conflict between moderation and extremism in the Palestinian movement in a special way: "We must guard against a new generation of Palestinians all becoming Abu Nidal-type hit men," she said. "I fear my own children could one day turn to terrorism if this situation continues," she confessed in an April 1986 interview with

Newsweek. She was especially worried about her son Musab, an articulate seventeen-year-old. ''To me, Rome and Vienna was a butcher's game,'' said Musab, ''but sometimes it seems that the only way to get anyone's attention about Palestine is to kill someone, like Abu Nidal does.''

He should know. After all, Abu Nidal killed his father.

11

The American Connection

The turning point came in October 1985. A single shot caused a dramatic change in the foreign policy of the United States and in the way it responded to international terror. Leon Klinghoffer, a seventy-year-old Jew from New York, embarked on a leisurely cruise to the Mediterranean, with a planned stopover in Israel. With another 450 tourists from the United States, Europe, and South America, he and his wife boarded the Italian liner *Achille Lauro* in Genoa. After a restful four-day cruise in the quiet waters of the Mediterranean, the ship anchored in Alexandria, Egypt. A large number of passengers left the ship for a short tour of the city, to be followed by a bus trip to Port Said, where they were to rejoin the ship. They were scheduled to sail from there to the last port of call: Ashdod, Israel.

Leon Klinghoffer was unable to leave the ship, as he had been partially paralyzed three years earlier following heart problems. Confined to a wheelchair, he had to forego the tour. It was this fact which sealed his fate.

Close to midnight on October 8, 1985, when the ship was about fifty miles off Port Said, it was taken over by four Palestinian terrorists. Armed with grenades, revolvers, and explosives, they threatened to blow up the ship and all its passengers unless Israel released fifty of their comrades who were in Israeli jails.

A few hours later, some of the hijackers pushed Klinghoffer's wheelchair to the stern of the ship, and ordered their youngest member, a seventeen-year-old, to

173

shoot the invalid. The youngster drew a revolver and fired once into Klinghoffer's head. The terrorists claimed he had died of a "heart attack." But the world refused to believe them, just as it refused to believe other announcements by the Palestinian terrorist organizations; especially as evidence soon emerged which clearly refuted their claims.

The evidence was supplied by the monitoring services of Israeli military intelligence, and it was sent to the American intelligence services. Israel had recorded a radio-telephone conversation between the terrorists on the ship and the leader of the organization which had sent them to carry out their nefarious deed. The leader turned out to be Abul-Abbas, head of the Palestinian Liberation Front, a small, ideologically radical, anti-Syrian and pro-Iraqi splinter group, which, unlike most other militant terrorist organizations, had agreed to cooperate with Yasser Arafat.

On the recording one can clearly hear Abul-Abbas giving orders to his terrorists and warning them not to do anything stupid. The Israeli intelligence services are convinced that Abul-Abbas was in charge of the operation. They are equally convinced that this was with the full knowledge and agreement of Yasser Arafat, in spite of Arafat's repeated denials and his attempt to portray himself as being opposed to terror. Abul-Abbas also attempted to deny his complicity, but Israel's hard evidence overcame these protestations of innocence.

After negotiations lasting more than 24 hours with Yasser Arafat and Abul-Abbas, who both portrayed themselves as "honest brokers," who were in no way involved in the hijacking, the hijackers gave themselves up to the Egyptian security forces. In return, President Hosni Mubarak guaranteed them "free passage." They chose to fly to Tunis, where the P.L.O. headquarters are located—another proof of the links between the P.L.O. and the hijacking. The American intelligence services, however, with indirect aid from the Israelis, had other plans.

The United States was incensed. One of its citizens who had wished no more than to spend a tranquil vacation on a cruise ship had fallen victim to Palestinian terrorists wanting to strike at Israel. The dramatic accounts by the news media in the United States, which reported on the whole incident fully and at length, had a great impact on both American public opinion and the American government. The United States ambassador to Egypt, Nicholas Valiotis, who followed the hijacking attempt closely, labelled the terrorist involved in the shooting "a son of a bitch," and his words were broadcast over one of the television networks. President Ronald Reagan decided to act.

The four terrorists, together with their leader, Abul-Abbas, received an Egyptian government Boeing aircraft at an Egyptian military airport, so that they could be flown to freedom in Tunis, as they had been promised. The Egyptian government attempted to conceal all the details of the proposed flight, but, utilizing ultra-secret monitoring equipment, Israel and the United States were able to follow all the preparations being made for it.

At 12:10 A.M. on Friday night, as the plane carrying the terrorists was over the Mediterranean near Italy, a number of interceptor planes were launched from the decks of the U.S. Sixth Fleet, and these forced the Egyptian plane to land at a NATO base in Sicily. This was a dramatic turn in the history of the United States' struggle against terror. For the first time the United States government had taken a concrete, active step, rather than simply condemning acts of terrorism. This was considered by the heads of the intelligence services of the United States, Israel, and other Western countries as a major shift in U.S. policy. Even though the outcome was not ideal, this did not change the new reality.

Immediately after the Egyptian plane with the terrorists on board landed in Sicily, the Italian authorities hastened to place the terrorists under arrest. But to the amazement of all, rather than putting them all in prison, Italy decided to free Abul-Abbas. Not only that: it placed a special plane at his disposal and flew him to Yugoslavia. He made his way from there to Iraq. The other four terrorists were arrested and sentenced to relatively short prison terms.

Acting on the large amount of information supplied by
Israel on the involvement of Abul-Abbas in the hijacking
of the *Achille Lauro* and other terrorist acts, on Saturday,
October 12, 1985, the United States had asked the Italian
government to apprehend the terrorist until the United
States had time to file a formal extradition request. But
even a direct and moving phone call by President Reagan
himself to Premier Bettino Craxi of Italy had been to no
avail. Italy permitted Abul-Abbas to escape.

The information supplied by Israel, and especially the
recording of Abul-Abbas' telephone call, had persuaded
the State Department that there was at least *prima facie*
evidence to send him to trial. Its legal experts had formulated a detention order against him, and had asked the
Italian government to detain him until all the pertinent
materials had been gathered. The Italians, however,
claimed that all the preliminary evidence sent to them was
inadequate.

The reason for Italy's stubborn refusal to keep Abul-
Abbas in detention pending an American extradition
request was a counter-request by the Egyptian government. President Hosni Mubarak contacted Premier Craxi
and explained to him that he, Mubarak, had personally
pledged to the terrorists that they would be freed if they
would surrender themselves. "I must keep my promises,
otherwise there will be far-reaching consequences in the
future when we come to similar negotiations with terrorists," he explained. "Otherwise they will not believe our
word."

Craxi was also pressured by his friend Yasser Arafat,
who accompanied his appeal with threats to the effect that
should Craxi not give in, Italy would be a future target
for revenge by the terrorists. Once again, Italy preferred
to submit to the blackmail of terror rather than to cooperate with the United States. As for Abul-Abbas, he is
now in Baghdad and is threatening to take revenge against
the United States.

In spite, however, of all Washington's anger—the
United States sent a formal protest note to the Italian government—American government officials, and especially
its intelligence community, were not able to conceal their

satisfaction. For the first time since international terrorism began attacking Western targets about twenty years ago, the major power in the world was doing something about it. Israel was especially overjoyed. The prime minister, Shimon Peres, sent a telegram complimenting Reagan on the United States' success in forcing down the plane carrying the hijackers. In his messages, Peres wrote:

"Dear Mr. President,
    We salute your courageous decision and the decisive action. We congratulate you and the U.S. Navy on the flawless implementation. A major contribution to the international struggle against the double plague of cold-blooded murders and outright lies by both the perpetrators and their superiors. Your action is a landmark in the fight to eradicate terrorism and a shining example of your resolve."

The Israeli leaders also permitted themselves the luxury of smiling at the historic irony involved and how fate had taken its turn. Prior to the hijacking, the head of the P.L.O., Yasser Arafat, was slated to address the annual U.N. General Assembly in October 1985, at a meeting called to commemorate the fortieth anniversary of the founding of the world body, and the United States would undoubtedly have continued to move closer to the P.L.O., even to the extent of ultimately recognizing it. Now the United States informed the U.N. that it opposed Arafat's being granted the right to address its General Assembly after a hiatus of eleven years, and even threatened to cut off all financial support to the U.N. should Arafat be allowed to speak.

But Israel realized just how strange the situation was. Scarcely two weeks earlier, most countries in the world had censured Israel when its air force planes bombed the P.L.O. headquarters in Tunis. A week before that, on September 25, 1985, the Jewish Day of Atonement, three Israelis had been slaughtered in cold blood as their yacht lay anchored in the Cypriot port of Larnaca. The three terrorists involved, two Palestinians and a British mercenary named Ian Davidson, gave themselves up to the

Cypriot authorities, and were all sentenced to long prison terms.[1] During their interrogation, they claimed the three Israelis, a man and wife and their friend, were "agents of the Mossad," but their claim was soon shown to be baseless. The three Israelis were all in their 50's, and belonged to the Haifa yachting club.

It became apparent in the course of the interrogation that the terrorists belonged to Yasser Arafat's Special Unit of Force 17, and that their motive had been revenge for the capture by Israel a number of months earlier of a Palestinian ship, one of whose passengers was Faisal Muhammad Abu Sharah, the deputy commander of Force 17.

Following the murders in Larnaca, Israel decided to respond forcibly. In a daring and complicated action, American-made Israeli F-15 and F-16 airplanes flew about 1500 miles from Israel to Tunis and back. Refueling in midair, they attacked those buildings in the Hamman a-Shat quarter near Tunis which were serving as the P.L.O. headquarters. Yasser Arafat barely escaped in time. Rather than staying at his command center, he had preferred, for security reasons, to sleep in a different office not far from the headquarters.

Despite their understanding of Israel's action, all the Western European nations resounded with the by-now standard criticism of the bombing. A spokesman for the British Foreign Office stated that Britain could not agree to Israel's reprisals. The White House, too, deplored the incident, but in a restrained fashion. President Reagan went so far as to state that he always had the highest regard for Israel's intelligence capabilities. All this had happened just two weeks earlier.

Now, in mid-October, due to the single shot that murdered Leon Klinghoffer, the United States had changed its traditional policy towards international terror. For many years the United States had marched in a lockstep with the Western European nations, under the banner of "ap-

[1] As these words are being penned, rumors abound that Cyprus is working on an exchange whereby, in return for freeing the three terrorists, Cypriots held in Lebanon will be released.

peasement at all costs.'' Washington had believed that it was important to understand the motivation for terror and the sources feeding it.

Every time that Israel reacted with military reprisals for attacks against its citizens, the Western European nations criticized its actions. Israel was accused of being the guilty party, with its occupation policy on the West Bank, the Gaza Strip, and the Golan Heights being the root cause of Palestinian terrorism.

For many years the United States maintained a soft policy toward terror and those states which assisted terrorists. The United States also found it difficult to free itself from the trauma caused by the aborted attempt to free the American hostages held in the U.S. embassy in Teheran. The fiasco in the Iranian desert on April 25, 1980, when United States commandos were forced to terminate the action to free the hostages due to technical problems caused by defective gear, was a painful experience.

The Iranian fiasco dealt a crippling blow to the morale of the United States army and its deterrent ability. Once bitten, twice shy. This defeatist attitude continued for a number of years, even after there was a change of administration in Washington. In spite of Ronald Reagan's conservativism and his willingness to take bigger risks than had his predecessor, Jimmy Carter, this was not translated into operative language. While the rhetoric emanating from Washington differed under the new president, the lack of any actual response remained unchanged.

On April 19, 1983, a driver who belonged to one of the extremist Shi'ite organizations drove an explosives-laden car into the courtyard of the U.S. Embassy in Beirut and deliberately blew himself up with the car. Forty of the embassy staff, including senior officials of the C.I.A., were killed, and another eighty were wounded. The United States did not react. A few months later, in October of that year, 244 U.S. Marines were killed in a similar explosion in their military barracks in Beirut.

This time, President Reagan could no longer remain silent. Israeli intelligence immediately supplied him with reliable information which corroborated what the American intelligence services knew themselves. The terrorist attacks had been carried out by Shi'ite suicide squads, but they had been fostered by Syrian military intelligence while their ideological support came from Teheran.

President Reagan directed the planes of the Sixth Fleet to attack terrorist bases in the Bekaa valley, in Lebanese territory controlled by Syria. But this was too little, too late. Even worse, one of the planes was downed and the pilot was captured by the Syrians. (He was later freed after the Rev. Jesse Jackson intervened.)

In June 1985 a TWA airliner was hijacked by Shi'ite extremists in a flight from Athens and forced to land in Beirut. The United States did not react this time, either, in spite of the hints that it had dropped concerning its readiness to take military action to free the plane and its passengers. Instead, it was forced to use the "good services" of moderate Shi'ite leaders such as Nabih Berri, and persuaded Israel to undertake to free Shi'ite prisoners held in Israeli prisons.

But all these actions had a cumulative effect on the United States. The U.S. administration awakened, as it were, from a long sleep, and began to reach the conclusion that a proper response was necessary to all the different types of international terror: Arab, Shi'ite, Palestinian, and European. Until October 1985 the administration discussed the best ways to deal with the problem. From that month, though, there was a major change. From being a theoretical and conceptual exercise, planning was elevated to the operational level. The question as to whether to react became how to react. The Washington decision-makers decided that the standard responses, primarily by diplomatic means, were insufficient. Terrorism was still prospering.

As soon as this conceptual turnabout occurred, the way was open for the formulation of an operative plan. President Reagan ordered all the administrative agencies to change their approach in the war against terrorism. The C.I.A. was asked to increase its intelligence-gathering on the terrorist organizations; military intelligence was instructed to examine the ties between various countries suspected of aiding different terrorist organizations; and the National Security Agency was ordered to increase its monitoring of the messages emanating from Syria, Libya, Iraq, and South Yemen, and their communications with their consulates in Europe.

At the same time, the cooperation between the intelligence services of Israel and the United States increased. For years the two countries had exchanged political and military evaluations and technological and intelligence information. From 1973 on, following the Yom Kippur War, Israel's acquisition of American military equipment and arms increased dramatically, and the industrial and technological ties between the two were reinforced. Israel rushed to pass on to the United States the lessons it had learned while using American weapons in battle against the Arab states—both to the manufacturers of the weapons and to the U.S. military which was using similar arms.

In 1981 the defense ministers of both countries, Caspar Weinberger and Ariel Sharon, signed a memorandum of understanding for strategic cooperation. From time to time joint maneuvers were held between the Israel Defense Forces and the U.S. Sixth Fleet. On the intelligence front, the contacts were conducted along two planes: between the two countries' military intelligence departments, and in communications between the Mossad and the C.I.A.

Up to October 1985 Israel would also periodically send the United States information on various Palestinian terrorist groups, and would especially send warnings when it had received information on plans to hit American targets or interests. From October on,[2] the frequency of the exchange of information on the terrorist groups increased markedly. Amiram Nir and the late General Gideon Mahanaymi, the Israeli prime minister's advisers on counter-terrorism, visited Washington and New York on numerous occasions, and exchanged assessments with

---

[2] This cooperation continued in spite of the "crisis" brought about by the arrest of Jonathan Pollard, who worked in the research department of the U.S. Navy, and who was revealed to be a spy for Israel. Israel apologized, dismantled the unit involved, and Pollard was put on trial in Washington.

officials of the Department of Justice and the C.I.A., both of which are responsible for the battle against terror.

Israel was convinced that this drastic change in Washington would bring about operative change as well. The impression of the Israelis was that President Reagan had decided to inflict a blow on the terrorists and the countries aiding them, and he was only seeking a propitious moment to justify this in the eyes of public opinion.

Reagan was given that opportunity at the end of December 1985. The attacks by the Abu Nidal group on the El Al counters in the Rome and Vienna airports, while not aimed directly at the United States but rather at Israel, killed a number of United States citizens.[3] Even more: proof was found clearly linking the terrorist organization carrying out the murders to the countries which aided it. It was found that Libya had supplied the Tunisian passports which enabled the terrorists to enter Austria and Italy, and that the terrorists had trained in the Damour camp near Damascus, leaving on this assignment from Syria, via Budapest to Vienna and via Zurich and Belgrade to Rome.

The United States decided to act, and it chose to attack Libya's Qaddafi. Libya openly supports terrorist organizations, and has specifically announced its support for the Abu Nidal group. It finances international terrorism and its embassies supply logistic aid—the transportation of weapons and explosives in diplomatic pouches, the transfer of instructions, etc. Syria, on the other hand, is considered a more difficult target. It too aids terrorism and even initiates it, but unlike Qaddafi, with his "revolutionary" rhetoric, Assad prefers to work quietly. An Israeli official defined the difference between them as follows: "Qaddafi and Assad both belong to the same zoo, but Assad is a fox while Qaddafi jabbers like a monkey."

Washington accordingly chose the easier target of Libya. This is a small country whose ability to retaliate against the United States is limited. Colonel Qaddafi has

[3]One third of the victims of terrorism since 1968 had been American citizens.

no real allies, and the few that cooperate with him—Syria and Iran—will not come to his aid.

Before the United States decided to act against Qaddafi, Washington had only one problem: the USSR. But the Societ reaction was foreseen as well. The State Department, the Pentagon, and the C.I.A. reached the conclusion that Moscow would not come to the aid of Qaddafi. For the Soviets as well he was only a limited ally: they regarded him as an unpredictable person whom it was difficult to control. Unlike the Syrians, with whom Moscow is able to coordinate positions and cooperate in different ventures, the Kremlin finds it difficult to keep track of Qaddafi's exploits. And there is another difference: the Soviet Union has an important defense treaty with Syria, which it does not have with Libya.

Israel was more than delighted with the change of U.S. policy. For years it had been sounding the alarm against international terrorism, asking the international community to react suitably to the threat it faced. It was not sufficient merely to take defensive steps against the possibility of terrorist attacks. Action was needed against those states which supported terrorism. "Whoever wishes to wipe out international terrorism must hit those countries which aid terror, initiate it and stand behind it," the Israeli Foreign Minister, Yitzhak Shamir, stressed on numerous occasions. Binyamin Netanyahu, the Israeli ambassador to the United Nations, was a strong proponent of this idea.

Netanyahu, a former soldier and businessman, and a brilliant diplomat, has a strong personal reason for his concern with the subject. He is the younger brother of Lieut. Colonel Yonatan Netanyahu, leader of the daring Israeli commando unit that rescued all but three of the more than one hundred hostages captured by a combined band of European and Palestinian terrorists, and flown to Entebbe, Uganda, in July 1976. The Israelis lost only one of their men during that raid, but that was Yonatan Netanyahu.

Ambassador Netanyahu views the overall results of Entebbe as a lesson to be widely applied today. He believes that international terrorism is not a sporadic phenomenon born of social misery or frustration.[4] It is rooted in the political ambitions and designs of expansionist states and the groups that serve them. Without the support of such states, international terrorism would be impossible. He therefore proposes that the West take appropriate and effective countermeasures against terrorism and the states that support it. This should include:

a) military action

b) economic pressure—most of the countries supporting terrorism desperately need Western goods, weapons, or credit. Economic pressure could be a combination of boycott and embargo.

c) political pressure—this could range from international condemnation to cutting off diplomatic relations, as the United States and Britain did with Libya.

But the question remains: to what extent was Israel influential in the change which took place in the United States? The answer to this question brings us back to the classical question of cause and effect. It is possible that Israel's position as expressed by Netanyahu and others was a factor in motivating the U.S. administration to change direction; certainly Israel's determined decision to fight terror fitted in very well with the new concept being formulated in Washington. The United States came to the conclusion that its international presence was in great danger because of terrorism. Both its official deployment—embassies, military bases, and other government institutions—and its civilian deployment—American corporations, citizens, and tourists—were in danger. The presence of these bodies and individuals throughout the world is certainly the longest extension of, and an extremely important tool for increasing, American influence in the world.

The conclusion was clear. President Reagan could not afford the political price of further humiliation at the hands of international terrorism. There was only one possible solution: to choose a target and hit it. Since the United States is a superpower, its decision-making pro-

---

[4] Binyamin Netanyahu (ed.), *Terrorism: How The West Can Win* (New York: Farrar, Straus and Giroux, 1986).

cess is complicated. As a superpower, the United States thinks and acts in terms of strategic considerations, and finds it difficult to utilize tactical means. Everything is slow and ponderous. So are its responses. This was certainly true when the United States was not sure of itself and wished to receive the support of other states, first and foremost of Israel.

In March 1986 William Casey, the Director of the C.I.A., along with senior members of the State Department, toured the Middle East in connection with American efforts to curb terror and to strike the terrorists and those countries which offer them shelter. Casey and President Reagan proposed that the United States and Israel embark on a joint military venture against Libya.

To Washington's chagrin and surprise, Israel rejected the proposal. The Israeli political and military leadership held intensive discussions on the Amercian proposal, but the firm opposition of Prime Minister Peres and Defense Minister Rabin carried the day. "Libya is not one of the states which most endangers Israel," was the way Rabin put it. "Israel has more than enough enemies and does not need to add another one to the list. If we attack Libya, we will have to face an additional new front. The entire Mediterranean will then become an arena of confrontation."

At the same time, Israel indicated that it would be willing to grant any other type of aid necessary for the success of the United States action. U.S. and Israeli intelligence and political sources explained that the gigantic apparatus of the C.I.A., which in recent years alone has recruited an additional 3000 agents and is constructing two more seven-story buildings at the Langley center near Washington, is still not capable of transmitting to the American president and administration the type of information needed to adopt decisions for a comprehensive struggle against terrorism. Israel, on the other hand, has the needed information, and even though the United States was disappointed by Israel's refusal to be involved militarily, it still received a great deal of vital information from Jerusalem.

At the end of March 1986, the United States reinforced
its Mediterranean fleet and sent it on what were termed
"military maneuvers." In practice, though, this was
meant to be nothing more than a provocation against
Libya. The "maneuvers" were held near the Libyan shore
in the Gulf of Sidra, which the United States considered
to be international waters, in spite of Libya's territorial
claim to the gulf. Qaddafi promptly proclaimed that anyone entering the gulf beyond a line corresponding to the
northern-most point of the Libyan coast would be killed.
He named this the "death line."

On March 23, 1986, ships of the U.S. fleet crossed the
"death line," and U.S. planes began patrolling the coast
off Libya. Libya's response was to fire surface-to-air missiles at the planes, but they all missed their targets. The
United States finally had the "provocation" it had sought.
President Reagan ordered an immediate response, and the
next morning U.S. planes and ships fired on the new
SAM-5 missile bases which Libya had just received from
the Soviet Union, and which were operated by Soviet
technicians. A number of patrol boats of the Libyan navy
were also hit.

Colonel Qaddafi was stunned. For the first time since
he had begun aiding international terrorism he had been
punished for his actions. But he soon recovered from this
shock and declared a "war of terror against the United
States." Sabri al-Banna also announced that he was placing his men at the disposal of "Brother Qaddafi" and the
"Libyan revolution." It was not long before the
response—revenge against the United States—was forthcoming.

TWA Flight 840, a Boeing 727 flying from Rome to
Athens with 115 passengers and 7 crew members, had
already begun its descent into Athens International Airport. It was a sunny day, April 2, 1986. Twenty minutes
before the plane was due to land, as it flew at an altitude
of 15,000 feet over Argos, near the ancient town of
Mycenae, an explosion shook the aircraft. At first the
pilot, Captain Richard Peterson, aged 56 and a 30 year
veteran, thought the problem was a broken window,
though he later likened the sound to that of "a shotgun

going off next to your ear." Neither the crew nor most of the passengers knew at the time that moments after the explosion four of the passengers had been sucked out of the 9 by 4 foot hole blown in the fuselage near the right wing. Thirteen minutes later, Peterson landed the plane safely, to the cheers and applause of his passengers and crew.

The bomb aboard Flight 840 had taken four lives, far fewer than the 166 killed two days earlier when a Mexican jetliner had crashed into a mountainside in central Mexico,[5] but it was one of the most chilling episodes in the almost two decades of airborne terrorism. It demonstrated that neither governments nor airlines have yet found the means to make air travellers safe from terrorist attacks.

It was quite clear to American intelligence that this had been an act of revenge perpetrated by Colonel Qaddafi, but there were problems in establishing which terrorists had placed the bomb on board. The Israeli prime minister, who happened to be in Washington at the time, provided the answer: "We know from our most reliable sources that it was a joint operation by Abu Nidal and Abu Musa."

On the day of the explosion an anonymous caller had telephoned a Western news agency in Beirut and claimed that the bomb was planted by a little-known group named the Izz al-Din Qasam unit of the Arab Revolutionary Cells. (Izz al-Din Qasam was a Palestinian Arab slain by the British police during the Arab revolt in Palestine in 1936. His name has been frequently used by Abu Nidal's terrorist units.) This name rang a bell in the different intelligence services, for, as we have seen, the words "Arab Revolutionary" are used quite extensively in operations by Abu Nidal.

[5] The Abu Nidal group also took responsibility for the Mexican air crash. Both Revolutionary Egypt and the Arab Revolutionary Brigades, cover names used repeatedly by Abu Nidal, claimed in Beirut that they had taken action in revenge for the shelling of Libya.

The caller claimed the bombing had been in retaliation for the U.S. missile attacks on Libya the previous month. A four-page handwritten statement repeating the claim and promising further attacks on U.S. targets ''across the world'' was later delivered to Beirut newspapers.

It is not surprising that Abu Nidal, acting on behalf of Colonel Qaddafi and with the aid of Syrian intelligence, was responsible for this act of revenge against the United States. What was unusual was the method used. The smuggling of plastic explosives which cannot be detected by airport X-ray machines onto an airplane was a new technique for the group. Abu Nidal learned this technique from another Palestinian terrorist group, the Arab Organization of May 15, whose leader, Muhammad al-Amri, is an explosives expert. Al-Banna met with al-Amri in the early 1980's, and was very impressed by his personality and unusual terrorist methods, which include sending group members to befriend or even marry European women who are later used as agents. Al-Amri has specialized in sophisticated bombs, including pressure-sensitive barometers used for setting off explosives in suitcases once an airplane has reached a certain altitude. Abu Nidal has evidently decided to adopt the methods of Abu Ibrahim, and the TWA explosion was just the beginning.

Nor is there any feeling that the war against terrorism is being won on the ground. Two days after the TWA explosion, a bomb went off in ''La Belle,'' a West Berlin nightclub frequented by American soldiers. An American soldier and a West German woman were killed, while more than 200 people were injured.

As has been his custom for many years, Colonel Qaddafi praised the attack on the nightclub as a revolutionary act, thus again giving the United States an opportunity to blame him as being directly responsible for it. American intelligence claimed that it had recorded secret broadcasts between Tripoli and the Libyan embassy in East Berlin, in which Libya had ordered the bombing.

A vigorous investigation by the West German authorities brought about the apprehension of a number of suspects in the bombing of the nightclub. One of them, Ahmad Hazi Hindawi, confessed that he had received the explosives-laden suitcase which he had left in the night-club from Syrian diplomats in East Berlin, and not from the Libyans, as the United States had claimed. The police found in his possession the phone numbers and sketches of other nightclubs in Berlin which are frequented by American servicemen.

But nothing could have prevented the Reagan administration from pursuing their goal. Once they decided, they would not allow the facts to kill their long-desired plan. The United States hurriedly sent emissaries to the various West European capitals to try to persuade them to mount a joint military action against Libya. None of these countries, however, found the evidence produced by the United States intelligence services to be sufficiently convincing. Italy, France, and West Germany rejected the American request, and only Margaret Thatcher of Britain offered aid to the Americans.

12

The British Policy

On April 15, 1986, the United States Air Force launched a surprise attack on Qaddafi's headquarters in the Bab al-Aziz quarter of Tripoli, as well as on the new missile batteries installed by the Soviets in Benghazi. More than a hundred Libyans were killed, most of them civilians, including one who was claimed to be Qaddafi's adopted daughter. (There are those, though, that claim that the dead child was not Qaddafi's, and that the statement that she was his daughter was no more than a propaganda ploy.) Two of the Libyan leader's children were injured when a bomb struck his headquarters, which is also used as his residence. Qaddafi himself survived the bombing but suffered from shock, and for two days was unable to make a public appearance.

The United States planes had left from bases in Britain, but had to fly two thousand extra miles when both France and Italy barred their airspace for the flight. The United States was extremely dismayed. Not only had its allies deserted it, but Qaddafi, who had been the main target of the raid, had miraculously survived.

The British readiness to assist the American attack should not have been surprising. Ever since the Conservative party had won the elections in May 1979, the cooperation between the two countries had continued to grow. Even more than by the conservative ideology shared by the two governments, the special relationship was shaped by the excellent understanding between the two leaders. Margaret Thatcher and Ronald Reagan come from dissimilar backgrounds but have adopted a similar view of the world. They see eye to eye on many topics. In economics, both are believers in the free market concept and in monetarism. They are not pleased with the welfare state, and see it as a burden on society. Both Thatcher and Reagan are intent on limiting the intervention of the central government in the economy. And their views on foreign policy are close to one another. President Reagan described the Soviet Union as an "evil empire," while Prime Minister Thatcher regards communism as a growing threat. They feel the same about international terrorism and state-sponsored violence. Both believe that terror must be combatted by all the means available to the West: diplomacy, economic sanctions, and, if necessary, military actions.

There is no doubt that the special "chemistry" that has developed between the president and the prime minister influenced the latter's decision to allow American planes to use British bases on their way to Libya. Margaret Thatcher acted unhesitatingly as soon as the American administration asked for her help. She was ready to endure the criticism that the Labour opposition and the media ultimately heaped on her. Her opponents claimed that the air raid would induce Colonel Qaddafi to take revenge, and would thus act to increase terror. In their view, the British involvement had made Britain and its diplomats and subjects abroad easy targets. Another claim was that the operation itself had not been overly successful, and that terrorism cannot be fought by conventional means. What were needed were totally different methods. But the Iron Lady proved once again that she was a "convinced politician," and it was impossible to persuade her to change her mind.

The basis for the British government's decision to allow United States F-111's to attack Libya from bases in the United Kingdom was the 1951 agreement signed by President Harry Truman and Prime Minister Clement Attlee, which was endorsed the following year by Truman and Winston Churchill. Details on the agreement regarding U.S. bases in Britain have always been shrouded in secrecy. The relevance of the agreement to the current situation appears to lie in Harold Macmillan's address to the House of Commons on December 12, 1957, in which he stated that "the use of bases in an emergency was accepted to be a matter for joint decision by the two governments in the light of circumstances prevailing at the time."

Only hours after the U.S. action against Libya, Prime Minister Thatcher told the House of Commons that the agreements "have been the same for well over thirty years and have not changed." Her government's approval soon followed, although clear reservations were voiced by senior ministers, including Defense Secretary George Younger.

In the House of Commons, former premier Edward Heath disclosed that Washington had asked his government for similar approval to use British bases during the 1973 war between Israel and both Egypt and Syria. "Our reply was, 'No,'" he told M.P.'s. But with Margaret Thatcher the policy has been dramatically changed. The justification for the U.S. attack on Libya was its supposed intelligence-gathering on terrorism sponsored by Mu'ammar Qaddafi. However, Mrs. Thatcher also told the House of Commons[1] that "I have seen and examined our own intelligence," which indicated that the Government Communications Headquarters (GCHQ) at Cheltenham and its Cyprus outstation also monitored Libyan activities.

Mrs. Thatcher also stated that she concurred with the U.S. assertion that its action was legally justified under Article 51 of the United Nations Charter. In addition, the fifth article of the North Atlantic Treaty Organization charter states that "the parties agree that an armed attack against one or more of them in Europe or North America shall be considered an attack against [all of] them."

In another statement, Prime Minister Thatcher explained: "I think we are safer in the long run from terrorism. . . . If a terrorist knows that he can use force indiscriminately against our people anywhere at any time and that he will never be met with force in defense of our

[1] April 15, 1986.

own interests, then he will go on doing it and more people will lose their lives in the longer run.''[2]

The British government's resolve to fight against terrorism was not confined to words alone, but was supported by deeds as well. Its readiness to exercise force in the international arena was expressed not only in the overt aid offered to the American planes but also in more covert fashion. All intelligence branches entrusted with combatting terrorism, including the police Anti-Terrorist Squad, M.I.5, the Special Branch, and M.I.6, had begun to prepare themselves to confront this new enemy. From the time that the intelligence community became aware that Britain had turned from a base country to a target country[3] and to an objective of the Palestinian terrorist organizations, they were forced to improve their knowledge about these organizations. Earlier, on June 3, 1982, after the terrorists who had attempted to assassinate Ambassador Argov had been caught, precious time had been wasted because the investigators of the Anti-Terrorist Squad were unfamiliar with the fine differences between one Palestinian terrorist organization and another. They could not, for example, distinguish between the Abu Nidal group and Fatah, and this lack of knowledge enabled the suspects to stall and thereby gain time, during which they hoped their comrades would be able to flee and conceal their tracks. If the organization responsible for the terrorist attack had been identified at an earlier stage, the investigators would have been able to draw certain conclusions on the *modus operandi* of the group. Since then, the British intelligence services have delved much more deeply into the question, and have improved consistently in correlation with the increased threat.

Those who are responsible for the struggle against terror have acquired greater knowledge and understanding of the Palestinian and Muslim terrorist groups. Considerable effort has been expended in penetrating these groups, in

[2] In an interview with Granada Television, April 21, 1986.
[3] A *base country* is one in which terrorists or foreign agents act against third parties, while a *target country* is one against which terrorists act, both on its soil and against its interests abroad.

planting agents within them, and in locating informers, so
that information can be gathered on the groups' intentions
and plans. Police officers who were able to converse in
Arabic were recruited, so that suspects could be interrogated without the need for a translator. Security was
stepped up at the airports, and greater attention was paid
to foreigners from the Middle East entering Britain. In
addition to the elite units of the S.A.S., other contingents
were also trained to fight terrorism and to react speedily
in a hostage crisis. There was increased cooperation with
other European countries, the United States, and Israel.
Already during the investigation of the attempted assassination of Ambassador Argov the head of the investigating team, Superintendent John Paul, flew to Israel to
utilize the information that the Israeli secret services had
accumulated about the Abu Nidal group and about the
three terrorists. Since that time, the ties between Britain
and Israel have been further strengthened, and Israel has
furnished the United Kingdom with information of great
value on Arab or Palestinian terrorists who managed to
enter Britain and planned to commit terrorist acts in it.
Britain, for its part, was able to reciprocate by transmitting reports on the interrogation of dangerous terrorists
such as Rasmi Awad and Nezar Hindawi, and on another
squad of Abu Nidal that planned to kill the Israeli ambassador to Britain.

This change in British policy is even more noticeable
if one compares it to the British attitude in 1970. That
year, Leila Khaled, a female member of the P.F.L.P.,
became internationally notorious when one of her hijack
attempts over Britain was foiled by an Israeli security
guard. A Palestinian who had been born in Haifa in 1946,
Khaled had fled with her family to Tyre, Lebanon, when
she was two years old. Following the Arab defeat of
1967, she joined the left-wing P.F.L.P. On September 6,
1970, Khaled and a South American comrade who had
joined the Palestinian cause, Patrick Arguello, tried to
hijack an El Al Boeing 707 bound for New York from
Amsterdam. At 1.50 P.M., as the plane was over the
south of England, the two terrorists tried to force their
way into the cockpit. There was a brief struggle in which

an Israeli cabin steward was shot in the stomach (he later recovered) and Arguello was shot dead by an El Al security man. Khaled was overcome by a male passenger, who hit her forcefully on the head. She did manage to throw a grenade, which miraculously failed to explode. The plane made an emergency landing at London's Heathrow airport, where Khaled was handed over to the British police.

A few weeks later, though, when P.F.L.P. gunmen hijacked three airliners including a British plane to Dawson's Field in Jordan and a fourth to Cairo and held more than three hundred passengers and crew members hostage, Khaled was one of a handful of Palestinian terrorists in several European countries who were released in return for the safety of the hostages. She was flown out of Britain to Cairo on a Royal Air Force Comet jet on September 30, 1970. She continued to be heavily involved in terrorism, and was spotted near Amsterdam's Schipol airport in August 1972.

The submission by Britain and other European countries to the terrorist demands was merely the beginning of a long period during which Palestinian and international terrorism was appeased.

It is true that the violence of the Middle East had spread to Europe even earlier, immediately following the 1967 Middle East war. On August 18, 1969, Palestinian terrorists had placed an explosive device at the entrance to one of the Marks and Spencer stores in London, but the major turning point in the spread of terrorism came after September 1970.

Over the course of time London became a focus of terrorist acts against Arab targets. The tough British extradition laws made matters easier for the terrorists and limited the risks involved in their activities. From the middle of the 1970's London was one of the more important centers in Europe offering refuge to political exiles from Arab countries.

At the same time, London had become one of the key tourist attractions for Arabs. Sheikhs with petrodollar fortunes and Iranian businessmen occupied some of the most expensive suites in the fanciest hotels or owned homes in

the smart suburbs as they patronized the brothels and luxurious casinos that had sprung up to provide every syba-
ritic pleasure. Londoners, who are not known for their
love of foreigners and even less for their love of those
with a Middle Eastern appearance, took to complaining
that the British capital had become an "Arab city." It was
natural that such a concentration of wealth, pleasures,
perversion, and political intrigue would make the city a
prime target for various Middle Eastern terrorist groups
bent on revenge and murder.

British intelligence officers believe that at that time, in
the 1970's, almost every Middle Eastern group had its
presence in London, ranging from the P.L.O. through its
archenemy, Abu Nidal; from political exiles opposed to
Anwar Sadat and Hosni Mubarak through enemies of the
Shah of Iran, including some leaders of the Kurdish
national movement. While much of the action in these
groups was of a political nature and entirely legal, there
were also acts of terrorism, murder, extortion, kidnappings, and "work accidents." In April 1977, for example, the former North Yemeni prime minister, Abdullah
al-Hejini, his wife, and the minister at the Yemeni
embassy were gunned down in cold blood at the entrance
to their hotel. Toward the end of that year, two Syrians
would be found lying dead near their car, having been
murdered in cold blood. And a few days later, Sa'id
Hamami, one of Yasser Arafat's close friends, would be
killed.

The conversion of London into one of the world's
"terrorist capitals" forced the authorities to establish new
forces that would be able to deal with the plague. What
exacerbated the situation even further was the arrival on
English shores of Irish terror.

The Anti-Terrorist Squad had originally been set up in
response to terrorist attacks by an anarchistic group known
as the "Angry Brigade," a gang which had attacked various targets which symbolized to it the "capitalist establishment," such as the residence of the home secretary.
When first set up, it was known as the Anti-Terrorist
Department, and its original function was to defuse
bombs. Later, when the attacks by Irish terrorists

increased, the Home Office decided that a small department was insufficient for its needs. The sophistication of the I.R.A. operations, the use of booby-trapped cars and plastic explosives, and the boldness of execution (the climax of these actions in a later period being in 1979 the killing of Lord Mountbatten by a bomb placed on his yacht and the attempted murder of Margaret Thatcher in Brighton in 1984) led to a decision being taken in 1974 for the formation of a larger unit to combat terror. From that time on, over the course of years, the squad's aims have undergone a change. Once London became one of the central venues for international terrorism, the squad began shifting its focus from the Irish terrorism to Middle Eastern terror.

A report prepared for the squad for the years 1983–1985 shows that 80 percent of its activities were directed at violent groups from the Middle East. The tenacity and the professionalism of the British forces combatting this terror, which improved year by year, proved themselves in the summer of 1986 in three separate cases related to the Abu Nidal group and the Arab states which support it.

The Spanish Link: A Libyan citizen wearing a false beard and dark glasses in order not to be identifiable appeared in the Central Criminal Court at the Old Bailey in September 1986, where he testified against two of his comrades who had been accused of attempting to smuggle explosives and grenades into Britain. The appearance of the Libyan, who was in actuality a police agent, was the dramatic climax of a plan that had been foiled due to good intelligence.

In August 1985, one of the two weekly flights from Tripoli of Arab Airlines, the Syrian national airline, landed at Heathrow airport. The plane carried, in addition to its passengers and their luggage, a small box of chocolates. The Libyan air crew handed the box to a Libyan national who was waiting for it at the terminal. The "mystery man" placed the box into a brown attaché case, and tried to leave the area as fast as he could. Underneath a layer of chocolates lay four Russian-made hand grenades. The man was supposed to go to an underground station in south London two days later and to meet two of his contacts there. He was to identify them by means of a password. By the Abu Nidal group's policy of compartmentalization, the person who had received the grenades at the airport did not know those to whom he was to hand the package.

What the officers of the Libyan security services did not know, however, was that their agent in London was an opponent of Qaddafi's regime and had agreed to become a double agent, to betray his employers, and to work for British intelligence. The Libyan agent contacted his British case officer, met him, and handed him the ''chocolate grenades.'' The grenades were then replaced by duds. The double agent went on to meet his contacts at the underground station. The person who appeared was Dr. Rasmi Awad, while his comrade, Nasser Muhammad, waited for him in a car whose engine had been left running. A police ambush that had been laid on in the area immediately arrested Dr. Awad and prevented Muhammad from escaping. During the subsequent interrogation, it was found that Dr. Awad, who was forty-three years old, was a Palestinian doctor with a Jordanian passport, and had lived in Madrid for a number of years—and Madrid had served as an important center for Abu Nidal. After Dr. Awad began to cooperate with the police, documents relating to the organization were found in his home, as was a list of potential targets, which included NATO bases, ''Zionist'' targets, and so-called reactionary Arab regimes, such as Jordan and the United Arab Emirates. Nasser Muhammad, aged twenty-six, carried an Iraqi passport and claimed to be a student. Although neither during their detention nor at their subsequent trial was any mention made of the use to which the grenades were to be put, the London police believe that they were meant to be used in an attack on the El Al counters at Heathrow.

Dr. Awad, who had arrived in London from Madrid just to receive the grenades, was sentenced to twenty-five years' imprisonment, while the Iraqi ''student'' was cleared of the charge of conspiracy and was ordered to leave Britain immediately after his trial. By foiling this plot, Scotland Yard believes it broke up a cell of the Abu Nidal organization as it was about to be activated in London for attacks in Britain and on the Continent.

In spite of its fears of retaliation by Libya or Abu Nidal, the British government decided at the beginning of October 1986 to terminate all flights of the Libyan airline to British airports. This was but one of a series of decisions taken by the Thatcher government against Libya. Earlier, immediately after the murder of Policewoman Yvonne Fletcher in St. James's Square by bullets fired from the Libyan embassy in April 1984, Britain had broken all diplomatic ties with the regime of Colonel Qaddafi. The "Libyan People's Bureau," which had been used as a cover for terrorist attacks and for propaganda against opponents of Colonel Qaddafi, had been closed down, and the sale of all arms to Libya had been forbidden and other commercial ties had been restricted.

The Swedish Link: During the first two weeks of October 1986, Special Branch officers arrested and questioned six men suspected of being members of the Abu Nidal group. Three of the men carried Jordanian papers, two had Iraqi documents, and the sixth was a Swedish national, although he had been born on the West Bank of Jordan, now under Israeli occupation.

The six were arrested due to intelligence information conveyed by Israel to the British authorities. As, however, at the time of their arrest they had not been carrying any weapons, grenades, or explosives, they could not be charged. The apartment of the Swede, though, was found to contain clippings from the *Jewish Chronicle* which detailed the daily routine, public appearances, and other reports on the Israeli ambassador, Yehudah Avner. The attempted assassins of Ambassador Argov, Avner's predecessor, four years earlier had made similar use of newspapers and the media as rough intelligence material, this being a characteristic *modus operandi* of the Abu Nidal group. In the end, all six were expelled from Britain. The Swedish national was expelled to Sweden, where he was interrogated by the Stockholm police as to possible involvement in the murder of Swedish Prime Minister Olaf Palme, but after a short examination he was cleared of this charge and released. Ambassador Avner expressed his heartfelt thanks to the British government for unveiling the plot, while senior officials in the British intelligence community complained that Sweden, due to its liberal policy toward immigrants and refugees from the Middle East, had become a safe haven for terrorists, who used it as their embarkation point for attacks launched in Europe. The British complaints were supported by the Israeli authorities, who with great trepidation had organized a trip by Minister of Defense Yitzhak Rabin to Stockholm in November.

The Syrian Link: Through three hours of courtroom testimony on October 7, 1986, she had barely raised her voice above a whisper. Now thirty-two-year-old Ann Marie Murphy fixed her gaze on the Jordanian defendant, Nezar Mansur Hasi Hindawi, and unleashed the rage she had nursed since April 17, the day she had been detained at Heathrow airport with a four-pound bomb and a detonator in her luggage. Pounding her fists against the witness box, she screamed at the defendant: "How could you do this to me? I hate you! I hate you!" Tears of rage ran down her face as she shouted: "I could kill you for what you did, you bastard!" Hindawi, also aged thirty-two, appeared unmoved by the outburst. As his trial began in early October at the Old Bailey, Hindawi faced charges of trying to blow up an El Al jet by planting a time bomb in the carry-on bag of his pregnant fiancée. Had the plot succeeded, Murphy and the remaining 385 passengers on Flight 016 from New York to Tel Aviv via London would have perished at 1:04 P.M. somewhere over Austria, two hours after takeoff. Declared the prosecutor, Roy Amlot: "It was one of the most callous acts of all time."

It was certainly no more than a coincidence, yet it is difficult to ignore how history has a habit of repeating itself. The judge in the Hindawi case was William Mars-Jones, who had also sat on the bench in the case of the attempted assassins of Ambassador Argov, and Roy Amlot was the prosecutor in both terrorist trials. In the Argov case, Amlot spoke of "the Baghdad connection," while in the Hindawi case time after time he exposed "the Syrian link."

Nezar Hindawi, while not a full member of the Abu Nidal group, had in the mid-1970's been an inactive member of Wadi' Haddad's terrorist group. Afterwards he lived in London with some of his family members, but, together with his brother, was a frequent visitor to Libya. The brothers were in Tripoli, Libya, in August 1985 and offered their assistance to Colonel Qaddafi's intelligence services. In December 1985 Nezar sent a letter offering his services to Abu Musa's splinter group, which cooperates with Abu Nidal.

In the guise of a journalist writing for various Arab publications, Nezar Hindawi made numerous trips to Eastern Europe. In addition to a number of visits to Warsaw, where his former wife, Barbara, lived, he also visited East Berlin and Bulgaria. His Jordanian passport was stamped with entry visas to Egypt, Italy, and West Germany. All these trips were made on behalf of Arab terrorist groups, primarily that of Abu Nidal.

The brothers Nezar and Ahmad Hasi received a certain amount of basic training in an isolated Abu Nidal house located in Ba'albek, in the Lebanese-Bekaa valley.

It is perhaps not surprising that the Hindawi brothers became terrorists. Their family home in Baaquare, a small village in northern Jordan, was damaged in an Israeli air raid after 1967. Following this, some members of the family became sworn enemies of Israel and joined the P.L.O.

After Abu Nidal decided that Nezar Hindawi could be trusted, he sent his name to Syrian intelligence, which was seeking new recruits.

In his interrogation by the police, Hindawi told how he had been recruited by Syrian intelligence. Surrounded by armed guards, he had been taken to a building in Damascus and presented to Brigadier General Muhammad al-Khuli, commander of Syrian air force intelligence. After a short preliminary talk with the general, Hindawi was taken under the protection of Colonel Haithan Sa'id, one of General al-Khuli's assistants, and of another officer named Muphir Aquard. Hindawi told the police that the Syrian colonel had been the one to plan all the details of the action, and had met with him at least twice in Damascus in February and March.

On February 26, the colonel had supplied him with a fictitious Syrian passport that resembled those used by government officials and issued under the name of Issam a-Share. The a-Share family is a very prominent one in Damascus, one of its members being the Syrian minister for foreign affairs. The passport had visas in it valid for travel to Italy, France, West Germany, and Britain. Another Syrian agent had prepared the explosives that had been smuggled into Britain by a crew member of the Syrian Arab Airlines.

While still in Damascus, Hindawi had been shown the carry-on bag that was to be used, with a false compartment for the explosives, and had been taught how to activate a calculator that had been rigged up to detonate the explosives. Colonel Sa'id had been the one to choose the objective, an El Al plane, and he had suggested the means for accomplishing the deed: to use Hindawi's girl friend as a human "time bomb."

Hindawi returned to London, lived on and off with Ann Murphy, an Irish chambermaid who worked in the Hilton Hotel, and from time to time vanished for secret meetings with Syrian intelligence personnel. Murphy was totally in love with him. The Jordanian was everything she had dreamed of—handsome, charming, wealthy, a man of the world. He promised exotic "Arabian nights," a far cry from the life she had shared with five brothers and three sisters on a council estate seven miles south of Dublin. Hindawi lived with her for about eighteen months. When she told him he had made her pregnant, he vanished. Some time later he reappeared and said: "We are going to get married." Murphy was overjoyed. On her own admission in court, Ann Murphy accepted without question Hindawi's absences during which he did not maintain contact with her. She also accepted his claims that he was divorced from his Polish wife. She didn't think twice when he told her that they would be marrying in a foreign country. Her parents told of how he had asked her to buy a bridal gown, and had even given her two hundred pounds for the expenses involved. Hindawi claimed he had bought her a carry-on bag, and had "lovingly" packed it for her himself.

The timer and detonator were concealed in the specially rigged calculator. Murphy told how, on the way to the airport in a taxi, she had seen Hindawi take out the calculator and place a battery in it, thus activating the device. The prosecutor, Roy Amlot, mentioned that Hindawi had given two different accounts after his arrest. In his first version, he had claimed he had been given the bag in Syria and had been told it contained drugs. In another account, he claimed he had been given the bag in London by a man that he named.[4] Hindawi also told the police that he had returned from the airport in a car belonging to a member of the Syrian airlines, and reported to the ambassador. The ambassador transferred Nezar to two other Syrian diplomats, who were in reality intelligence officers. They found him accommodations in their apartment in south London and dyed his hair. They also promised to try to smuggle him out of Britain. The next morning, when Nezar looked out the window, he saw a black Syrian embassy limousine parked outside the building, and he was convinced that the Syrians planned to liquidate him. As a result, he fled the apartment and moved to a hotel, before finally giving himself up to the police. He preferred being jailed in Britain to being killed by the Syrians.

Ann Marie's carry-on bag was found to have a false bottom, and the compartment underneath it contained about four pounds of a Czech-made plastic explosive called Sematex, an explosive which the East European countries export in large quantities to the Palestinian terror groups. Dark orange in color and claylike in consistency, Sematex can only be detected by trained dogs, but apparently not by existing airport equipment, which consists primarily of X-ray machines.

High-technology weapons have created a terrifying dilemma for airport officials in their war against terrorists. New guns have already been developed made entirely of

[4] As a result of its investigation, the British government expelled three Syrian diplomats.

plastic. These do not show up on X-ray machines. Easily concealable hand guns, along with hard-to-detect putty-like explosives made of readily available ingredients, give air pirates an edge that officials are finding increasingly difficult to counter. But Israel's state airline, El Al, which sets the world standard for security, prefers to rely mainly on people rather than on machines to spot danger. While El Al's thoroughness sometimes infuriates passengers who must endure a check-in ritual that includes hand searches of carry-on luggage, minute scrutiny of passports, and rigorous quizzing of passengers about the contents of their luggage, the results in the case of Ann Marie Murphy justified El Al's methods.

The discovery of the booby-trapped bag not only pre-vented an explosion on the Boeing 747 which would have led not only to the death of all its passengers and crew, but also inevitably to a new war in the Middle East, for the investigation by the British authorities, who were aided by the expertise of the Israelis, soon showed a clear "Syrian link."

Immediately after Murphy was caught by the El Al personnel, she was questioned by the anti-terrorist squad of the London police. When questioned, the Irish woman stated that she had received the bag from her Palestinian boyfriend, Nezar Hindawi. She mentioned that Hindawi had become her lover, and after she had become pregnant he had promised to marry her. They were to be married in Israel, where, according to Hindawi, his family lived. He asked her to fly to Israel alone on El Al, while he would take a later flight from Paris to Tel Aviv. As a Palestinian, he told her, it would be difficult for him to fly on the Israeli airline, and he therefore preferred to fly on a different carrier. Ann Marie believed him, and received the bag from her lover without knowing its true contents.

Nezar Hindawi told the police that after he learned of the failure of the bomb plot, he had gone directly to the Syrian embassy in Belgrave Square and had given an envelope to the Syrian ambassador personally. The ambassador then called Damascus for further instructions. Amlot said that the ambassador, Loutouf al-Haydar, had apparently "greeted him warmly that day." At the end of Hindawi's interrogation by the police, he singled out the picture of the Syrian ambassador among pictures of various people.

At the trial, the prosecutor stated that Hindawi had been working on behalf of a group calling itself the Revolutionary Movement for the National Salvation of Jordan, with the stated aim of shedding Jewish blood. (Hindawi had also told the police that the group was opposed to King Hussein.) He had travelled to Damascus and seen the head of Syrian intelligence, and alleged he had agreed to carry out attacks on Israeli targets in return for cash and for guaranteed places for Jordanian students in Syrian universities.

The intelligence community of the Western states and of Israel have never heard of this group, and believe it is a fictitious name for a non-existent organization. Hindawi has learned well the lessons taught by Abu Nidal, who constantly uses the word "revolutionary" in the titles of the fictitious organizations which he invents to take responsibility for the terrorist acts of his group. This version is supported by the statement of Abu Iyad in Paris. Arafat's deputy arrived in the French capital on October 5, 1986, in order to help the local authorities find the perpetrators of the bombings within the city in the previous month. He specifically blamed Syrian intelligence, which acts with the aid of Palestinian organizations, such as that of Abu Nidal or Abu Musa, which carry out terrorist acts and then lay the blame on non-existent revolutionary organizations.

The fact that Nezar Hindawi had often visited Eastern Europe, including Bulgaria and East Germany, was further evidence, based on previous precedents, of the involvement of these states in international terrorism, a fact established earlier in this volume.

It appears that Nezar Hindawi and his brother Ahmad Hasi, of Berlin, and a cousin, Awni Hindawi, who was arrested in Genoa, Italy, had attempted to establish a "family" terrorist ring. Nezar, a mercenary sworn to shed Jewish blood "until the end of the world," is also believed to have been involved in the La Belle disco bombing in West Berlin which prompted the American air raid on Libya.

Documents found in his brother Ahmad Hasi's apartment in Berlin showed details of the disco where the blast occurred. West Berlin police suspect the two brothers of direct involvement, but so far they have insufficient evidence to charge them. "But if they did not do it, we have no idea who else was behind it," a security source said.

While involvement in the disco bombing must remain a strong suspicion, German intelligence officers are sure that Nezar, and, it is alleged, his brother, did bomb the German-Arab Friendship League in West Berlin in March 1986, injuring nine people. Ahmad Hasi was due to stand trial in Germany for this bombing.

Even in prison, Nezar Hindawi plotted terrorist acts. He smuggled a letter from his prison cell to his cousin Awni Hindawi in Genoa, urging the taking of British hostages for whom the Jordanian brothers could be exchanged.

What is more, he recommended that the kidnappings take place when Mrs. Thatcher was visiting Israel in May 1986. This has fuelled press speculation that there was a plot against the British prime minister, but intelligence sources say the idea has no foundation.

Genoa's anti-terrorist police had been monitoring Awni's mail, and the letter was intercepted. Italian anti-terrorist officers arrested Awni and charged him with "membership of an armed band," a standard catch-all charge in Italy, invented to deal with the Red Brigade. While questioning Awni, Italian police and two Scotland Yard anti-terrorist detectives secured further evidence of Syrian terrorist involvement.

They discovered that Nezar and Awni had been trained in the same camp near Damascus by officers of Abu Nidal and Syrian intelligence. Then Nezar settled in London and Awni in Genoa, while Nezar's brother was establishing himself in West Berlin. Their aim was to operate as terrorist mercenaries.

After forming the Revolutionary Movement for the National Salvation of Jordan, they started to offer themselves as mercenaries for the Palestinian cause, mainly to the Abu Nidal organization.

In the summer of 1985, they sought backing from Libya, and it is believed they were told to prove themselves. The attacks on the German-Arab Friendship League and the disco were the result, and it was the success of these bombings which convinced Abu Nidal that Nezar Hindawi and Syrian intelligence were worth using for the El Al plot. It was only the speedy cooperation of Israel, Britain, West Germany, and Italy that exposed this link and nipped the group in the bud, before it had had time to carry out any further terrorist acts.

Hindawi, his lawyer, Gilbert Grey, and the Syrian government attempted to disprove the allegations made against him and the Syrian government. Nezar changed his story and claimed in court that he had thought the carry-on bag he had given Ann Murphy contained drugs and not explosives. Afterwards, through Gerald Grey, he claimed that the British and Israeli intelligence services had concocted the case against him, in order to establish a *casus belli* for a military action against Syria. Hindawi's defense was so similar to that of the Syrian government that one felt the versions of the two had been coordinated in advance.

When Hindawi was asked by the police why he had spent the few nights before his attempted action in the company of the Syrian air crew, he answered that "all Arabs are comrades." Hafez Assad, the president of Syria, used similar reasoning. He stated:

"We have learned that he [Nezar Hindawi] is a Jordanian. He worked for one of the Arab newspapers published in London. He came to Syria once, a year before the incident, and said he had a Jordanian passport which had expired and which the Jordanian authorities declined to renew. He requested a Syrian passport. It was granted—an ordinary matter that happens often in Arab countries."[5]

The Syrian president denied that Syria had anything to do with the attempted bombing of the El Al airliner, and charged that Hindawi's actions were part of an Israeli plot to discredit Damascus:

"Syria has no interest. Blowing up an airplane does not cause the end of Israel. Does Syria feel proud before the world that it has downed a civilian Israeli plane? . . . This is merely an allegation without evidence. It is logical to conclude that some intelligence services, in the forefront the Israelis, are behind such acts because they benefit from them."[6]

This far-fetched allegation was echoed by Loutouf al-Haydar, the Syrian ambassador to Britain, whom Hindawi had implicated in the El Al plot. Al-Haydar reportedly dismissed the allegations as "a setup to defame Syria." In addition, the state-controlled Damascus Radio charged that U.S. and Israeli agents were responsible for "a major campaign against Syria."

It is indeed difficult to try to fathom what could have motivated Syria to embark on such a bloodthirsty action. The Israeli intelligence services also found it difficult to explain the motivation involved. This action might have been taken in retaliation for the forcing down of a Libyan plane in February 1986, one of whose passengers was the vice-chairman of the Syrian Ba'ath party. Another possible explanation is that the action was taken without the approval of President Assad, even though General al-Khuli is a very close friend of the president, dating back to the time when Assad was the commander of the Syrian air force. The latter hypothesis would seem to indicate that Assad is losing his grip on the government.

The timing of Syria's abortive bomb plot may have indicated an intention to "punish" Israel and America for the raid on Libya two days earlier. But evidence in court suggested that plans for the bombing of the jet were in hand before the air raid, and this, coupled with a closer look at one or two of the Syrian personalities, points to another, more devious motive.

Western and Israeli intelligence sources have long been aware of a "hawks and doves" split in the Damascus administration. President Assad is, for the moment, a

[6] *Ibid.*

dove. His long-term plans are for war with Israel, but he wants "strategic parity" first and acknowledges that he is not yet ready.

But had the bomb in Ann Murphy's bag blown apart the El Al jet with the loss of everyone on board, with Syria shown to be the guilty party, the obvious result would have been the beginning of war in the Middle East, and a heightening of tensions between the two superpowers.

Israel would have been forced to retaliate with strikes on Syrian bases or even on Damascus itself. (Israel hit Damascus in the 1973 war.) And Syria would have had the excuse to respond with attacks on Tel Aviv or Haifa.

This may well have been the intention of the Syrian "hawks"—a section of the Syrian military who believe that, even if they did not win a war with Israel, they could at least conclude a peace gaining them their main objective, the return of the Golan Heights.

The hawks calculate that their strength lies in their possession of new Soviet missiles, which would allow them to hit Israeli civilian targets, and an assumption that Israel would not use its nuclear weapons for fear of retribution from Russia.

A conclusion that the "hawks" gave the go-ahead for the El Al bomb to provoke the war, without the assent or knowledge of President Assad, is supported by the evidence as it emerged during the three-week trial of Nezar Hindawi, and, in particular, the part played by Colonel Haithan Sa'id and his superior, General al-Khuli.

In any event, the denials did little to allay growing Western convictions that Damascus supports terrorism, even if it does not actively engage in attacks, in its struggle against Israel and Jerusalem's Western allies.

In Hindawi's trial, Roy Amlot told the twelve jurors that Hindawi "was acting in concert with the Syrian government." What Amlot did not reveal in court was other, secret proof of Syria's involvement in terror. The monitoring services of G.C.H.Q. and of M.I.5 intercepted all telephone conversations of the Syrian embassy in London. Not only were incoming and outgoing calls taped, but also the typing of electronic typewriters and personal conversations in the embassy itself.

The British intelligence services were even able to record the sound of what seemed a small explosion on April 17, 1986, the day planned for Hindawi's attack. After careful analysis, they decided that this was not an explosion, but rather the pop of a champagne bottle being opened. A number of British intelligence officers believed that the Syrian embassy staff was celebrating Hindawi's attack. But that appears an exaggeration. April 17 is also Syria's National Day, and the members of the embassy had probably broken out the bottles in honor of the occasion. The day of the planned attack may nevertheless have been chosen for its symbolic value. The Syrian leadership may have sought a reason for a celebration, and the downing of an El Al plane might have been a perfect—macabre—reason.

But not only the British security services were busy tapping the Syrian lines. Israel's intelligence services also recorded an increased volume of communication between Damascus and its London embassy in the days preceding the planned attack. They believed this heralded a planned attack on an Israeli target in London. Security was stepped up on Israeli institutions and diplomats, and the El Al security guards were placed on alert—and it was El Al security that averted the calamity.

On October 24, 1986, the twelve jurors found Nezar Hindawi guilty, and Judge Mars-Jones sentenced him to an unprecedented forty-five-year prison term. As Hindawi stood motionless, the judge said that Britain would not tolerate terrorist acts, which "will be tracked down and brought to justice. They can expect no mercy from our courts."

And indeed the British government proved that it is not willing to tolerate terror. Already in May 1986, in her visit to Israel, Prime Minister Thatcher expressed her "shock" at the attempted terrorist act. But Thatcher, who at the time received intelligence reports from Israeli intelligence officers on the Syrian involvement in international terror, did not wish, due to the principle of *sub judice*, to react publicly. When the court sentenced Hindawi, however, the government hastened to react. Three hours after the sentence had been passed, the Syrian ambassador, Loutouf al-Haydar, was invited to the Foreign Office and was informed, in a five-minute conversation, that Britain had decided to break diplomatic relations with Syria.

Damascus was staggered. President Assad was furious, and ordered the British diplomats in Syria to vacate the country within seven days, as opposed to the fourteen days the British had allowed the Syrian embassy staff in London. Syria closed its airspace and its territorial waters to British planes and ships, while its foreign minister claimed Thatcher was a Zionist agent. Damascus promised to find a way to retaliate against Britain and to "pay it back."

The Syrian threats were supported by Colonel Qaddafi, who was in reality the only Arab leader who came to the aid of Syria, by also closing his airspace to British planes flying to Africa.

The British security forces take the Syrian threats seriously, and all British embassies throughout the world have been alerted to a possible Syrian attack.

Until the trial of Nezar Hindawi, evidence that Syria was backing terrorist outrages had always been murky. With the knowledge that the finger of guilt can now incontrovertibly be pointed at Damascus, it was inevitable that Mrs. Thatcher's reaction would be swift, in the light of her strong public stance against terrorism.

The United States and Canada, in endorsement of Britain's stand and in appreciation of its determined resolution, called back their ambassadors from Damascus, but without formally breaking relations with it. To Britain, this was but token consolation. Western Europe, and especially West Germany and France, did not follow the British lead when it broke diplomatic relations with Syria. France announced that it would continue to maintain relations with Syria and even planned to sell it arms. Its stand aroused the wrath of both Israel and Margaret Thatcher.

But even Israel and the United States could not plead complete innocence. Shortly before the release in November 1986 of David Jacobson, an American who had been held hostage in Lebanon by pro-Iranian Shi'ite Muslims, a Danish freighter reported to be carrying military supplies left the Israeli port of Eilat bound for Bandar-Abbas, Iran. According to officials in Jerusalem and Washington, it was the latest episode in a secret program by the Reagan administration to use shipments of military equipment for two purposes: in the short run, to buy freedom for American hostages; and in the longer term, to maintain contact with moderate elements in the Iranian army, in the hope of repairing relations with whatever follows Iran's aging fundamentalist leader, Ayatollah Ruhollah Khomeini.

Reports of the arms deliveries surfaced after the Iranian press agency revealed that Robert McFarlane, the former White House national security advisor, flew to Teheran on a secret mission earlier in the fall of 1986, carrying a cake shaped like a key and a Bible signed by President Reagan—peace offerings of a sort. Mr. McFarlane declined to comment, but whether or not the bizarre details were true, experts figured that such a trip would not have been made without encouragement from some Iranian political faction.

It also caused a great deal of embarrassment to the United States and developed a deep split between the White House and the State Department. The secretary of state, George Shultz, was the first senior official to restate the U.S. policy of denying arms and spare parts to Iran. The McFarlane mission has all the hallmarks of a White House operation. Reports in Washington said that Lieutenant Colonel Oliver North of the National Security Council played a key role in setting up the trip. Colonel North is said to have made several trips to Europe and the Middle East, sometimes in disguise or using an alias, to meet informers and possible intermediaries in the hostage crisis. He was assisted by the Israeli prime minister's advisor on counter-terrorism, Amiram Nir, who brought in, with the full knowledge of the Israeli cabinet, former intelligence agents who managed to establish business and military links with Teheran. Colonel North and his Israeli counterparts have been acting under the direct instructions of the national security advisor, Admiral John

Poindexter, who took over control of the small administration group in charge of the hostage crisis. Mr. McFarlane performed the same task before he resigned. During the secret contacts, Iranian officials were told that the U.S. would not object to third countries, such as Israel, selling surplus American weapons and spare parts to Iran, if it could help to secure the release of U.S. hostages.

There is always a certain slippage between principle and pragmatism in foreign policy, but rarely has the point been illustrated so dramatically. That a tough-talking Israeli and American are apparently willing to pay ransom for innocent Americans who are grabbed in Beirut raises some knotty questions and poses some risks. The impression may be created that Washington and Jerusalem are prepared to buy favors from states that control terrorist organizations. This could have also undermined the strong determination shown by the British government.

There is no doubt that, with the information which Israel has of the direct Syrian involvement in this attempted bombing, Israel could not have failed to respond had the plane indeed exploded. It is assumed that Israel would have attacked Syria, and it is quite possible that a new war would have broken out in the Middle East. But even though war was averted, there is still great danger.

This time Syria was caught red-handed. The proof against it is conclusive, and in spite of Syria's vehement denials of complicity in the affair, Damascus is afraid of reactions by the United States and Israel. In fact, official Syrian spokesmen have even stated that there is a "division of labor" between the two allies, where the United States will take care of Libya while Israel has been assigned to deal with Syria.

It was no surprise to the Americans when they decided to put a halt to Qaddafi that Syria has continued to be involved in terrorist acts. When the Israeli defense minister, Yitzhak Rabin, turned the spotlight on Syria, the United States administration was not particularly pleased. As far the Americans are concerned, Syria is different from Libya, and is a much harder target to hit. Information has accumulated over the years as to the role played by Syrian military intelligence in planning, implementation, and logistic assistance to terrorists who are affiliated with Syria, and yet additional facts keep emerging. In fact, the information gleaned in London was but the tip of the iceberg. There is a clearly defined policy underlying the terrorism which is orchestrated by Syria. Damascus is trying to achieve by terror—primarily through Abu Nidal—both political and military gains. Militarily, in spite of Syria's boast of attaining a "strategic balance" with Israel, it is still far from reaching that goal, and it thus tries to subvert Israel's power by attempting to undermine its morale, its citizens, and its economy.

It is not very difficult to visualize what effect the explosion of the El Al plane and the murder of close to four hundred people would have had on the Israelis. And this terrorist campaign has another goal as well, a political one. Syria wishes to prove to the United States that no Middle East moves toward peace can succeed without Syrian participation.

All the terror stemming from the Middle East, including the attempted assassination of Ambassador Argov, and especially the terror emanating from Ireland, have made Britain the leading country in the European Economic Community in its resolve to fight terror. Unlike various other European countries, Britain does not limit itself to expressions of political sentiments and in operational plans to thwart terror, but also wishes to bring about genuine and true cooperation between all countries of the E.E.C., as well as between Europe and the United States.

Already in October 1985, the home secretary, Douglas Hurd, in a speech to the Police Management Association, emphasized the British government's commitment to international cooperation to combat terrorism. He listed the objectives of the British and other governments as:

—to promote an acceptance among friendly countries of a common interest in fighting all kinds of terrorism, since a terrorist success in one country makes it more

likely that attempts to repeat the success will be made
in other countries;
—to create an international climate in which state-sponsored terrorism is unacceptable and in which states
tempted to use terrorism realize that this will harm, not
advance, their interests;
—to secure agreement that no substantive concessions
should be made to terrorist demands;
—to ensure that diplomatic immunities are not abused
by states which support or condone terrorism;
—to take fitting action against such states in conjunction with other friendly countries;
—to ensure that consistent and effective measures are
taken to prevent the hijacking or sabotaging of aircraft;
—to create an international environment in which it is
difficult for terrorists to operate (for example, by denying them arms and money);
—to impede the movement of international terrorists
from one country to another by the use of immigration
measures;
—to ensure that there is full cooperation among security services, police forces, and other organizations, so
that intelligence and information about terrorists, terrorist organizations, and diplomats connected with terrorism is exchanged. The aim, among other things, is
to prevent acts of terrorism, bring the perpetrators to
justice, and expel or exclude those involved, including
diplomats, from all friendly countries.
Half a year later, when the United States raid on Libya
was fresh in mind, the foreign and commonwealth secretary, Sir Geoffrey Howe, briefed the House of Commons about the meeting of the Foreign Affairs Council of
the European Economic Community and about its resolutions, which included:
—a severe cut in the size of the People's Bureaus
throughout the community;
—confining members of those bureaus to the city where
they are officially assigned;
—restricting the size of other official Libyan bodies to
the minimum necessary for their stated business;
—applying a much stricter visa regime to Libyans;

—ensuring that any Libyan expelled from one member state will be expelled from the community as a whole.[7]

The twelve member states also reaffirmed their ban on arms sales to Libya, and decided to press other countries to join it. They agreed to look urgently into further action on the abuse of diplomatic immunity, while the interior ministers of the twelve members would try to concentrate the closest possible cooperation between interior ministers, the police, and security services. Transport ministers were asked to step up urgently their cooperation on aviation security.

Another milestone in the battle against international terrorism came in Tokyo, when President Reagan and Prime Minister Thatcher persuaded their colleagues to accept further decisions.

On May 5, 1986, the industrialized democracies pledged themselves to "maximum efforts" in the fight against terrorism and gave the green light to unilateral action to halt it. In their summit meeting in Tokyo, they also singled out Libya as a supporter of terrorism. In a "Statement on International Terrorism," they specified a group of six measures "open to any government" to apply "in respect of any state which is clearly involved in sponsoring or supporting international terrorism, and in particular of Libya."

The participants in the Tokyo summit asserted that terrorism "must be fought relentlessly and without compromise" through "determined, tenacious, discreet and patient action" which combines "national measures with international cooperation." The separate statement on terrorism was approved by President Reagan and the leaders of France, Italy, West Germany, Great Britain, Japan, Canada, and the European Economic Community.

The specific concrete actions open to individual governments include:

—an embargo of arms shipments to nations which sponsor or support terrorism;

—tighter restrictions on diplomats and official establishments of such nations;

[7]Statement made in the House of Commons, April 23, 1986.

—denial of entry to all known or suspected terrorists;
—improved extradition procedures;
—stricter immigration and visa controls;
—closer cooperation between police and security forces.

An additional expression of Britain's policy may be found in the resolutions adopted in a meeting of the interior ministers of the European Economic Community known as the Trevi Group. The key figure at this meeting was the British Home Secretary, Douglas Hurd, who at the time served as president of the group. Hurd explained that the key to counter-terrorism lay in the fullest possible sharing and joint analysis of all information available. "We must pool more effectively our knowledge of who they are, where they are, and what they are planning," he asserted.[8]

The meeting has been described by officials and experts as the biggest intelligence-coordination operation ever mounted in Europe to counter terrorism.

Police and security services began to compile a blacklist of the most dangerous terrorists who threaten the security of Europe. With over forty different groups either based in Europe or using E.E.C. capitals, the European intelligence services anticipated a need to monitor at least two hundred persons known to be assassins, planners, and arms dealers. The blacklist would include the leaders of the I.R.A. command and many of the most dangerous Arab and Palestinian terrorists, and would be headed by Sabri al-Banna and all the top echelon of his organization. According to British intelligence sources, the Trevi Group agreed to set up arrangements for regular up-to-date assessments of terrorists' threats, to target the major leaders and organizers of terrorism, and to begin a new system of speedy and secure communications between European police forces. It was decided that this vital information would be sent to all E.E.C. security services via a secure coded facsimile service. This would merely involve the picking up of the phone on a guaranteed secure line, and would ensure that urgent information

[8] Presidency Statement by the Home Secretary, Douglas Hurd, September 25, 1986.

would be available to everyone at the same time. The ministers were concerned that if the coded communication system were too sophisticated several countries, such as Portugal, Spain, and Greece, which are used extensively by Abu Nidal and other Palestinian groups, would not be able to benefit, as their computers were not as advanced as those of Britain, France, West Germany, Holland, Belgium, or Italy.

These new measures would help to target terrorists' movements, money supplies, arms, and equipment, so that the security services could break the terror networks. It is a pity that these resolutions, like others in the past, were adopted under pressure, and in the light of bloody and brazen murders by terrorists. The attacks in Paris, Karachi, and Istanbul were renewed reminders that terror still thrives and continues to remain active.

13

Istanbul, Karachi: The Terror Continues

"Do you recognize him?" the young Palestinian was asked. He took the photograph, brought it up close to his eyes, and peered at it intensely for a few seconds. Two other terrorists were asked the same question. At least one of the three identified the picture: "Yes, I recognize him. We trained together in our base in the Lebanese Bekaa valley. I don't know his name, but only his underground pseudonym. We called him Abu Izam."

The interrogator and the interpreter of the Italian police force smiled with satisfaction. They offered their prisoner another cigarette, allowed him to finish smoking it, and then returned him to his cell. A liaison officer of the Italian police hastened to pass the information on to the police forces in Western Europe and Israel.

The three prisoners included Attab Hassan, who is serving a fourteen-year sentence in one of the top-security prisons in Italy for his part in the grenade attack in September 1985 on the offices of the British Airways in Rome; Ahmad al-Hussein, known as Abu Sarj, serving a sentence for tossing grenades into the Café de Paris in Rome in April of that year; and Muhammad Sharham, who is awaiting trial for the attack on the El Al counter at the Rome airport.

This meeting between Hassan and the investigators took place on one of the first days of September 1986. A few days later, in the course of his visit to the United States, the Israeli minister of defense, Yitzhak Rabin, was able to announce that ''we have reason to believe that Abu Nidal was responsible for the attack on the synagogue in Istanbul,''[1] and to repeat this allegation a fortnight later in an interview with Turkish television. ''We have some pieces of information which identified those who took part in the attack as members of Abu Nidal,'' he continued.

Until the confirmation by the terrorist held in Rome, the investigators of the Turkish police found it difficult to identify the attackers, and—even more—they were in shock at its barbarity.

Two Arab terrorists, posing as photographers, had entered a newly refurbished synagogue in the Jewish quarter of Istanbul during Sabbath services on Saturday, September 6, 1986. After locking the doors with iron bars, the attackers had sprayed the congregation with submachine guns and hand grenades. Twenty-one worshippers, including seven rabbis, were killed in the massacre, and four others, including the chief rabbi of Istanbul, were wounded in the blaze of gunfire and explosions that went on for three to five minutes and left the synagogue on fire. The bodies of the gunmen were found in the carnage.

Witnesses described scenes of horror as bullets from automatic weapons raked the benches, worshippers in prayer shawls screamed and fell, and blasts shook the Neve Shalom Synagogue, the city's largest.

Bodies and parts of bodies lay all about the synagogue, and many of the dead could not be identified immediately. The bodies were taken away in pine boxes.

Nave Shalom, which means ''Dwelling-Place of Peace,'' had been extensively renovated in the months prior to the attack, and that morning's service was the first after the completion of the work. Istanbul, Muslim Turkey's largest city with 5.5 million people, has a Jewish population of about 22,000 Turkish nationals, mostly descendants of those Jews who fled the Spanish Inquisition in the late fifteenth century, and who still speak a Spanish dialect known as Ladino.

[1] The Israeli daily Ha'aretz, September 14, 1986.

The area around the synagogue is normally a bustling commercial center with small shops and offices, but many were closed for the Sabbath and the neighborhood was quiet that morning.

More than thirty members of the congregation had gathered inside the synagogue and had just begun services when the terrorists entered at about 9:15 A.M. It is unclear how many gunmen entered. Turkish officials said two terrorists apparently took part, although earlier reports had mentioned as many as five.

The gunmen gained entry, witnesses said, by posing as photographers who wanted to take pictures of the newly refurbished synagogue. At least two members of the congregation, including the synagogue warden, entered after the terrorists.

Once inside, the terrorists barred the main doors, then, shouting in Arabic, took up positions about ten yards apart and began opening fire and hurling grenades, killing and wounding worshippers as they scrambled over benches and chairs. The only uninjured survivor of the attack said he had pretended to be dead to escape the bloodbath.

Rafi Saul, seventeen years old, said the terrorists shot their victims, including his father Moise, then poured gasoline on the bodies and set them on fire. "When the fire started," he added, "I looked across from where I was hiding and saw they were starting to burn the corpses. They poured gasoline on them; I played dead and stayed still."

Outside, passersby and a few merchants heard the commotion. "There were screams and then I heard shots," another witness said. "I later heard an explosion, and the force of it threw a young worshipper—a man—out of the synagogue into the street."

"The shooting lasted from three to five minutes," said Oul Esin, who believed the explosions occurred later.

Istanbul's deputy chief of police, Mehmet Agar, said the gunmen then attempted to flee. Some may have escaped, but at least two were confronted outside the building by the police who had begun to arrive by that time. As a result, he stated, the gunmen ran back into the synagogue. "Then a loud explosion was heard. We are not sure whether they committed suicide or the bombs went off accidentally,'' he stated.

Turkish security officials said two Polish-made submachine guns, seven unexploded Soviet-made hand grenades, and more than a hundred spare cartridges were found inside the synagogue after the firemen managed to douse the flames in the one-story building.

Several anti-Israel terrorist groups claimed responsibility for the attack. An anonymous telephone caller in Beirut made a claim on behalf of the Muslim fundamentalist group, Islamic Holy War, and another on behalf of a group named Islamic Resistance, a pro-Iranian organization.

The Turkish authorities, while describing the gunmen as Arabs, did not immediately recognize any of the anonymous phone claims as valid. But Israeli counter-terrorist experts reached the conclusion—even without having the full details—that the attack bore Abu Nidal's marks.

The Target: Abu Nidal's organization is the only one of the Palestinian terrorist groups that has never refrained from attacking synagogues or holy sites. Since 1981 it has unhesitatingly attacked synagogues in Vienna, Brussels, and Rome. Sabri al-Banna and his officers have always claimed that synagogues serve as ''fronts'' for secret work of the Mossad, and they are thus regarded as legitimate targets.[2]

The Brutality: The stupefying cruelty, lack of any mercy, cold-blooded and unhesitating murder; all these are

---

[2] An official spokesman of the ''P.L.O.—Revolutionary Council,'' the official title of the Abu Nidal group, admitted indirectly in a conversation with a reporter of Radio Europe 1 that it was its men that had perpetrated the murder in Istanbul. The reporter met the spokesman, who identified himself as Atef Abu Bak'r, at an Abu Nidal base in the Lebanese Bekaa valley, and asked him why they ''attack Jews in synagogues in Istanbul and not in Tel Aviv.'' Abu Bak'r's reply, as broadcast on October 14, 1986, was that ''this is an answer to the Mossad that has extended the war to Europe in liquidating Palestinian personages.''

signs of the Abu Nidal organization more than of any other organization.

The Target Country: Turkey has in recent years become one of the most important targets of the organization. In a number of instances, Abu Nidal's terrorists attacked United States and Jordanian targets on Turkish soil, while in other cases the government authorities apprehended Abu Nidal activists who had planned terrorist acts.[3] Also, the fact that Turkey is geographically close to Iraq and Syria, both of which have granted asylum to Abu Nidal, and to Bulgaria, which has fostered relations with the terrorist organizations, has made the country an attractive center from which the Abu Nidal group has embarked on terrorist acts.

The Weapons: The use of Polish W.Z.63 submachine guns in the attack can also aid in drawing the conclusion that this action was taken by Abu Nidal. This small but efficient weapon has become very popular among the group.

And finally, the events of the day preceding the attack in Istanbul can also lead us to the conclusion that Abu Nidal had sent his men out on this mission.

The hijacking began on Friday, September 5, 1986, at 6:00 A.M. The four gunmen drove onto the Karachi airport in what looked like an airport security van, and

---

[3] On October 10, 1986, the Ankara police force apprehended four Palestinian terrorists who carried Jordanian passports, and charged them with membership in the Abu Nidal group and in involvement in the murder of a Jordanian diplomat in June 1985. The four were Bassam Lutfi Fa'iz Za'id al-Ahmad, Sami Rushdi Ahmad Washash, Na'ef al-Nabi, and Nadir Hasnin Habash. In the police interrogation it became clear that the planner of the attack was Ibrahim Ali Muhammad al-Haj, who had arrived in Turkey from Syria, and had contacted al-Nabi, a minor functionary in the Jordanian embassy in Ankara. Al-Haj, assisted by the four members of the cell, decided to murder the Jordanian diplomat, and immediately after the murder left Ankara. The cell is also suspected of involvement in and assistance with the attack on the Istanbul synagogue.

stormed aboard the Pan American World Airways jumbo jet on its way from Bombay to New York.

Demanding to fly to Cyprus in order to gain the release of a British and two Palestinian terrorists held in prison in that country, they held the parked Boeing 747 containing 389 passengers until 10:00 P.M., at which time they began shooting and detonating grenades inside the newly darkened cabin. The panic-stricken passengers, screaming and crying, many of them spattered with blood, tumbled down a vinyl chute that popped out when someone managed to open an emergency side exit. Airport security officials placed the number of deaths at sixteen: fourteen passengers, one member of the Pan American crew, and one ground-crew member. One hundred passengers were injured. A Pakistani passenger on the plane, Mohammed Amin, said that in the final minutes of the drama he had heard one of the hijackers say to another: "The moment for the last holy war has arrived."

There were a number of unexplained contradictions in the accounts of what the Pakistani commandos did in the last moments of the hijacking. Kurshid Anwar Mirza, chairman of the Pakistani Civil Aviation Authority, told reporters in a press conference that the hijackers appear to have panicked when the fuel ran out on the plane's electrical generator, causing the lights to dim and the air-conditioning system to shut off. At this point, he said, the hijackers herded the passengers into the middle of the plane, where they waited in the darkness as the gunmen grew increasingly edgy and nervous.

Earlier, Air Marshal Mirza had claimed that the Pakistani authorities had anticipated that the airplane power would dim and shut off. He said the commandos took this to be "their cue" to move toward the plane in the darkness for possible action against it. He also revealed that the tarmac lights had been turned off previously to facilitate the move.

But a few days later Mirza changed his story. He asserted that while the tarmac lights had been turned off, he and the others were surprised when the plane's lights began to dim. He said that at the time the commandos "were not in the vicinity" of the plane, and that it took

ten to fifteen minutes for them to arrive, ready to secure
the craft and capture the four hijackers.

But just a few hours later two Pakistani brigadier gen-
erals involved in the preparations for the rescue contradicted Mirza. "We saw smoke inside the plane and we
were there in two minutes," said Tariq Mahmoud, leader
of the commando squad, which officials said was spread
out in the scrub brush area behind the plane, near the tarmac.

Moreover, it was General Mahmoud and Brigadier
General Tariq Rafi, the latter in charge of the airport
security police, who announced that none of the hijackers
had been killed and that all four were alive.

All these comments are mystifying regarding Pakistani
intentions. It appears that some officials were hoping to
make sure that the public got the impression that the
commandos had not in any way provoked the hijackers
into firing on the passengers. It also seems clear that the
Pakistani authorities are ashamed of the way they handled
the hostage crisis and of the failure of their security,
which became clearer after all four of the hijackers were
arrested. By claiming that the anti-terrorist squad was not
in the vicinity, the Pakistanis evidently wish to explain
away an obvious failure in their attempt to rescue the
passengers unharmed.

At least six members of the Karachi airport security
force have been suspended for negligence in allowing the
hijackers to drive onto the tarmac in a van disguised to
look like an official security van. Three of the hijackers
wore security personnel uniforms, consisting of light blue
shirts and dark blue trousers. They were also apparently
able to obtain security badges or stars in a marketplace in
Karachi. In addition, the Suzuki van the hijackers rented
had apparently been painted the same blue color as the
official van used by the airport security force. They had
even added a light and a siren on the roof to help complete the picture.

The police investigation established that the terrorists
seemed to have spent considerable time preparing for the
operation. One of the hijackers had arrived in Karachi on
August 17, almost three weeks before the hijacking took

place. He had arrived carrying a Bahrain passport and had checked into the expensive Taj Mahal Hotel, where he apparently took care of preparations for the hijacking. He had originally been identified as Gomer Hussein, but later on hotel employees said his name was Bomer, and they displayed a number of checks that he had signed the latter way.

Investigators said that it was Hussein who rented the van for the hijacking from a private car-rental agency. He was also evidently "Mustafa," reportedly the leader of the hijacking, who had negotiated with officials at the airport command post.

In the first few days after the attack, the Pakistani authorities arrested another twenty-five suspects, all Palestinian students. Afterwards, all were freed except for Suliman Tariki, who had been detained at the Islamabad airport carrying a Libyan passport. The police are still searching for two of Tariki's accomplices, who had flown with him to Islamabad and had disappeared there. It soon became apparent that the three had made frequent flights between Islamabad and Karachi in the days preceding the hijacking.

All four hijackers and Taraki claimed in their interrogation that they had either been born or had lived in the Sabra and Shatilla refugee camps. At first, the Pakistani investigators, who were assisted by F.B.I. and C.I.A. experts, found it difficult to ascertain exactly what had happened. "They refused to cooperate and it was difficult to get them to tell the truth," was the way a spokesman for the Pakistani foreign ministry put it.[4] Four days after the hijacking, however, the U.S. defense secretary, Caspar Weinberger, was able to state that "there are strong indications derived from basic intelligence sources that it was an Abu Nidal activity. That doesn't necessarily mean only Abu Nidal was involved, but it seems to have been involved as far as we know."[5]

[4] A spokesman for the Foreign Office in Karachi, as reported on October 4, 1986, by the French News Agency.
[5] In an interview with the *Washington Post*, September 9, 1986.

The "indications" to which Weinberger alluded are numerous:

The Timing: This returns us to the Istanbul massacre. The fact that both incidents occurred within a day of each other can point to Abu Nidal. His organization is the only one to have carried out coordinated attacks either at the same time as or close to one another against different targets in different areas of the world. Thus, on October 11, 1976, there were attacks on the Syrian embassies in Rome and Islamabad, and on December 27, 1985, at the El Al counters in Vienna and Rome.

The Professional Skill: Abu Nidal's organization has the professional ability to carry out complex operations, even though he is aided by logistic support from the Libyan and Syrian embassies.

Careful Planning: The operations of the group are characterized by careful preparation, sometimes over a lengthy period of time. Due to the group's adherence to the principle of compartmentalization, various squads are sent to prepare the action. Another squad smuggles in the weapons. Finally, the hit men who are meant to carry out the action arrive at their destination. Compartmentalization and secrecy are observed scrupulously, and no squad comes in contact with another.

Infrastructure: Abu Nidal has for years had an infrastructure in place in the Indian peninsula, including Pakistan. It aided him in attacking ten targets in the Indian peninsula during the years 1976 to 1986, including diplomats and embassies of Kuwait, the UAE, Syria, Iraq, and Britain; four of these attacks occurred in Pakistan and the remainder in India. In these ten years the organization was able to link up closely with local radical organizations, including the family of Zulfikar Ali Bhuto, the Pakistani president killed by President Zi'a al-Hak. Bhuto's children are aided in their opposition to the Pakistani regime by Libya, which has served as the contact between them and Abu Nidal's organization, and in 1981 one of the members of the family was involved in the hijacking of a Pakistani plane that landed in Damascus.

Barbarity: The readiness to open fire on passengers and to kill indiscriminately is a characteristic of the Abu Nidal group.

Why was the Abu Nidal group involved in the hijacking of a United States airliner in Pakistan? And in the massacre at the Istanbul synagogue?

Abu Nidal's organization coordinates and leases out its services to radical Arab regimes which support terror, first and foremost Libya. As Libya finds it difficult to organize complicated terrorist attacks, it has already approached Abu Nidal a number of times in the past and asked him to carry out attacks on its behalf. Similarly, in the case of the Pan Am plane, this action was carried out at the request of Colonel Qaddafi. It is not that Abu Nidal needs any special encouragement to hate the United States, but in the case of the Pakistani hijacking, he was acting as a "subcontractor" on behalf of Libya.

Libya often offers a general "contract," without specifying details, and leaves the specific target to Abu Nidal. For such actions, Abu Nidal is paid in cash. On other occasions, Libya has approached criminal elements in Europe to carry out terrorist acts on its behalf, but in such cases the target is a specific one, such as the killing of an exiled political opponent of the Libyan president.

Abu Nidal does not always use his own men for his actions. Israeli intelligence sources noted that in 1986 Abu Nidal began using terrorists of other groups. As part of his cooperation with the Abu Musa terrorist group and with Ahmad Jibril, Abu Nidal hired killers to carry out his missions, paying their organizations in cash. We know that he has included in certain attacks members of Lebanese and Muslim terrorist groups. That is evidently what he did in the attack on the Istanbul synagogue, which was one made on his own initiative. This cooperation points to a new direction of terrorist attacks by Abu Nidal. Robert Oakley, who was in charge of the counterterrorist bureau of the U.S. State Department, revealed that a "terror summit" had taken place in Teheran in August 1986. It included representatives of Abu Nidal, Abu Musa, and Lebanese Shi'ite terrorist groups which were linked to Hizballah and were under Syrian and Iranian control and influence. At this meeting, Oakley alleged, a new strategy was discussed to defeat the means adopted by the various Western powers against international terrorism, primarily against Arab and Muslim terror.[6] The "terror summit," like other events, proves that terror continues. It is thus essential for the Western states to remain on guard against it. The United States and Britain have shown that they are willing to invest a great deal of resources—political, military, technological, and financial—so as to supply a suitable response to terror, and they are in the forefront of the struggle against it. It appears, though, that most European countries, not to speak of such countries as Turkey, Pakistan, and India, which are also victims of terrorism, and other countries in Asia and Africa, have not yet formulated a clear and decisive policy.

[6] In an interview with the Italian magazine *Panorama*, September 4, 1986.

14

The Soft Response

Talking of terrorism, one is reminded of the old English joke about the dreadful weather in that part of the world: Everybody talks about it, but why doesn't anyone do anything about changing it?

Airport security in Western Europe, the United States of America, Asia, and Africa continues to be inadequate. It demonstrates once again that neither governments nor airlines have yet found the means to make air travel and holy shrines safe from terrorist attacks. Nor is there a sense that headway is being made in the war against terrorism. Western nations refuse to take strong and appropriate countermeasures. They refuse to follow Margaret Thatcher's and Ronald Reagan's firm actions. Each pays lip service to the war against terrorism; each finds its own excuse to do nothing. When it comes to terrorism, we are always at square one. International terrorism is still a dominant factor in our daily routine. It seems that governments and airline companies have not learned their lessons and, perhaps more precisely, have extremely short memories. Despite the terrorist attacks against TWA and Pan Am, the Vienna and Rome airports, and Hindawi's London attempt to blow up an El Al plane, most of the airports throughout the world continue to use X-ray machines which have been shown time and again to be ineffective in detecting plastic explosives and the plastic guns which are in widespread use by terrorist organizations. And new improved plastic guns are being developed which do not show up on conventional X-ray machines. Easily concealable hand guns, such as the Gluck 17, are legally available in the United States. The Gluck is a 9-mm. partially plastic gun made in Austria. When disassembled, it does not look like a firearm. The polymer handgrip, trigger guard, and ammunition clip do not set off any security devices. East-bloc countries have provided the Czech-made plastic explosive known as Sematex in large quantities to Syria, Iraq, Libya, and South Yemen, all of which sponsor terrorism, and the terrorist organizations have even found ways to purchase the Gluck 17. Intelligence reports in Israel and Western Europe suggest that Abu Nidal is engaged in a major effort to arm his organization with this new equipment.

Most of the airlines refuse to learn from the Israeli experience, which prefers to rely on people rather than machines to spot danger. In addition to body searches where the security guards deem this necessary, El Al, the national Israeli air carrier, also employs armed sky marshals on its flights. It is true these methods cause inconvenience and contradict the "commercial philosophy" of other airlines, but nevertheless Israel's safety record is excellent. El Al can boast that none of its planes has been hijacked since 1968. It is therefore amazing to discover the wide discrepancy between the strong rhetoric used by the politicians and executives and their weak actions. This is even more true for governments, than for airlines.

The beautiful words on a "war to the finish on terrorism" are not always backed up in deeds. After Nezar Hindawi's aborted attempt to blow up the El Al plane, the workers at the Manchester airport demanded that the El Al counter be moved to the furthest point in the terminal. They claimed that their lives were in danger, and therefore did not wish to deal with the Israeli airline. A similar dispute arose at the Frankfurt airport. The local authorities in Frankfurt attempted in the summer of 1986 to move the El Al counters to a closed and special section. The Israeli airline refused, and its workers stated, "We will not go down to the cellar," but the local authorities attempted to enforce this change by a court order. Finally, the director-general of El Al, Rafi Har-Lev, warned that the company would discontinue its flights to Frankfurt, at which point the airport authorities backed down. These examples show how only those who employ resolute security measures or are considered targets for terrorism are penalized by those countries that pay little more than lip service to the need to combat terror. Rather than seeking to destroy the source of the terror, they wish to cower behind "simple solutions," such as moving an airline counter.

The double standard employed and the blatant hypocrisy shown are even more evident with national governments. The European Economic Community has tried to flex its muscles publicly. The meeting of the Trevi Group in London is a good example of this. At this conference, it was stated that a list of two hundred of the most dangerous terrorists would be compiled. Abu Abbas of the P.F.L.P. was clearly included in this list. Yet after the *Achille Lauro* was seajacked in October 1985 and the Italian government had him in its hands, it allowed him to fly to Yugoslavia and thus to escape the imprisonment he so obviously deserved. Nor were the pleas of the United States to hold him in detention of any avail.

The French government has also carried on negotiations with the terrorists for years. The international media have carried reports of deals and of efforts to make deals between French government officials and representatives of various terrorist groups, especially those of the Middle East. Official spokesmen of France always denied the reports and labelled them "unfounded." But in the summer of 1986 they were confirmed by the highest possible authority. Pierre Marion, who headed the French external secret service (D.G.S.E.) from 1981 to 1983 under the Socialist government of François Mitterand and who was removed from office due to differences of opinion, revealed remarkable details in an interview with Radio Europe 1. For example, after the murder of Jews at the Goldenberg restaurant in Paris in August 1982, six terrorist cells were located by his service. These were being used as transfer points for terrorists, and acted under a simple principle: The weapons and explosives arrived in the diplomatic pouches of Syria, Libya, and Iraq. The terrorists arrived by plane or train. Their case officers found them accommodations, gave them the weapons and explosives, and informed them of their targets.

Marion conveyed this to President Mitterand and handed him a list of ten people who headed these terrorist cells, some of them diplomats of the above three countries and others Palestinians who did not enjoy diplomatic immunity. "I suggested that we liquidate them. I told him there was no other way to get rid of them, but the president refused. Nor did he permit us to attack a school for terrorism in Beirut from which terrorists were sent out for attacks in Paris. Another proposal that we brought was that French agents act in an operation to liquidate terrorist branches in neighboring countries in Europe. This too was rejected."

Marion stated that he had no choice, and instead of a military operation against the terrorists, he was forced to compromise and to appease them. "I arranged a meeting with the brother of the president of Syria. Rif'at Assad asked me to come without any bodyguards to his rustic villa near the Versailles Palace. I passed through a flock of bodyguards all armed from head to toe, and found myself face to face with the one who is considered to be the head of the terrorist orchestra in the Middle East."[1] The meeting lasted five hours, and another was set for the following week. At the second meeting, General Assad promised that Abu Nidal would not carry out any terrorist attacks on French soil. The promise was kept. Dr. Issam Sartawi was in France at the time, but by orders of his Syrian masters Abu Nidal postponed his plan to assassinate him. Sartawi enjoyed another eight months of grace until murdered by Abu Nidal's terrorists in Portugal, after having left Paris.

France has made the appeasement of terrorists a permanent part of its policies. President Mitterand and his Socialist prime ministers forced the heads of the French secret services to keep communication lines open with the terrorist leaders and with the secret services of those countries which aid them.

[1] In a news broadcast of Radio Europe 1, September 13, 1986.

In February 1986, the French suddenly freed two Abu Nidal terrorists who had killed a P.L.O. representative eight year earlier. The French, who had suffered a "bloody Christmas" of explosions throughout Paris, believed that by freeing the two they would be taking out an insurance policy against further terrorist attacks, but they soon found out how wrong they had been.

The terrorist attacks were renewed in the summer of 1986, and even at a greatly intensified level. In September there were eleven terrorist attacks in Paris, in which ten people were killed and about sixty injured. The responsibility for these attacks was taken by the exact same organization as had taken responsibility for the earlier attacks in December 1985: a group which labelled itself the Committee for the Freeing of Prisoners.

The very first attack in this new series was marked by failure. On September 4, 1985, at 6:30 P.M., scores of people jammed into each crowded carriage of the R.E.R., the suburban railroad line known as "the Metro of the unfortunates." The train itself carried hundreds of people from the center of the city to the suburbs to the east. A few minutes after the train entered the long, dark underground tunnels, one of the passengers heard a small pop under his seat, and a thin stream of white smoke emanated from a package underneath the seat. The passenger pulled the emergency cord, and the train ground to a halt. Police that were summoned cleared the train. In the package, the police found thirteen sticks of dynamite, which had not gone off due to a defective detonator. An anonymous caller contacted the French News Agency that same evening and announced that the Committee for the Freeing of Prisoners assumed responsibility for the aborted attack and that this was "just the beginning." The caller announced that the attacks would continue.

The French security services were staggered. After all, they had already appeased Abu Nidal, so why were the attacks being renewed? They had to find another answer. Their search did not continue for very long. Another explosion took place a few days later at the post office branch of the Hotel de Ville in the municipal building, at a time when Prime Minister Jacques Chirac, who is also the mayor of Paris, was but meters away in his office conducting a meeting. A week later another explosion rocked a bar named the Renault, on the Champs-Elysées. Two policemen and a security man were injured badly as they attempted to defuse the bomb. Another anonymous caller for "the Committee" warned that the attacks would continue until three specific prisoners were freed. These included Georges Ibrahim Abdallah of Lebanon; Anis Nakash, who had tried to assassinate the exiled prime minister of Iran, Shaipur Bahtiar; and the Armenian Varoujian Garbidjian of A.S.A.L.A., who had been involved in an attack on the counters of the Turkish airline at Orly airport. The investigators, however, were convinced that the primary aim of these attacks was to gain the release of Georges Ibrahim Abdallah.

Abdallah, aged thirty-five, was detained by the French security authorities on October 25, 1984, in the city of Lyons. He had entered a police station on his own to ask for protection, claiming that Mossad agents were out to kill him. The police are very interested in people that the Mossad wishes to kill, and Abdallah underwent a thorough interrogation. He finally broke and revealed his true identity. Abdallah was born in Qubayat, in northern Lebanon. He was an Orthodox Christian with a broad education, who spoke French and had a deep understanding of political thought. The Abdallah family is one of the most prominent in the village, with one of Ibrahim's brothers having earned a doctorate from the Sorbonne, and another a lecturer in the Tripoli university in Lebanon.

From his earliest youth, Abdallah showed a tendency to communism, and he was fully aware of Leninist-Marxist doctrine. He spent a considerable amount of time studying in Communist China, and was a member of the Syrian Populist party of Lebanon, which believes that Lebanon, Israel, and Cyprus should all be annexed to a "Greater Syria." In the 1970's, he was a member of the P.F.L.P. of George Habash, and was sent for training in Algeria. For a short time in 1978 he was in prison for having robbed a Beirut bank, and he then joined the splinter group of Wadi' Haddad. Later on, at the beginning of the 1980's, he founded his own organization,

known in English as the Lebanese Armed Revolutionary
Factions (L.A.R.F.).

He was fascinated by the terrorist leaders such as Carlos and Abu Nidal, as well as by the many myths surrounding them. He decided to emulate them and to
establish his organization along similar lines, these being
secrecy, compartmentalization, careful preparation, surprise, and ties with the secret services of radical countries.

The ideology of his group is a conglomeration of
Marxism mixed with Syrian nationalism. The group
believes in a world revolution and is vehemently opposed
to "Zionism, Israel, and American imperialism."

Whenever L.A.R.F. made an announcement that it took
responsibility for a terrorist act, it always included a quote
from Jean-Jacques Rousseau, showing how great an influence the philosopher had on Abdallah.

Appropriately, L.A.R.F. came to life in Lebanon, the
crossroads between Europe and the Arab world, in 1980.
Most of its small force are Lebanese Christians from two
small northern villages, Qubayat and Andraqat. To judge
from its record of attacks, it believes in international terrorism as a force, and the sole aim is to strike at American, Jewish, or Israeli targets in Europe. In religion and
politics, it has connections with the P.F.L.P. through the
latter's leader, George Habash, who is both a Christian
and a Marxist. It seems likely that on occasion L.A.R.F.
carries out missions on his behalf. Certainly the fact that
most of its attacks have been in Italy and France con-
vinces intelligence sources that the Lebanese group works
in conjunction with the Italian Red Brigades and with
Direct Action in France. The use of such a title as the
"Lebanese Armed Revolutionary Factions" gives a clue
to its aspirations to be considered a part, however small,
of the European Red Army conglomerate.

L.A.R.F. first attracted attention in 1981 when one
of its gunmen tried to shoot Addison Chapman, then
the U.S. chargé d'affaires in Paris, as he left home on the
way to the embassy. With great presence of mind the
diplomat dived under this car and escaped unhurt as
the hit man fired six rounds at him. At first there was lit-

tle inclination to believe the claim from a hitherto-unknown organization, and blame was placed on better-known groups.

The existence of L.A.R.F. was soon confirmed when its men used exactly the same methods in January 1982 and succeeded in murdering Lieutenant Colonel Charles Ray, the American assistant military attaché, with a single shot in the head as he left his home in Passey, Paris. A letter written in Arabic and delivered in Beirut justified the killing by accusing the United States of leading a "fascist, Zionist, reactionary alliance" against the Lebanese people.

Within a few weeks the same organization turned its attention to Israelis abroad. In April 1982 a girl assassin shot dead with three bullets Yacov Bar-Simantov, an Israeli embassy second secretary. When his seventeen-year-old son, Avi, gave chase, she ordered him in French: "Stop, or I'll shoot." That incident was followed by two more attacks in Paris in the same year: A parcel bomb delivered to the American commercial attaché killed two police officers, and a bomb in the car of an Israeli diplomat injured a number of others.

The group claimed no more outrages until February 1984, when in Rome one of its gunmen killed Leamon Hunt, an American diplomat who was director-general of the multi-national peacekeeping force in Sinai. This attack was followed by a failed attempt on the life of the U.S. ambassador in Strasbourg.

Until the summer of that year very little information had come to light about the composition of the mysterious L.A.R.F., such a small and obscure though dangerous organization. New facts came to light with the arrest of Abdallah Muhammad al-Mansuri, a nineteen-year-old Arab travelling on the Orient Express through Yugoslavia to France. He carried a false Moroccan passport and about seventeen pounds of explosives. Under interrogation, he revealed the names and addresses of collaborators, and international investigators were able to piece together some picture of L.A.R.F. activities.

The French police followed this up by raiding an apartment in Lyons where they arrested the group's leader,

Georges Ibrahim Abdallah, who unlike the bosses of most terror groups had himself gone operational. In Rome the Italians arrested a Lebanese woman named Josephine Abdu. In a Paris raid on an apartment, police discovered an arsenal of arms and explosives. Among the weapons there were a Czech-made 7.65 automatic pistol which was proved by ballistics tests to have been used in the murder of both Lieutenant Colonel Ray and Yacov Bar-Simantov.

L.A.R.F. has also displayed a new side to international terror, almost a new strain—the "family terror." The group has never numbered more than twenty to thirty people, all relatives or childhood friends of the leader.

Ibrahim was sentenced in June 1986 in the court in Lyons to four years' imprisonment for having a weapon in his possession and for using forged documents—in his apartment police had found five passports with fictitious names, the passports stemming respectively from Algeria, the South Yemeni republic, Malta, and two from Morocco. On the other hand, he was not indicted for involvement in the murder of the diplomats Ray and Bar-Simantov. Police investigators and the prosecution claimed that "we do not have any eyewitnesses or direct proof" to enable them to link him to the murders. It appears, though, that the very question of whether Abdallah would be indicted for murder was a matter of secret negotiations between the French government and the terrorist group. On March 23, 1985, five months after Abdallah was detained, members of L.A.R.F. kidnapped the French cultural and arts attaché in Beirut. They demanded that Abdallah be released in exchange for the hostage. The Socialist government conducted negotiations with them by means of Syrian and Algerian intermediaries. The French hostage was freed a week later, in return for certain obscure promises that have not been clarified. It is possible that the French government promised L.A.R.F. that it would not charge the group's leader at all, or that it would only charge him symbolically. In any event, the French justice ministry was inclined not to invest a great deal of effort in seeking a conviction of Abdallah. Somebody did not like this tendency and made a point of leaking to the press that the police had found new evidence

in the case which linked Abdallah directly to the murder
of the diplomats on French soil. The Ray family also
became involved, and by means of the U.S. government
threatened to go to court to force the prosecution to charge
Abdallah with involvement in the murder of the diplomats. When it became clear to L.A.R.F. and especially
to Abdallah's brothers that the French government was not
keeping its side of the deal and was about to force Abdallah to stand trial in February 1987 for the murders they
established the Committee for the Freeing of Prisoners.
At the same time, they turned to General Al-Khuli of
Syrian air force intelligence. The general, who already
knew the Lebanese group from past experience, put it in
touch with the Abu Nidal group, as well as with
A.S.A.L.A. and with the Iranians. Abu Nidal in turn
made the connection between the group and the French
Direct Action. Asala supplied logistic support in Paris
using its own infrastructure, and in return the committee
added the Armenian terrorist to the list of those it wanted
freed, while Iran, by means of its secret services and its
embassy in Paris, offered other aid, hoping thereby both
to gain the release of Anis Nakash, who had tried to
assassinate Bahtiar, and to try to persuade France to terminate its massive aid to Iraq.

The French government, as is its wont and in accordance with its tradition in the past few years, spoke with
a forked tongue. The double standard was revealed to all
when, at the same time that Jacques Chirac was deploring
terror, he secretly sent emissaries to Syria. Ministers,
officers of the security services, and even the Arab arch-
bishop Hilarion Capucci, who had been expelled from
Israel at the beginning of the 1970's for gunrunning on
behalf of the Palestinian terrorists, were asked to mediate
and appease the terrorists and those offering them sanctuary. And indeed the appeasement worked. The French
begged and pleaded, the Syrians issued orders, and the
family terror ceased in October as if nothing had ever
happened. In spite of the cloak of secrecy that was placed
about the entire process, it appears that this time too the

French government gave L.A.R.F. promises which evidently satisfied it.[2]

Yet none of these private dealings with terrorists prevented the French minister of the interior and public safety from participating in the deliberations of the Trevi Group, deploring terror, and voting for all the resolutions that were adopted. But in addition to the French and the Italians, who have shown the complete absence of any backbone when confronted by Middle Eastern terror, the conference was also attended by other interior ministers as well; for example, by the Greek minister of the interior, whose country has become a refuge for terrorists. Athens is one of the most important centers of Abu Nidal. In it he has attacked British objectives without the Greek government being able to find the perpetrators.[3]

The Portuguese minister of the interior was also at the meeting, but made no mention of the fact that the murderer of Sartawi is still walking around free, after his country freed the man.

Europe stands completely exposed. It finds itself unable to combat the madness of a few dozen terrorists. It has shown itself unwilling to once and for all chop off the heads of this hydra which keeps it awake at night.

---

[2] The French *Le Monde* claimed that a "deal" was struck, with the mediation of various dubious Lebanese characters, whereby L.A.R.F. was promised that in Abdallah's forthcoming trial, matters "might turn out in his favor" provided that the terrorist acts ceased. The truce was also reportedly accompanied by a threat: that if the Abdallah clan did not respect the truce there would be physical reprisal by agents of the Syrian secret services.

[3] On October 20, 1986, Brigadier Munzar Abu-Gazala, one of the most senior P.L.O. officers, was killed when a bomb exploded in his car. The Athens investigators believe that the cause of the blast was an accident that occurred as Abu-Gazala was transporting explosives from one place to another. The P.L.O. blamed the Mossad for the blast, while Abu Nidal claimed responsibility for the deed.

Epilogue: The Future of Terrorism

What is terrorism?

It would be highly desirable if all discussions on terrorism, its motives and inspiration, its specific character, its modes of operation, and its long-term consequences, were based on a clear, exact, and comprehensive definition of exactly what terrorism is. Ideally, there should be agreement as to whether terrorism is simply violence in general or whether it is a specific form of violence.

Agreement on a definition does not, alas, exist, and there is no reason to believe that such an agreement will emerge in the near future. Few people nowadays succumb to the romantic picture of the terrorist as a gallant idealist. But many still see "one man's terrorist as another's freedom fighter." Most experts, however, agree that terrorism is the use or the threat of use of violence as a method or strategy to achieve certain goals; that its aim is to induce a state of fear in the victim; that it is ruthless and does not conform to humanitarian norms; and that publicity is an essential factor in terrorist strategy.[1]

Yet there is little, if anything, in common between the Russian terrorists of the nineteenth century and Abu Nidal; a definition trying to cover both these types of terrorism as well as other modern-day types would have to be either very vague or misleading. But the absence of an

[1] Walter Lacqueur, "Reflection on Terrorism," *Foreign Affairs*, Fall 1986.

exact definition does not mean that we do not know in a general way what terrorism is; it has been said that it resembles pornography—while it is difficult to describe and define, it is easy to recognize when one sees it.

What we see today is something new and different from what was seen in the past. A new era has opened in the history of terror. Since the Lebanese war we are witnesses to the "fragmentalization" of the Palestinian terrorist organizations. The P.L.O. has broken up and its central authority has vanished. In its place, we find the birth of various small organizations without a coherent ideological identity, such as the Abu Nidal group, L.A.R.F., or family terrorist groups such as that of Nezar Hindawi.

These organizations are characterized by great secrecy. They have the ability to carry out operations successfully, and insist on compartmentalization so as to avoid penetration by hostile elements wishing to learn more about them.

Modern terrorist groups are willing to hire themselves out as "subcontractors" and to accept mercenary missions on behalf of the security services of different states. In return for these services rendered, the terrorist groups receive funds, logistic support, diplomatic passports, safe houses, means of transportation, arms and explosives.

Modern-day terrorism is far more brutal than its predecessors. It is interested in causing as large a number of casualties as possible.

Nowadays, terrorists are no longer necessarily individuals or small groups operating within a single country. They are more and more members of organizations which operate across national frontiers and have access to substantial sums of money, arms, equipment, technical knowledge, and training. A world-wide system of competitive arms salesmen makes weapons more easily available to terrorist groups. Mass communications assure instantaneous publicity. Travel has become easier between different countries, and border controls are diminishing.

The organizational and logistical support backing the terrorist is often a smooth-running and effective mechanism. The terrorists and their equipment, including weapons and explosives, easily pass through borders and barriers. They utilize the means put at their disposal by states and embassies.

A common element of most of the terrorist acts in the past few years has been their anonymity. As opposed to the practice in the 1970's, when many different organizations hastened to take responsibility for every terrorist act, terrorist acts today often remain "unclaimed." Alternately, the claim of responsibility is made by an unknown—and often non-existent—organization. By maintaining anonymity, the terrorists wish to keep the security services of the different countries guessing—and at the same time to create even greater panic among the general public, which by its nature fears the unknown. At first blush there appears to be a contradiction here: since one of the aims of terrorism is to carry out "propaganda by means of acts of violence," as far as the terrorist is concerned it is essential that the perpetrators of a given act be known. Yet in the past few years this "propaganda" aspect has lost much of its value, especially as terrorism has more or less "stabilized" throughout the world: the organizations and the states responsible for terrorism are well known, so that even if they do not assume responsibility publicly, they can still be identified by their handiwork. On the other hand, the very "anonymity" of the terrorists, the fact that they are "invisible," and the uncertainty in identifying them creates a feeeling as if they are to be found everywhere and are omnipotent.

The might of terrorism has always lain in its power of magnification, where an act too puny to be noticed if directed against the armed forces of a state can be turned into a psychological blow strong enough to shake a society if it is directed against a few ordinary and unarmed people. Thanks to the modern technologies of weaponry, television, and travel, the magnifying power of terrorism has never been greater. The self-proclaimed heirs of those nineteenth-century anarchists who invented "the propaganda of the deed" and would not dream of walking away from deeds that now yield so much propaganda are often willing to keep a country guessing—and unstabilized.

We are now faced by a change in the course and strategy of terror. This strategic turn to a large extent stems from the great involvement of certain states in terror.

If there has been a significant development in the last decade, it has been state-sponsored terrorism. There are certain new features to this that make it more dangerous and more pervasive than ever in the past. Terrorism has become more frequent and more brazen; first, because it is tolerated or ignored, mainly by those on the receiving end who suffer; and second, by the fact that resistance to state-sponsored terrorism has been weak and uncoordinated.

We should also recognize that weapons of mass destruction as well as increasingly lethal conventional armaments have made regular warfare potentially too costly; terrorism is therefore viewed by several countries as a cheap way to strike a blow at their enemies.

State-sponsored terrorism is mainly the instrument of dictators with ambitions far in excess of their power base. Today, many dictators in the Middle East and Central America rule small or relatively weak countries. Libya is an extreme example; but for its investment in terrorism it would not be much more important than the Fiji islands.

Libyan sponsorship of terrorism has been largely at the initiative of one man, Mu'ammar Qaddafi. In Syria and Iran, on the other hand, the support given terrorists has been more institutionalized. The Syrian and Iranian sponsors of terrorism have therefore been more discriminating in their targets and are therefore, within limits, more successful.

The attitude of the Soviet bloc has been more ambiguous. It has used terrorism as a weapon to destabilize certain countries, but only as a minor instrument in its general arsenal of political warfare. The Soviets will never extend open support; it has to be carefully laundered through a series of subcontractors and middlemen. But, as in the unique relationship between the Soviet bloc and Abu Nidal, for instance, this means that the Soviets cannot maintain full control over the terrorists; the gunmen may land them in situations which were not planned and which may be politically harmful. To engage in the support of international terrorism is to play with a fire that is difficult to control.[2]

The Soviet involvement, even though indirect and latent, opens new horizons to international terror. It can help the terrorist utilize unconventional methods. One can indeed ask why it is that unconventional terrorism has not spread any further. The technology and the know-how are around, and certain of the terrorist groups already have access to these. "Unconventional" does not necessarily imply "nuclear." It is true that when one maps out "worst-case scenarios," one speaks of terrorists having access to nuclear, chemical, or biological weapons. Nuclear weapons are something else, but there is no problem for the existing terrorist groups to escalate terrorism significantly. Why has this not happened until now? It is not because escalating terrorism significantly will hamper them in achieving their goals, because many terrorists have no hesitation in using means which do not further their declared intentions. The answer is evidently that the terrorist entrepreneurs are not always any more innovative than the governments and the states against which they are fighting. In other words, terrorists too tend to be conservative, frozen in certain methods and patterns which they repeat.[3]

About twenty years ago, a wave of innovation swept the terrorist world, as seen, for example, in the skyjacking of planes. These innovations were disseminated from the original groups to other groups. Now again conditions have become ripe for new terrorist innovators and the international conditions encourage the dissemination of a modern wave of terrorism that will be based on new methods.

Targets may change. As an example, terrorists may again move against symbolic targets of value, such as societal monuments, with shattering effects.

[2] *Ibid.*, p. 96.
[3] Yehezkel Dror, "Unconventional Terrorism—A Glance into the Future," in Eli Tavin and Yonah Alexander (eds.), *Terrorists or Freedom Fighters* (Fairfax, Virginia: Hero Books, 1986).

There can be escalation in the usual sense in weapons systems, such as with the use of new types of guns, grenades, and explosives.

Biotoxological possibilities are increasingly tempting.

There may be an escalation in tactics or strategy, as, for instance, overloading the defensive systems of a given society by many simultaneous acts, or by more sophisticated methods of threats.

There is therefore no escaping the conclusion that it is difficult to envision the end of the terror. And even if the West should adopt even better decisions, it is doubtful if it could eliminate this scourge.

Appendix A

A Letter to "Comrade Thabit"
(A letter found in the room of Na'if Rosan in Evelyn Gardens, London)

Dear Comrade Thabit

10 May 1982

We send our sincere *Nidali* (struggle) greetings, and wish you and all the dear comrades with you, success and speedy progress in fulfilling our revolutionary and nationalist aims, concerning the liberating unity and the establishment of a popular democracy.

1. We are sending you this letter by an authorized messenger—Comrade Wasfi—who will discuss with you your status in regard to the assignment given you, and which will be discussed in this message.

2. He will also explain to you our political and organizational situation and will give you $3000. Please act in a concentrated way against one target or more. The United Arab Emirates—strike them. Because the authorities there handed over to the Jordanian government a number of our imprisoned comrades, and contrary to their promise to free them and to give them to us. Hit a number of targets and without mercy. Let this be *the embassy and its employees* (emphasized), its financial or tourism institutions, or another official institution. Do not spare anyone. You can take care of this assignment by liquidating individuals or by planting bombs, provided that the objective is destroyed. Whatever means you use, be sure your security is ensured. You are to gather accurate infor-

mation on other targets that we will deal with later. We believe that the step taken by the United Arab Emirates is like a declaration of war against us. They are to be taught a lesson they will never forget. Dear comrade, we have not heard from you for a long time. Your telegram of March 8, 1982, which also contained your new address, was the last time we heard from you. We hope that everything is fine with you. We also hope that you have succeeded in obtaining valuable information about the agreed targets. Please send us a detailed letter through the messenger Wasfi, who will explain to you the latest developments. Our condition continues to improve.

Finally, our warm blessings to you and the comrades with you, and the best of wishes for your success. We hope to hear from you soon.

Revolution till Victory,

Your brother "Mutana"

Note: If Comrade Wasfi cannot see you in person, this will be done through Comrade Iman.

Appendix B

Names of the Organization
The organization led by Sabri al-Banna is normally known as the Abu Nidal group. Officially, though, it refers to itself as:

1. Fatah—the Revolutionary Council (F.R.C.). This organization took responsibility for most of the group's acts against Israeli targets.
2. The Palestinian National Liberation Movement (P.N.L.M.).
3. Black June—All actions against Syria, primarily under Iraqi direction, were carried out under this name.
4. Black September—All attacks on Jordanian targets during 1983–1985, which were directed by Syria, used this name.
5. The Revolutionary Arab Brigades (R.A.B.)—Used in attacks on Kuwait and the United Arab Emirates.
6. The Revolutionary Organization of Socialist Muslims (R.O.S.M.)—used in attacks on British targets.
7. The Egyptian Revolution—took responsibility for attacks on Israeli diplomats in Cairo and the hijacking of the Egyptian airliner at the end of 1985. Sometimes the term "Revolutionary Egypt" was used.
8. Al-Asifa (the Storm). Al Asifa had been the name of the military arm of Fatah. Abu Nidal, who claimed that he was following the true path of Fatah, also adopted this name for his use.
9. Al-Iqab (the Punishment)—This name was used in the very first attack attributed to Abu Nidal.

10. The Arab Nationalist Youth Organization (A.N.Y.O.)—This was founded by Libya in the early 1970's, and was led by Marwan Haddad. The organization was financed and operated by Libya, and its members were young Palestinians who had left Fatah and the P.F.L.P., many of whom joined the organization after Fatah disbanded the original Black September. Toward the end of 1973, there were certain links between this group and Abu Nidal in Baghdad. This was the name used by the terrorists when Abu Nidal contributed planning and personnel for the joint hijacking of the K.L.M. plane in 1973.

Appendix C

Transcript of Marwan al-Banna's Interrogation by Police
(Selections of the interrogation at Paddington Green, London, June 5, 1982—translated from the author's Hebrew notes)

Inspector Paul: What is your name?
Al-Banna: Marwan al-Banna
—Where were you born?
—In Nablus.
—Where is that?
—On the west bank of the Jordan.
—When did you arrive in London?
—In November 1979.
—From where?
—From Jordan.
—With whom did you arrive in Britain?
—I came by myself.
—For what purpose?
—To study.
—Where did you study?
—At Bedford College in Bedfordshire.
—What did you study there?
—I studied English there for three months, and after that I continued to study at Southeast London College.
—Are you still studying there?
—No, at present I am studying at Waxhall College.
—To whom do the suitcases in the car belong?

—The brown one belongs to me and I think the second belongs to Rosan, who wanted to give it to his friend.

—Do you know what we found in your room at the Y.M.C.A.?

—No.

—We found a suitcase full of grenades and weapons with ammunition. Did you know what was inside it?

—I only knew for a few days.

—Why didn't you tell the police about it?

—I was afraid to tell the truth.

—What did you see when you looked in the suitcase?

—I saw a machine pistol and I felt the grenades. Rosan asked me to look after them.

—Why did he ask you to do that?

—I already told you that I only knew about it for a few days and when I found out what was in the suitcase, I told Rosan to take it away immediately, and he promised to do so soon.

—Aren't grenades and weapons meant to kill?

—Yes, you are correct, but I didn't want to kill anyone.

—Wasn't your job to supply the weapons for the attack?

—No.

—Why did you, a Palestinian, keep in your room the addresses of so many Israeli organizations, including the car license numbers? What interest do you have in Israeli organizations in this country? There must be a reason.

—There is no reason.

—Why did you write it?

—I didn't write it.

—Are you saying this is not your handwriting.

—Only a few of the pages are in my handwriting.

—In these lists Henry Kissinger, a Jewish discotheque, Abba Eban, former foreign minister of Israel, the Israeli ambassador in Britain, Mr. Shlomo Argov, and the British-Israeli Commerce Chamber are all mentioned. Why did you list them?

—No reason. I didn't list them for any reason.

—Why are you, a Palestinian, interested in the Jewish Association for the Blind, for example?

—No, I am not interested in it.

—Why then did you list it, and, for example, the Institute for Jewish Affairs?

—Somebody told me to write them.

—Who asked you?

—I don't know his name.

—Was he an Arab like you?

—Yes.

—Is he a Palestinian?

—Yes.

—Why don't you know his name?

—I don't know his real name.

—By which name do you know him?

—It is the same man who gave me the grenades and weapons in the silver-colored suitcase. And I don't know his name.

—But you gave me his name before, didn't you?

—Yes, that is correct. His name is Jabbar.

—Is Jabbar the name of a place or of a person?

—The name of a person.

—If he asked you to prepare the list, why didn't you give it to him immediately?

—They wanted to know how many Jewish institutions there are in this country.

—How did you acquire the information?

—Most I found in the newspapers.

—And the rest?

—I found some of it by chance.

—Why aren't you telling the truth?

—I am now willing to tell the truth.

—Are you a member of an organization?

—I am not an active member, only a political member in the Palestinian National Liberation Movement.

—Tell me about the organization.

—It is al-Fatah.

—Go on.

—Al-Fatah until 1974, or a little before.

—And they separated?

—Yes.

—How did your group begin?

—They began with the P.L.O. but left it.

—Who is the leader of the group?

—It doesn't have a leader. Every decision is made after a meeting among the senior members of the movement.

—In other words, before you do anything, you discuss it?

—I don't know that. I am not an active member, only a political member.

—Have you heard of Abu Nidal?

—Yes, but his real name is Sabri al-Banna and he is a relative of mine.

—Is that also the name of the group, Abu Nidal?

—No. The group is known as the Palestinian National Liberation Movement.

—Does it have other names?

—No, but in the past we were also known as Black June.

—Are you a member of this group?

—Yes, I told you, only a political member.

—Is the group active in this country?

—I don't know. I only know Rosan.

—Do you not know other people for security reasons?

—Possibly.

—Tell me about the weapons.

—A member of the group arrived about a month ago and asked me to look after them because they said they were going to use them.

—What is his name?

—I don't know his name. His alias is Jabbar.

—Jabbar also asked you to prepare the lists?

—Yes.

—Were the names on the lists meant to be targets?

—No, not all.

—But you knew the group was planning against a number of targets?

—Yes, but most of the names were for the purpose of gathering information.

—Why don't you tell the whole truth?

—I am willing to tell the truth and you decide if you want to believe me.

—Fine.

—I am a political member of the P.N.L.M., not an active member. I came here to study and to complete my studies and that is all.

—Tell me about the assault.

—I was asked by Na'if Rosan to meet him at the Intercontinental Hotel. I arrived at 10.30 p.m. and Na'if was waiting for me outside the hotel and told me that the group was about to attack one of its targets that night.

—Na'if is higher up in the organization?

—Yes, he is higher than I, and I take orders from him. He told me to come and I came.

—So you admit that the aim was to attack?

—Yes. I agree that the aim was to attack and to blow up Israeli targets but also to do other things.

—Such as?

—To organize a general movement against Israel.

—We found a letter to Thabit.

—I don't know.

—That is an alias?

—I know nothing about that letter.

—Do you know Sa'id?

—Yes. He studied at Waxhall College but I known him as Abduh.

—He shot the ambassador?

—I know nothing about it.

—He shot him with the gun given him by Rosan?

—I don't know Sa'id.

Appendix D

A List of the Terrorist Attacks Attributed to the Abu Nidal Group

September 5, 1973—Attack on the Saudi embassy in Paris.

November 25, 1973—K.L.M. plane en route from Beirut to New Delhi and Tokyo hijacked over Iraqi air space, and diverted to Nicosia, Cyprus, and Valletta, Malta, airports. After lengthy negotiations, passengers and crew released. The hijackers were permitted to fly to Damascus. The Arab Nationalist Youth Organization claimed responsibility.

October 1974—An aborted attempt to assassinate the chairman of the P.L.O., Yasser Arafat, and member of the Executive Committee Abu Mazin.

November 22, 1974—B.E.A. plane en route from London to the Far East hijacked during a stopover in Dhubai. It was flown to Tunis. One passenger, a West German doctor, was killed, and after lengthy negotiations the passengers and crew were freed, and the hijackers were permitted to fly to Libya.

September 1976—Attack on the Semiramis hotel in Damascus, Syria.

October 11, 1976—Attacks on the Syrian embassies in Islamabad, Pakistan, and Rome, Italy.

November 17, 1976—Attack on the Intercontinental Hotel in Amman, Jordan, and the taking of hostages.

December 13, 1976—An attempt to attack the Syrian embassy in Istanbul was foiled.

December 27, 1976—An aborted attempt to assassinate the Syrian foreign minister, Abd al-Halim Khaddam, in Damascus.

October 1977—Another aborted attempt to assassinate the Syrian foreign minister. In the attack at the Abu Dhabi airport, Sayf bin Sa'id al-Ghubash, the foreign minister of the United Arab Emirates, was accidentally killed.

November 15, 1977—Assassination of the director of the Arab Library in Paris, Muhammad Salah.

January 1, 1978—The murder of the representative of the P.L.O. office in London, Sa'id Hamami.

February 18, 1978—Murder of the senior Egyptian journalist and head of the Committee for Afro-Asian Solidarity, Yusuf Siba'i. The attack began in the Hilton Hotel in Nicosia, and ended in a futile attempt to leave Cyprus by air.

June 15, 1978—The murder of the P.L.O. representative in Kuwait, Ali Yasin.

August 3, 1978—The murder of the P.L.O. representative in Paris, Izz al-Din Qalaq, and the Palestinian news agency correspondent, Adnan Hamid.

August 5, 1978—Attack on the P.L.O. offices in Pakistan.

June 9, 1979—Liquidation in Madrid of Muhammad Arif, a student who had been a member of the group and then left it.

November 13, 1979—Aborted attempt to kill Efraim Eldar, the Israeli ambassador in Lisbon. His Portuguese bodyguard was wounded in the attack.

November 20, 1979—A failed attack on the Peter Hotel in Salzburg, Austria, in which an exhibit was being held on Jerusalem, sponsored by the local Jewish community.

January 17, 1980—Murder of the director of the Arab Library in Paris, Yusuf Mubarak.

March 3, 1980—The mistaken killing of a Spanish lawyer, Adolfo Cottelo. The attackers had planned to kill Max Mazin, one of the leaders of the local Jewish community, who lived in the same building.

April 22, 1980—A failed attempt to kill Salah Khalaf, known as Abu Iyad, head of the Military Department of the P.L.O. and considered Yasser Arafat's deputy, in

Belgrade, Yugoslavia. A bomb was placed in his car, but he was not in the car when it went off. One of the perpetrators was caught by the Yugoslav police and handed over to Fatah, by whom he was tried.

July 27, 1980—An attack on the children of the Agudath Israel school for Jewish children, in Antwerp, Belgium.

July 1980—The police in Brussels, Belgium, foiled an attempt to attack an El Al plane. Explosives were found in the room of the suspect.

May 1, 1981—The murder of Heinz Nittal, head of the Israel-Austria Friendship League, in Vienna.

June 1, 1981—The murder of Na'im Khadir, P.L.O. representative in Brussels, Belgium.

August 1, 1981—An aborted attempt to kill Abu Da'ud, one of the leaders of Black September, in Warsaw.

August 29, 1981—Attack on the synagogue in Vienna, with two killed and nineteen injured.

September 23, 1981—The detonation of a bomb at the gate to the Shoham-Zim offices in Limasol, Cyprus. Five local employees were injured.

October 8, 1981—Aborted attempt to kill Abu Tariq, the P.L.O. representative in Libya, in Valletta, Malta.

March 1, 1982—The liquidation in Madrid of Nabil Arnaki, a member of the group who had left it.

June 3, 1982—Attempted assassination of Shlomo Argov, Israeli ambassador to Britain, in London.

June 4, 1982—Attempted assassination of a Kuwaiti diplomat in New Delhi, India.

August 23, 1982—Attempted assassination of a United Arab Emirates diplomat in Kuwait.

August 26, 1982—Aborted attempt to kill the consul of the United Arab Emirates in Bombay, India.

September 9, 1982—Attack on a synagogue in Brussels.

October 9, 1982—Foiled attempt to break into the Kuwaiti consulate in Karachi, Pakistan. One diplomat was wounded.

November 22, 1982—Two members of the group were detained on the Turkish-Greek border. Their car contained about ninety pounds of explosives which were meant for an attack on the Israeli embassies in Athens and Rome. The two—Muhammad al-Fayiz al Zomaria and Osama Abd al-Hayy, were sentenced to five years in prison.

April 10, 1983—Murder of Dr. Issam Sartawi in Portugal.

April 13, 1983—A booby trapped car blew up near the Saudi embassy in Athens.

June 7, 1983—A Fatah employee and his colleague wounded in Barcelona.

August 1983—The Egyptian police foiled attempted attacks on Israeli targets in Egypt and the Fatah offices in Cairo.

September 29, 1983—Gulf Air (of the United Arab Emirates) plane blown up in mid-air, with all 122 on board killed.

October 18, 1983—Attack on the Za'aran Royal Palace in Amman, Jordan.

October 25, 1983—Attempted assassination of the Jordanian ambassador in New Delhi, India.

October 26, 1983—Attempted assassination of the Jordanian ambassador in Rome. Both he and his driver were seriously wounded.

October 31, 1983—An explosives-laden car exploded near a Jordanian military installation in Zarqa.

November 7, 1983—Attack on two security guards of the Jordanian embassy in Athens; one killed and the other wounded.

November 9, 1983—A bomb found and defused near the Saudi travel agency in Amman.

November 10, 1983—A bomb found and defused near the Chinese embassy in Amman.

November 12, 1983—A booby-trapped car defused in the midst of a residential area of Amman.

December 19, 1983—Attack on the Jordanian embassy in Madrid; one person killed and another wounded.

December 29, 1983—A booby-trapped bomb defused near an American officers club and the French cultural center in Izmir, Turkey.

February 2, 1984—Murder of the United Arab Emirates ambassador in Paris.

March 1984—Threats on the life of Queen Elizabeth II during her visit to Jordan. Two days before her visit, on March 24, 1984, a bomb exploded outside the Intercontinental Hotel, while 20 British journalists who had come to cover the event were in the hotel.

March 28, 1984—The cultural attache in the British embassy in Athens, Ken Whitty, was killed. This was the first time that an organization referring to itself as the Revolutionary Organization of Socialist Muslims (R.O.S.M.) took responsibility for the deed.

May 5, 1984—Assassination of the chairman of the Arab Writers Union in Nicosia, Cyprus.

June 4, 1984—Zvi Kedar, a security guard at the Israeli embassy in Cairo was wounded by shots fired from a passing car as he was driving back from the local airport, where he had taken Eliyahu Ben Elissar, the then chairman of the Israeli Knesset foreign affairs and defense committee, and the first ambassador of Israel in Egypt. Two organizations, Al-Iqab (The Punishment) and Revolutionary Egypt, claimed responsibility.

August 4, 1984—A booby-trapped American diplomatic car parked near the American embassy in Amman blew up.

September 5, 1984—Three members of the Abu Nidal group killed the P.L.O. representative in Bucharest, Rumania. They managed to escape.

October 25, 1984—Attempted murder of the second secretary of the United Arab Emirate embassy in Rome.

December 4, 1984—Two Jordanian diplomats wounded by bullets in Bucharest.

December 29, 1984—Fahd Qawasma, the former mayor of Hebron, was murdered in Amman, Jordan, shortly after being nominated as a member of the P.L.O. Executive Committee. Qawasma had been expelled from the West Bank by the Israeli authorities, due to what the authorities claimed were "subversive and incendiary" acts.

February 22, 1985—A bomb discovered near the American cultural center in Amman.

March 9, 1985—A booby-trapped suitcase smuggled onto an Alia Jordanian Airlines plane. As the plane took off earlier than anticipated, the bomb blew up while the plane was on the ground at the Abu Dhabi airport. Damage was minor and confined to the plane itself.

March 13, 1985—Shots fired into the house of the Jordanian ambassador in Rome.

March 21, 1985—Grenade attack on the Alia Jordanian Airlines offices in Rome. Two workers were wounded.

March 21, 1985—A bomb exploded near the Alia offices in Athens. Three passersby were wounded.

March 28, 1985—A Beirut journalist kidnapped in Lebanon.

April 3, 1985—A rocket fired at the Jordanian embassy in Rome.

April 4, 1985—Two R.P.G. rocket launchers fired at an Alia plane about to take off from the Athens airport. The rockets hit the plane, but inflicted only minor damage, and the 100 passengers on board were miraculously saved.

April 23, 1985—Attempted assassination of the editor of the Kuwaiti *al-Siyasa* newspaper. The editor, Ahmad Jarallah, was wounded.

May 22, 1985—Foiling of an attempt to drive an explosives-laden car into the Cairo street where the U.S. embassy is located.

June 5, 1985—Attempted assassination in Athens of Mustafa Ali Mustafa, the P.L.O. representative in Greece.

July 1, 1985—Bombs exploded, as well as shots fired and grenades thrown at the Alia and British Airways offices in Madrid. One person was killed and 24 others wounded.

July 6, 1985—Two Palestinian members of the organization were arrested in New Delhi, as they planned to attack the P.L.O. representative.

July 11, 1985—Two major explosions in two cafes in Kuwait. Fifteen people killed and ninety wounded.

July 21, 1985—A bomb exploded at the Kuwaiti Airlines office in Beirut.

July 24, 1985—A Jordanian diplomat killed in Ankara, Turkey.

August 8, 1985—Bomb blast in the British-owned London Hotel in Athens. Thirteen British guests wounded.

August 20, 1985—Albert Atrakchi, first secretary of the Israeli embassy in Cairo, was killed, his wife and another Israeli woman were wounded, when they were fired upon from a passing car. The Egyptian Revolution claimed responsibility.

August 31, 1985—An armed Palestinian member of the group arrested outside the Jordanian embassy in Athens.

September 1, 1985—The Turkish authorities arrested a group of 12 members of the organization who had planned to attack Israeli, Jordanian, and American targets.

September 3, 1985—Grenades thrown at the swimming pool and gardens of the Glyfada Hotel in Athens, where a delegation of handicapped Britons was lodged. Two of them were killed and nine wounded.

September 15, 1985—An attempt to assassinate the editor of an Arabic weekly in Athens.

September 17, 1985—Two grenades thrown at the Cafe De Paris in Rome. Forty guests and passersby: British, German, Brazilian, and Argentinian were wounded.

September 18, 1985—Michel Namari, the publisher in Athens of the Arab News Letter, an anti-Syrian paper, was killed.

September 28, 1985—Three bombs thrown at the British Airways offices in Rome. Ten people were wounded.

September 30, 1985—A bomb exploded at night near the El Al offices in Amsterdam.

November 23, 1985—Hijacking of an EgyptAir plane on a flight from Athens to Cairo and its forced landing in Valletta, Malta. In an attempt by Egyptian commandos to free the plane, 59 passengers were killed and 10 wounded.

November 24, 1985—Hussein Ali Ibrahim al-Bitar killed in his home in Amman. The reason was a financial dispute with Sabri al-Banna, who claimed he owned the murdered man's home. Three assassins, bearing Jordanian passports, entered Jordan from Kuwait.

December 27, 1985—Attack on the El Al counter at the Vienna airport. One person was killed and ten wounded. Two of the terrorists were killed in the attack and the third was wounded and caught.

December 27, 1985—Attack on the El Al counter at the Rome airport. Seventeen people were killed and about thirty wounded. Three of the four terrorists were killed by Israeli security guards and the fourth was caught.

March 19, 1986—Etti Tal-Or, wife of an Israeli diplomat, was killed and three other Israelis (another diplomat's wife and two security guards) were wounded in Cairo upon leaving the Israeli pavilion at the International Trade Fair. They were shot from a passing car. The Egyptian Revolution claimed responsibility, stating in a press communique that they deplored President Mubarak's policy of peace with Israel; they promised to continue "the struggle against Israeli Mossad agents."

April 3, 1986—Four people killed aboard TWA Flight 840 from Rome to Athens during a mid-air explosion.

April 5, 1986—Two people killed and 200 injured when a bomb went off in "La Belle" nightclub in West Berlin.

April 17, 1986—El Al security guards in London's Heathrow airport prevented an attempt to blow up a Boeing 747 with 385 passengers aboard.

August 3, 1986—A rocket-and-mortar attack against the British air base in Akrotiri, Cyprus. The raiders used an 80-millimeter mortar gun and Soviet-built Katyusha rockets for hitting their targets. Three civilians were injured in the assault. A group calling itself the Unified Nasserite Organization claimed responsibility. The organization is believed to be the product of a merger of several Arab and Palestinian radical groups, including Abu Nidal, upholding the nationalist ideology and the philosophy of the late Egyptian president, Nasser, as well as that of the Libyan leader. The new merger is devoted to striking at American and British interests in retaliation for the April 1986 U.S.A. air raid with British assistance against Libya.

August 21, 1986—The West Berlin police announced the arrest of three Arab terrorists suspected of preparing to assassinate the United States ambassador to West Germany.

September 5, 1986—Twenty-two passengers and crew members killed and 100 injured in an attack on a Pan-Am airplane in the Karachi, Pakistan, airport.

September 6, 1986—Twenty-one worshippers killed and four others wounded in an attack on the Neve Shalom Synagogue in Istanbul's Jewish Quarter of Turkey.

September 10, 1986—Four Palestinians arrested in Ankara, Turkey, and charged as accomplices in the murder of a Jordanian diplomat in June 1985.

Appendix E

The Palestinian Terrorist Organizations

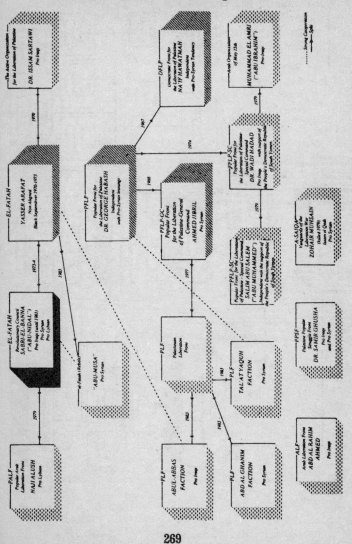

Appendix F

The Structure of the P.L.O.

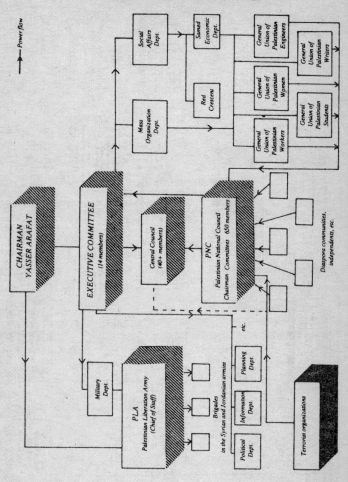

Appendix G

The Palestinian National Charter
The Palestinian National Charter as revised by the Fourth
PNC meeting, July 1968 (extracts)

Source: Leila S. Kadi, Basic Political Documents of the
Armed Palestinian Resistance Movement, Beirut: PLO
Research Center 1969, pp. 137–142.

Article 1: Palestine is the homeland of the Arab Palestinian people; it is an indivisible part of the Arab
homeland, and the Palestinian people are an integral part
of the Arab nation.

Article 2: Palestine, with the boundaries it had during
the British mandate, is an indivisible territorial unit . . .

Article 4: The Palestinian identity is a genuine, essential and inherent characteristic; it is transmitted from parents to children. The Zionist occupation and the dispersal
of the Palestinian Arab people, through the disasters
which befell them, do not make them lose their Palestinian identity and their membership of the Palestinian community, nor do they negate them.

Article 5: The Palestinians are those Arab nationals
who, until 1947, normally resided in Palestine regardless
of whether they were evicted from it or have stayed there.
Anyone born, after that date, of a Palestinian father—
whether inside Palestine or outside it—is also a Palestinian.

Article 6: The Jews who had normally resided in Palestine until the beginning of the Zionist invasion will be
considered Palestinians . . .

Article 8: The phase in their history, through which the Palestinian people are now living, is that of national struggle for the liberation of Palestine. Thus the conflicts among the Palestinian national forces are secondary, and should be ended for the sake of the basic conflict that exists between the forces of Zionism and of imperialism on the one hand, and the Palestinian Arab people on the other . . .

Article 9: Armed struggle is the only way to liberate Palestine. Thus it is the overall strategy, not merely a tactical phase. The Palestinian Arab people assert their absolute determination and firm resolution to continue their armed struggle and to work for an armed popular revolution for the liberation of their country and their return to it . . .

Article 10: Commando action constitutes the nucleus of the Palestinian popular liberation war . . .

Article 12: The Palestinian people believe in Arab unity. In order to contribute their share towards the attainment of that objective, however, they must, at the present stage of their struggle, safeguard their Palestinian identity and develop their consciousness of that identity, and oppose any plan that may dissolve or impair it . . .

Article 15: The liberation of Palestine, from an Arab viewpoint, is a national duty and it attempts to repel the Zionist and imperialist aggression against the Arab homeland, and aims at the elimination of Zionism in Palestine. Absolute responsibility for this falls upon the Arab nation—peoples and governments—with the Arab people of Palestine in the vanguard . . .

Article 19: The partition of Palestine in 1947 and the establishment of the state of Israel are entirely illegal, regardless of the passage of time, because they were contrary to the will of the Palestinian people and to their natural right in their homeland, and inconsistent with the principles embodied in the Chapter of the United Nations, particularly the right to self determination.

Article 20: The Balfour Declaration, the mandate for Palestine and everything that has been based upon them, are deemed null and void. Claims of historical or religious ties of Jews with Palestine are incompatible with the facts of history and the true conception of what constitutes statehood. Judaism, being a religion, is not an independent nationality. Nor do Jews constitute a single nation with an identity of its own; they are citizens of the states to which they belong.

Article 21: The Arab Palestinian people, expressing themselves by the armed Palestinian revolution, reject all solutions which are substitutes for the total liberation of Palestine . . .

Article 22: Zionism is a political movement organically associated with international imperialism and antagonistic to all action for liberation and to progressive movements in the world. It is racist and fanatic in its nature, aggressive, expansionist and colonial in its arms, and fascist in its methods . . .

Article 27: The Palestine Liberation Organisation shall cooperate with all Arab states, each according to its potentialities; and will adopt a neutral policy among them in the light of the requirements of the war of liberation; and on this basis it shall not interfere in the internal affairs of any Arab state . . .

Article 33: This Charter shall not be amended save by (vote of) a majority of two-thirds of the total membership of the National Congress of the Palestine Liberation Organisation [i.e. the PNC] at a special session convened for that purpose.

Appendix H

Bibliography

A. Primary Sources

Many of my interviews were related to the attempted assassination of Ambassador Argov in London. A number of people asked to remain anonymous.

1 Interviews with members of the anti-terror squad of the London police: Commander William Hucksleby, head of the squad; Superintendent John Paul, in charge of the investigation; Inspector Chris Berg; Constable Colin Simpson, assigned as Ambassador Argov's bodyguard.
2 Interviews with the public prosecutor in the trial, Roy Amlot; his assistant, Barbara Miles; and with the three defense attorneys.
3 Interviews with members of the Israeli embassy in London and with Israeli, American, and Western European officials of the intelligence community.
4 Interview with Dr. Issam Sartawi.
5 Conversations with Uri Avnery, editor of the Israeli weekly *Ha'olam Hazeh*.
6 Conversations with the Orientalist Professor Elie Kedourie, of the London School of Economics.
7 Transcript of the trial of the three terrorists accused of attempting to kill Ambassador Argov, held at the Old Bailey between January and March 1983.

8 Reports and articles from newspapers in Israel, the United States, Britain, Austria, Belgium, Spain, France, and English translations of Arabic articles dealing with Palestinian terror in general and Abu Nidal in particular.

9 Documents of the Shiloah Center of Tel Aviv University and of the Truman Institute, Hebrew University, Jerusalem.

10 The records of the Data Center, headed by Dr. Ariel Merari at Jaffe Center, of Strategic Studies of Tel-Aviv University.

B. Secondary Sources

Abu Iyad with Rouleau, Eric. *My Home, My Land.* New York: Times Books, 1981.

Adams, James. *The Financing of Terror.* London: New English Library, 1986.

Argov, Shlomo. *An Ambassador Speaks Out.* London: Weidenfeld and Nicolson, 1983.

Becker, Jillian, *The P.L.O.: The Rise and Fall of the Palestine Liberation Organisation.* London: Weidenfeld and Nicolson, 1984.

Ben-Ami, Shlomo. *Spain Between Dictatorship and Democracy, 1936–1977.* Tel Aviv: Am Oved, Sifriyat Ofakim, 1977. Hebrew.

Bloch, Jonathan, and Fitzgerald, Patrick. *British Intelligence and Covert Action: Africa, Middle East and Europe Since 1945.* Brandon (Ireland), Junction (London), 1983.

Brzezinski, Zbigniev. *Power and Principle: Memoirs of the National Security Adviser 1977–1981.* New York: Farrar, Straus and Giroux, 1983.

Cobban, Helena. *The Palestinian Liberation Organisation: People, Power and Politics.* Cambridge: Cambridge University Press, 1984.

Gilboa, Eitan, and Naor, Mordechai (eds.). *The Israeli-Arab Conflict: Factors, Confrontations, Chances.* Tel Aviv: Ministry of Defense Publications, 1981. Hebrew.

Haim, Sylvia G. (ed.). *Arab Nationalism.* Berkeley: University of California Press, 1964.

Harkabi, Yehoshafat. *The Lessons Learned by the Arabs from their Defeats.* A collection of translations from Arabic. Tel Aviv: Am Oved, 1969. Hebrew.

Ivienski, Ze'ev. *Individual Terror: Theory and Deed.* Tel Aviv: Hakibbutz Hame'uhad, 1977. Hebrew.

Kissinger, Henry. *Years of Upheaval.* Boston: Little, Brown and Company, 1982.

Laqueur, Walter. *Guerrilla.* Tel Aviv: Ministry of Defense Publications. Hebrew.

Laqueur, Walter. *The Terrorism Reader: A Historical Anthology.* New York: New American Library, 1978.

Laqueur, Walter. *Terrorism.* London: Weidenfeld and Nicolson. 1977.

Legum, Colin; Shaked, Haim; and Dishon, Daniel. *Middle East Contemporary Survey.* Vols. 1–4, 1976–1981. Tel Aviv: The Shiloah Center for Middle East and Africa Studies, Tel Aviv University. New York and London: Holmes and Meier.

Lodge, Juliet (ed.). *Terrorism: A Challenge to the State.* New York: St. Martin's Press, 1981.

Netanyahu, Binyamin (ed.). *Terrorism: How The West Can Win.* New York: Farrar, Straus and Giroux, 1986.

Rabinovitch, Itamar. *Syria under the Ba'ath 1963–1966: The Army-Party Symbiosis.* Jerusalem: Israel Universities Press, 1972.

Smith, Colin. *Carlos: Portrait of a Terrorist.* London: Sphere Books, 1976.

Snow, Peter, and Phillips, David. *Leila's Hijack War.* London: Pan, 1970.

Sterling, Claire. *The Terror Network: The Secret War of International Terrorism.* London: Weidenfeld and Nicolson, 1981.

Steven, Stewart. *The Spymasters of Israel.* London: Hodder and Staughton, 1980.

Tavin, Eli, and Alexander, Yonah (eds.). *Terrorists or Freedom Fighters: A Tool for the Full Understanding of Who They Are and How They Affect Civilization Today.* Fairfax, Virginia: Hero Books, 1986.

Tinnen, David, and Cristen, Dag. *The Hit Team.* New York: Dell, 1977.

Tomlinson, John. *Left-Right: The March of Political Extremism in Britain.* London: John Caldor, 1981.

Ta'ari, Ehud. *Fatah.* Tel Aviv: Lewin-Epstein, 1970. Hebrew.

Yodfat, Aryeh, and Arnon-Ohana, Yuval. *P.L.O. Strategy and Tactics.* London: Croom-Helm, 1983.

THE FATE OF THE EARTH IS IN OUR HANDS

THE FATE OF THE EARTH

JONATHAN SCHELL

"This is a work of enormous force. It compels us to confront head on the nuclear peril in which we all find ourselves." The New York Times Book Review

"Should be read by all Americans."
Walter Mondale, CBS-TV's Face the Nation

"A book that should be pondered by every citizen who participates in government, by every parent who has any hope for the survival of his children or his posterity." Philadelphia Inquirer

"There have been books that have changed our lives. This one may save our lives—provided it is read now and its warning heeded." Studs Terkel

An **AVON** Paperback 61325-5/$3.95 US/$5.50 Can

By the year 2000, 2 out of 3 Americans could be illiterate.

It's true.

Today, 75 million adults...about one American in three, can't read adequately. And by the year 2000, U.S. News & World Report envisions an America with a literacy rate of only 30%.

Before that America comes to be, you can stop it...by joining the fight against illiteracy today.

Call the Coalition for Literacy at toll-free **1-800-228-8813** and volunteer.

**Volunteer
Against Illiteracy.
The only degree you need
is a degree of caring.**

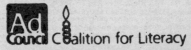

Ad Council   Coalition for Literacy